# PIPE FITTINGS

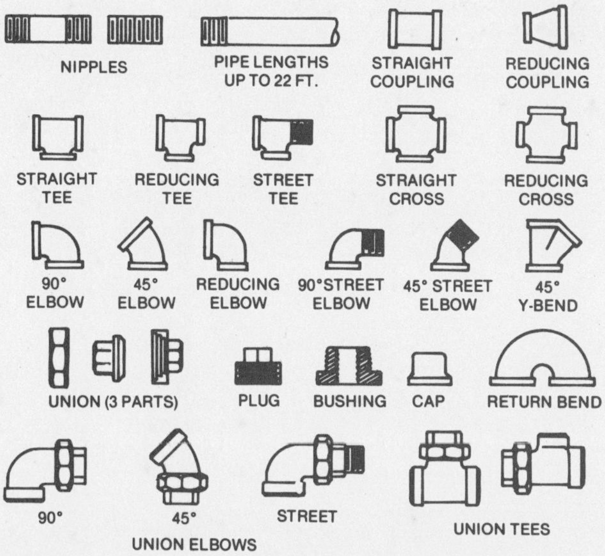


Here are the common steel pipe fittings. Nipples are simply short lengths of pipe threaded on both ends. Reducing fittings join two different sizes of pipe.

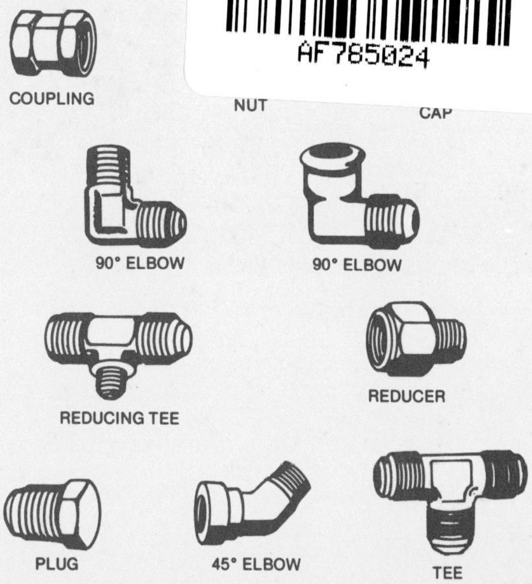


Compression fittings of the flared-tube type are the easiest for the novice to handle when working with copper tubing.

| STANDARD STEEL PIPE (All Dimensions in Inches) | | | | | |
|---|---|---|---|---|---|
| Nominal Size | Outside Diameter | Inside Diameter | Nominal Size | Outside Diameter | Inside Diameter |
| 1/8 | 0.405 | 0.269 | 1 | 1.315 | 1.049 |
| 1/4 | 0.540 | 0.364 | 1 1/4 | 1.660 | 1.380 |
| 3/8 | 0.675 | 0.493 | 1 1/2 | 1.900 | 1.610 |
| 1/2 | 0.840 | 0.622 | 2 | 2.375 | 2.067 |
| 3/4 | 1.050 | 0.824 | 2 1/2 | 2.875 | 2.469 |

## SQUARE MEASURE

144 sq in = 1 sq ft
9 sq ft = 1 sq yd
272.25 sq ft = 1 sq rod
160 sq rods = 1 acre

## VOLUME MEASURE

1728 cu in = 1 cu ft
27 cu ft = 1 cu yd

## MEASURES OF CAPACITY

1 cup = 8 fl oz
2 cups = 1 pint
2 pints = 1 quart
4 quarts = 1 gallon
2 gallons = 1 peck
4 pecks = 1 bushel

## WOOD SCREWS

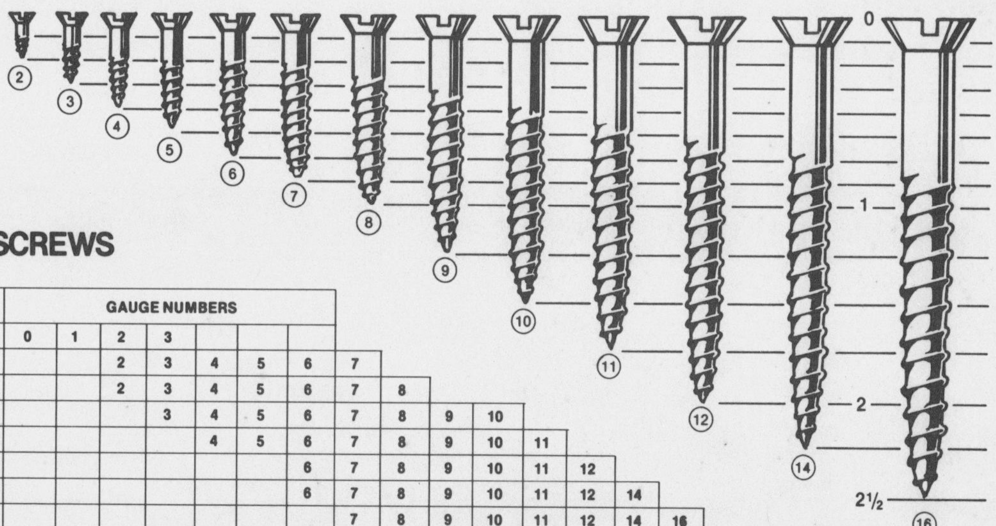


| LENGTH | GAUGE NUMBERS | | | | | | | | | | | | | | | | |
|---|---|---|---|---|---|---|---|---|---|---|---|---|---|---|---|---|---|
| 1/4 INCH | 0 | 1 | 2 | 3 | | | | | | | | | | | | | |
| 3/8 INCH | | | 2 | 3 | 4 | 5 | 6 | 7 | | | | | | | | | |
| 1/2 INCH | | | 2 | 3 | 4 | 5 | 6 | 7 | 8 | | | | | | | | |
| 5/8 INCH | | | | 3 | 4 | 5 | 6 | 7 | 8 | 9 | 10 | | | | | | |
| 3/4 INCH | | | | | 4 | 5 | 6 | 7 | 8 | 9 | 10 | 11 | | | | | |
| 7/8 INCH | | | | | | | 6 | 7 | 8 | 9 | 10 | 11 | 12 | | | | |
| 1 INCH | | | | | | | 6 | 7 | 8 | 9 | 10 | 11 | 12 | 14 | | | |
| 1 1/4 INCH | | | | | | | | 7 | 8 | 9 | 10 | 11 | 12 | 14 | 16 | | |
| 1 1/2 INCH | | | | | | | 6 | 7 | 8 | 9 | 10 | 11 | 12 | 14 | 16 | 18 | |
| 1 3/4 INCH | | | | | | | | | 8 | 9 | 10 | 11 | 12 | 14 | 16 | 18 | 20 |
| 2 INCH | | | | | | | | | 8 | 9 | 10 | 11 | 12 | 14 | 16 | 18 | 20 |
| 2 1/4 INCH | | | | | | | | | | 9 | 10 | 11 | 12 | 14 | 16 | 18 | 20 |
| 2 1/2 INCH | | | | | | | | | | | | | 12 | 14 | 16 | 18 | 20 |
| 2 3/4 INCH | | | | | | | | | | | | | | 14 | 16 | 18 | 20 |
| 3 INCH | | | | | | | | | | | | | | | 16 | 18 | 20 |
| 3 1/2 INCH | | | | | | | | | | | | | | | | 18 | 20 | 24 |
| 4 INCH | | | | | | | | | | | | | | | | 18 | 20 | 24 |

WHEN YOU BUY SCREWS, SPECIFY (1) LENGTH, (2) GAUGE NUMBER, (3) TYPE OF HEAD—FLAT, ROUND, OR OVAL, (4) MATERIAL—STEEL, BRASS, BRONZE, ETC., (5) FINISH—BRIGHT, STEEL BLUED, CADMIUM, NICKEL, OR CHROMIUM PLATED.

# In this volume . . .

**IF YOU'VE ALWAYS** wanted a conversation piece for your living room or study, this coffee-table aquarium is the answer. It is indeed unique, and isn't nearly as difficult to build as it appears. The table is divided into six separate compartments, each of which is sealed and completely independent of the others. The dry center well is also sealed, and is an ideal location for the air pump, regulating valves and light fixture. In the same article you'll find plans for another aquarium, a spellbinding in-the-walk tank. See the article on page 810.

**BUILD A CHARMING** colonial trestle desk. Because of its classic simplicity it is relatively easy to make, and fits into almost any style of decorating. Plans start on page 951.

**LEARN HOW TO SAW** firewood on the double with a two-man saw in the article on page 878.

**HERE'S A BEAUTIFUL** contemporary coffee table that leads a double life. Its illuminated top offers color-corrected viewing of your slides. A built-in dimmer softly illuminates decorative objects when the table is not in use for slide sorting. See the plans on page 806.

**HERE'S A LITTLE** colonial charmer—an attractive dry sink from yesteryear. Use it to store odds and ends and show off your plants. See page 1050.

**YOU CAN MAKE** a patio, pool deck or basement floor come alive by coloring it through any one of four methods: stain, paint, mix-in integrally, or dusting color on. Learn how on page 840.

# Look what you'll find in other volumes!

**KNOW WHAT TO DO** when trouble strikes your dishwasher. Take a look at the authoritative article on page 1002 of Vol. 7. In pull-apart drawings it shows you exactly where trouble may occur. Step-by-step charts start with the symptoms of the trouble, then move on to the possible causes, and the action to take to overcome the trouble. A large drawing identifies all the common components of the dishwasher. This article can save you a considerable sum in repair costs.

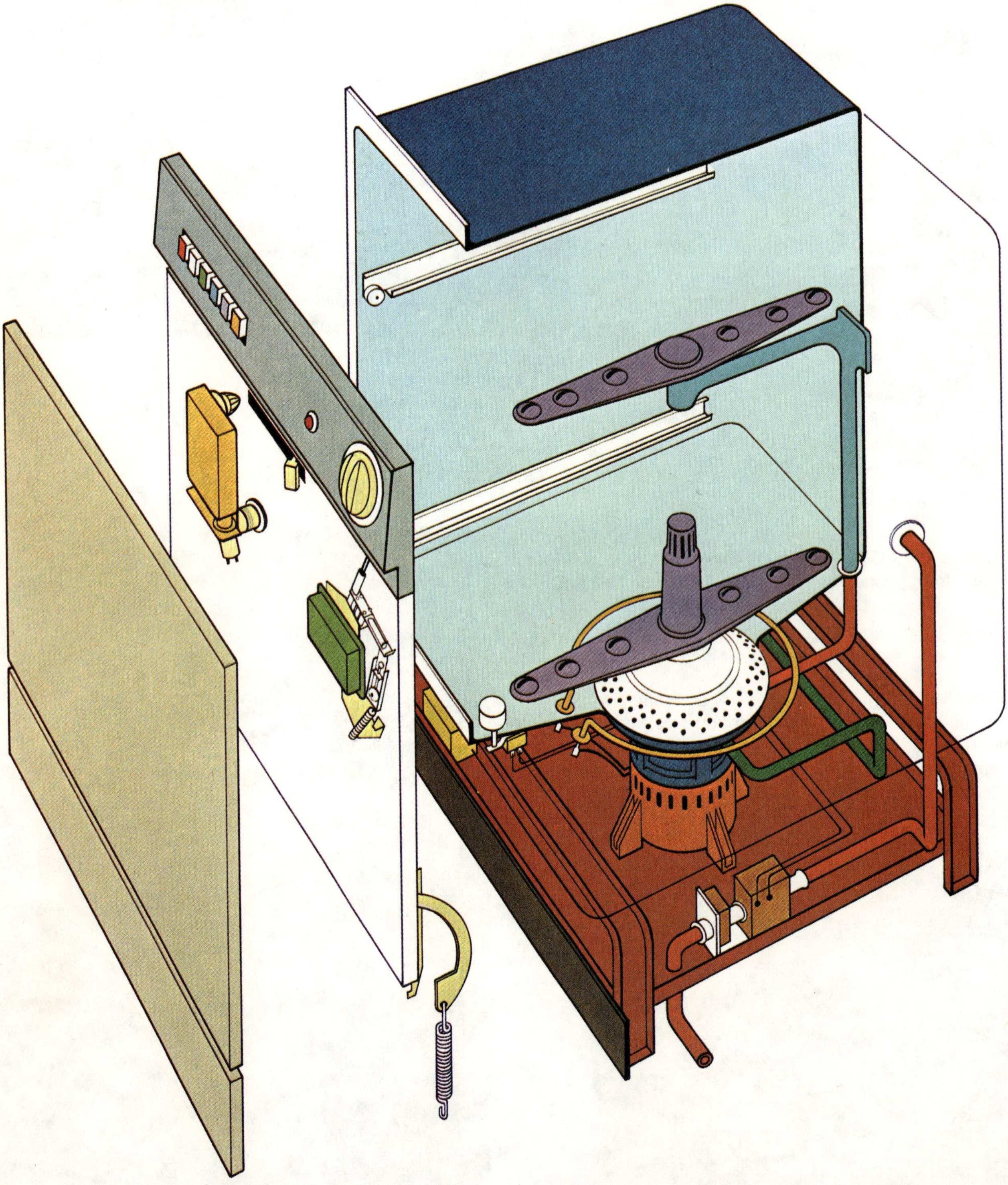

**FINE ART** at a price you can afford? Yes, if you use high-quality reproductions of fine paintings, and frame them yourself. You'll learn how in Vol. 8, page 1264.

**TO ENJOY** a fireplace to the utmost, learn how to cut wood and lay a fire properly. See Vol. 8, page 1229.

**THIS BEAUTIFUL TRESTLE TABLE** with matching benches, all of hand-pegged construction, could become an heirloom. See page 998.

**REMODELING YOUR HOME?** There are dozens of dramatic changes you can make yourself, such as opening up an entire room to the outdoors. See the article in Vol. 16, page 2416.

**PRIVACY SCREENS** not only make good neighbors, but draw admiring glances because they enhance the appearance of your home. You'll find two others in Vol. 15, page 2334.

**HERE A MODULAR** piece of furniture is an attractive room divider. You'll also find the same piece used as a hutch, hobby bench, sewing center, and vanity. See page 1890 of Vol. 12.

**YOU NEVER KNOW** what's made of hardboard these days. This stunning wall, believe it or not, is covered with hardboard panels. Learn all about hardboard panels in Vol. 13, page 2054.

**THIS FALSE A—CEILING** is installed right over an old ceiling. Ducts and wiring are routed above it. The hollow beams are made of red oak. See page 2416 of Vol. 16.

**THE LANDSCAPING OF ANY HOME** is its most important exterior attribute. Check the sensible guidelines in "Down-to-earth principles of landscaping" in Vol. 11, page 1675.

Popular Mechanics

# do-it-yourself encyclopedia

a complete how-to guide for the homeowner, the hobbyist—
and anyone who enjoys working with mind and hands!

## All about:

home maintenance
home-improvement projects
wall paneling
burglary and fire protection
furniture projects
finishing and refinishing furniture
outdoor living
home remodeling
solutions to home problems
challenging woodworking projects
hobbies and handicrafts
model making
weekend projects
workshop shortcuts and techniques
hand-tool skills
power-tool know-how
shop-made tools
car repairs
car maintenance
appliance repair
boating
hunting
fishing
camping
photography projects
radio, TV and electronics know-how
clever hints and tips
projects just for fun

volume 6

ISBN 0-87851-071-0
Library of Congress Catalog Number 77 84920



MANUFACTURED IN THE UNITED STATES OF AMERICA

# contents

## VOLUME 6

# Build a stool table

SEE ALSO

**Bridge tables . . . Butcher block furniture . . . Game tables . . . Occasional tables . . . Paneling, hardboard . . . Party tables . . . Snack tables . . . Stools . . .**

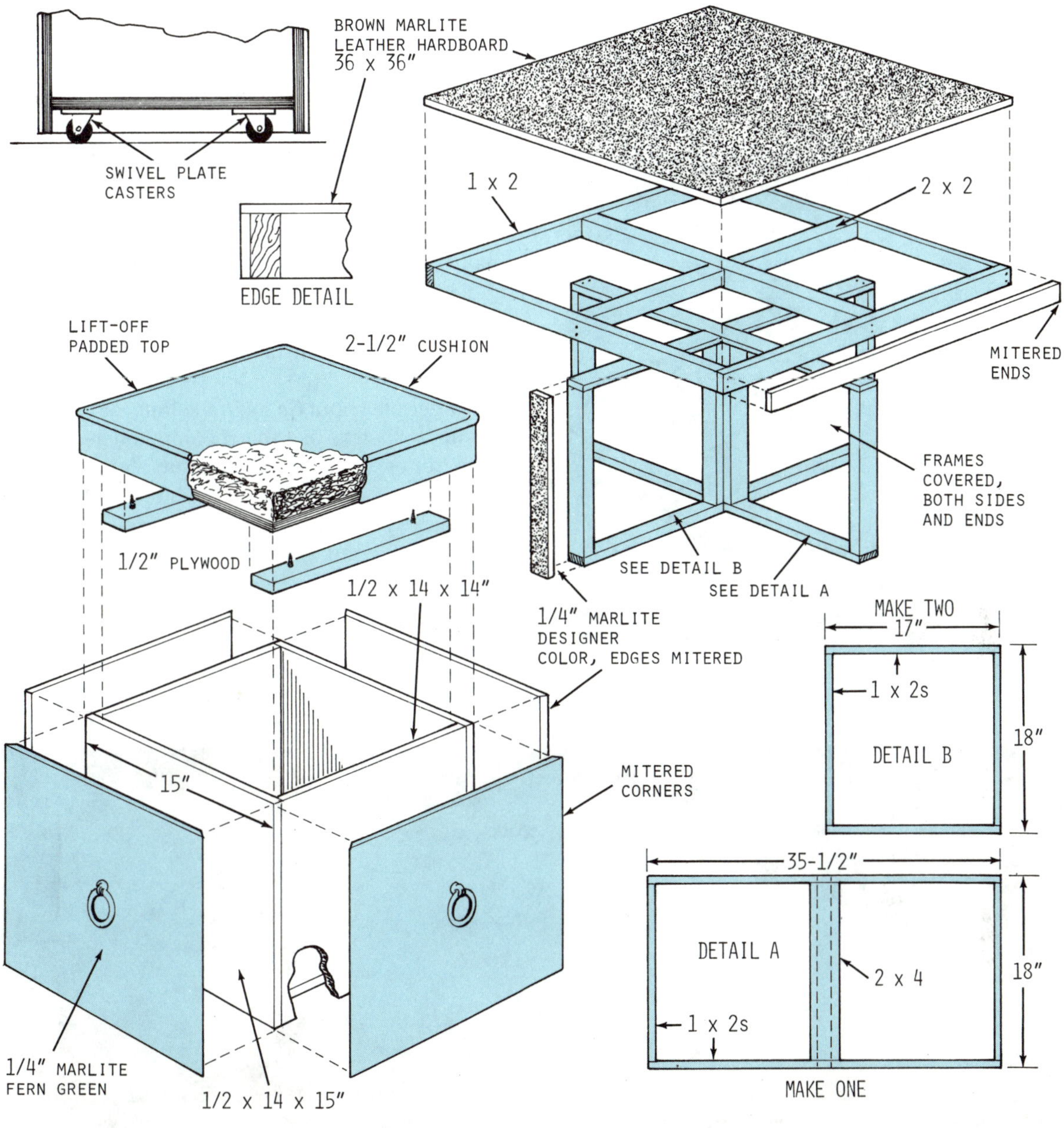


A REAL MISER when it comes to saving space, this table makes every inch count. Four box stools tuck under its top to provide instant roll-out seats, and each stool offers wonderful hidden storage under its lift-off cushion.

As a coffee table you'll find it the handiest thing ever for late-show snacks. As a game table it's marvelous for the kids' room. You'll even find the stools handy for extra seating when entertaining.

To top it off, it's an elegant looking piece of furniture for it is completely covered with both a textured and a slick plastic-finish hardboard paneling from Marlite.

The ⅛-in.-textured leather top is supported by a 35¾-in.-sq. frame of 1x2s and 2x2s, glued and nailed together. The 2x2s are notched.

The tabletop, in turn, is supported by a criss-cross base consisting of three 1x2 frames joined together at the center. The brown leather top laps at the edges of the hardboard strips applied to edges of the frame, while the joints of the fern-green members covering the base are mitered at outer corners. Regular panel adhesive is used to cement the hardboard in place.

The stools are made alike, starting with a box of ½-in. plywood. The bottom is recessed so that ball casters, such as Shepard's, will raise the stool about ½ in.

The padded seat is foam rubber placed on top of a 15-in. square of plywood and covered with a fitted vinyl top which is tacked to the underside.

# Build a coffee-table slide viewer

■ IF YOU SHOOT slides seriously, you need a light box to sort them on. Commercially made slide-sorter boxes are available but they have several shortcomings. For one, they don't hold very many slides. Also, their reddish light gives a false impression of your slides' color. And finally they're not attractive enough to leave out in plain sight between your sorting sessions.

This light box, though, is another story altogether. Its 900-sq.-in. viewing surface can hold more than 200 2x2-in. slides—many more than most people shoot on even the longest vacation. Its light—if you use the recommended fluorescent tubes or their exact equivalents—is the same 5000 K (Kelvin) bluish-white light that professional photographers and engravers use to judge slide color quality.

SEE ALSO

**Darkrooms . . . Game tables . . .**
**Illuminators, slide-copy . . . Lightboxes . . .**
**Occasional tables . . . Photography . . .**

**NAILING** jig cut from scrap helps align the side pieces with the end section.

**RECESS** clearance required for rewind mechanism by using a router or a chisel.

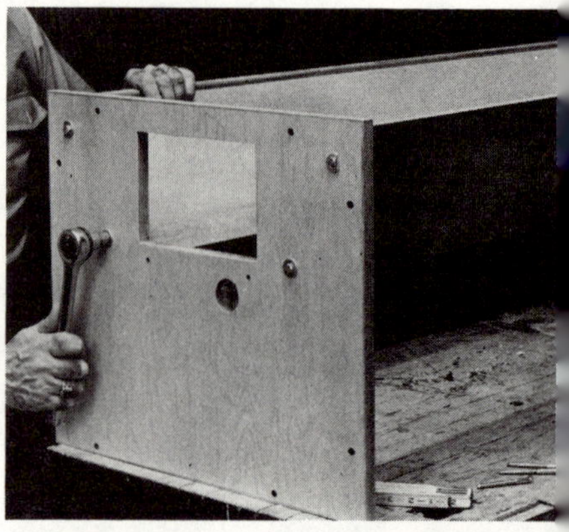

**ASSEMBLE** the table with glue and lagscrews turned into predrilled holes.

**MOUNT** rewind mechanism to blocks fastened to the end section.

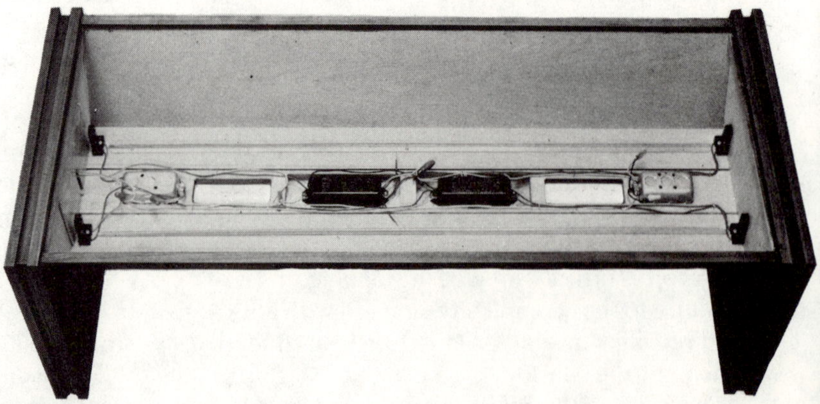

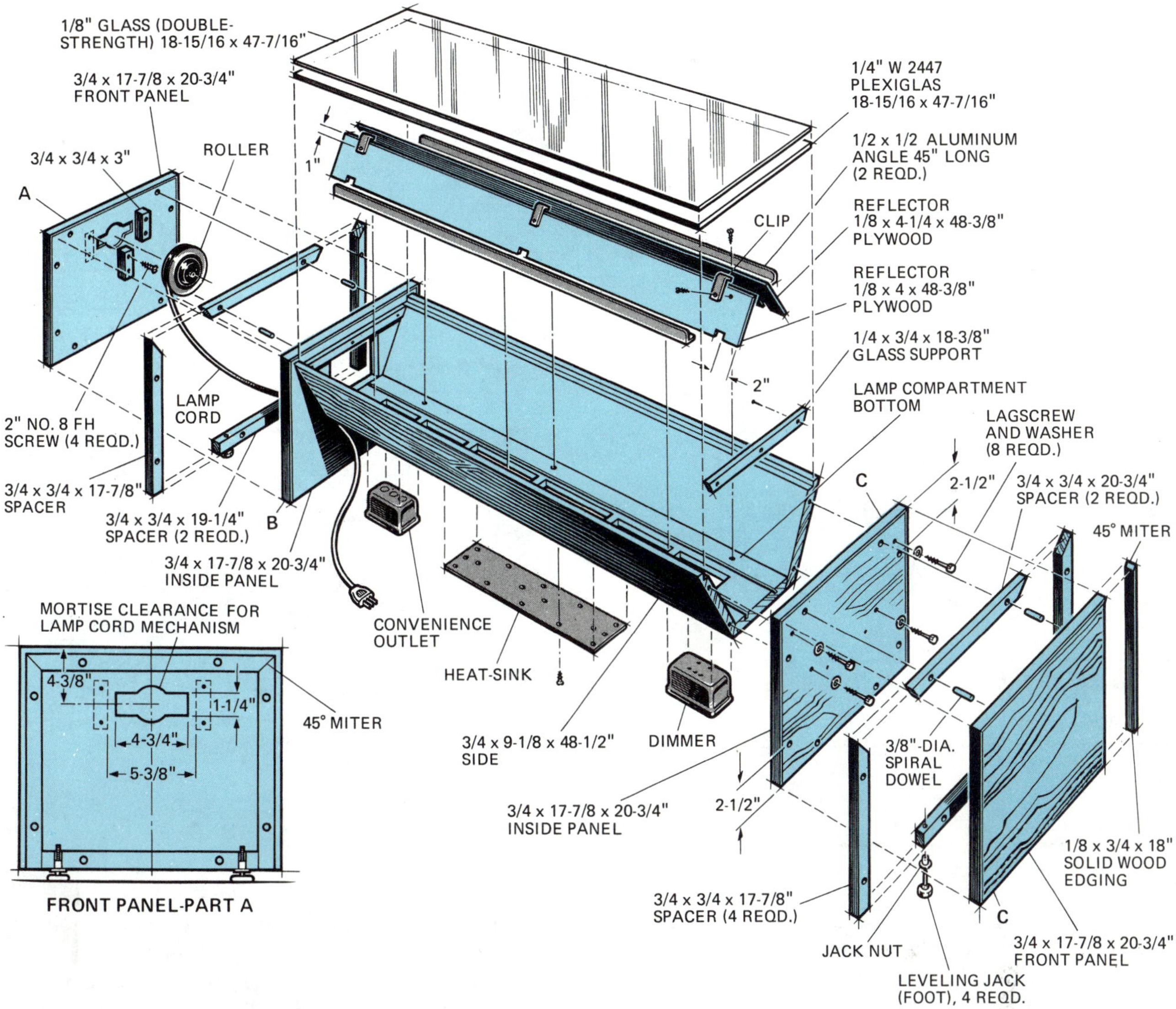

FRONT PANEL-PART A

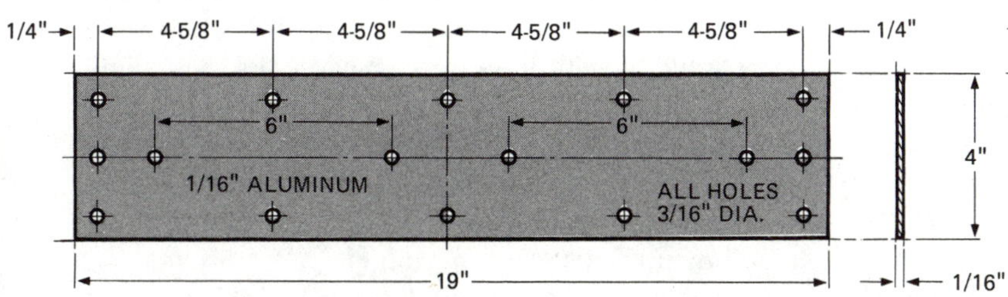

HEAT SINK

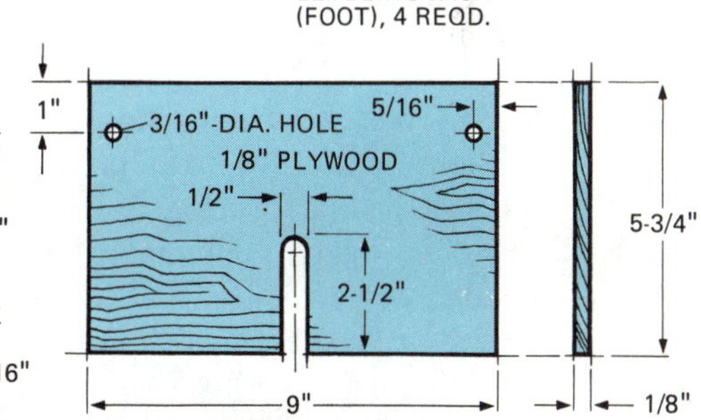

REWIND COMPARTMENT COVER

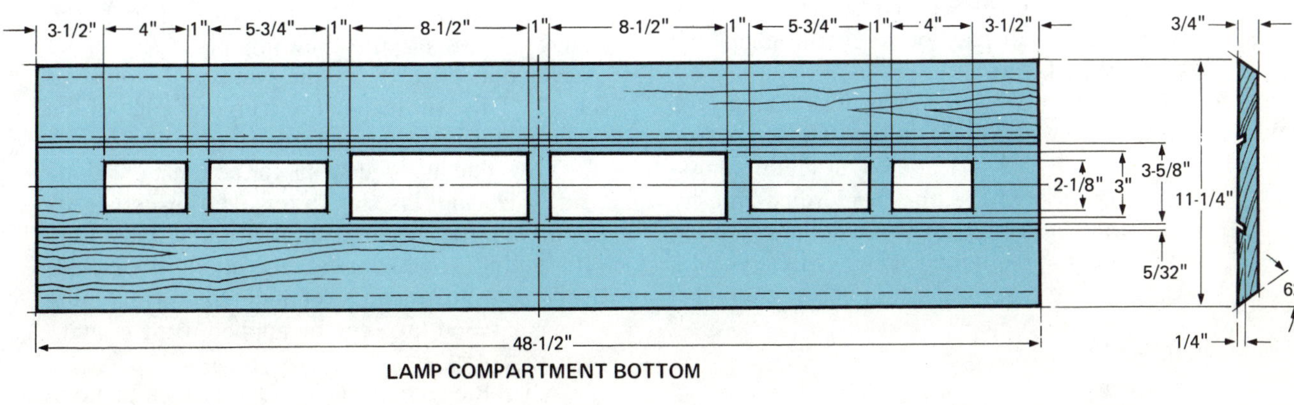

LAMP COMPARTMENT BOTTOM

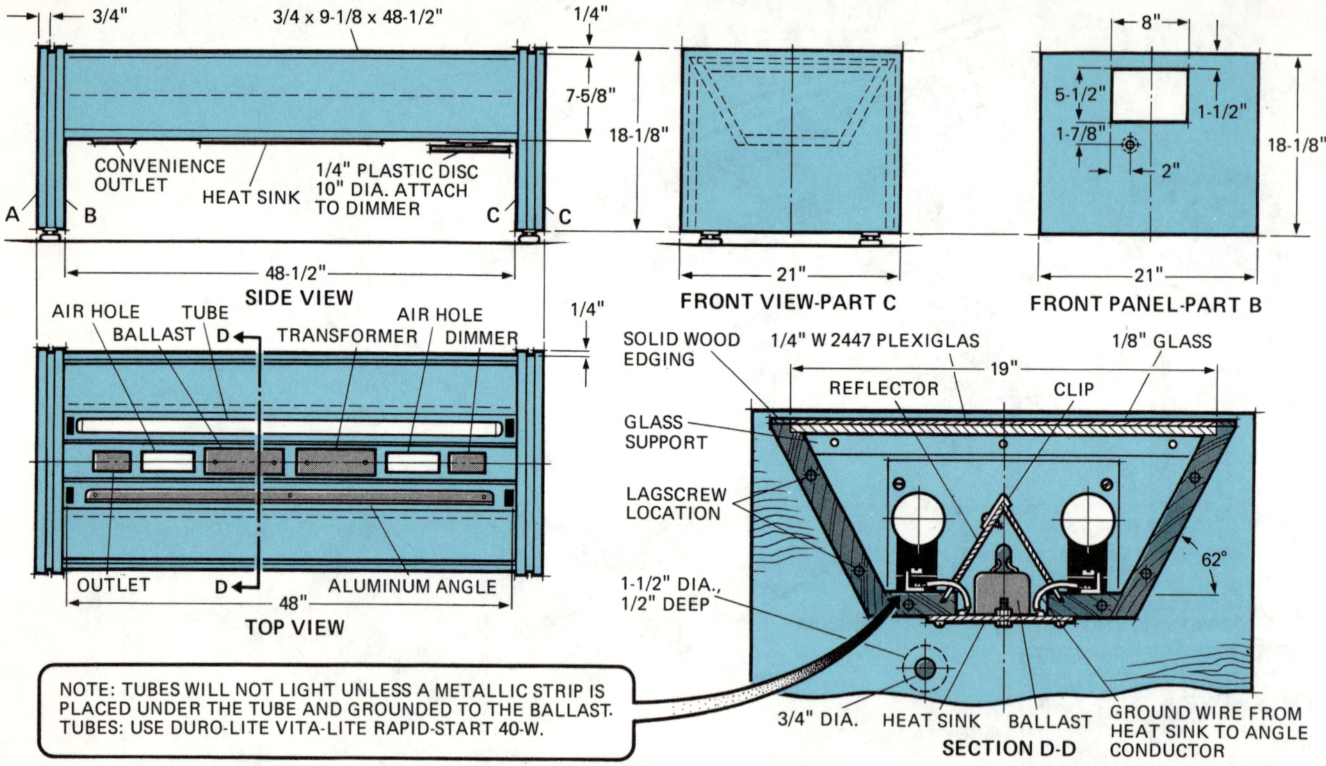


*coffee-table slide viewer, continued*

The bonus here is that this slide viewer has been built into the top of a handsome, modern coffee table.

The lighting of this tabletop is exceptionally even, thanks to the reflector design which is our version of those used in the Matrix line of professional light boxes. We've added two additional features to the Matrix design: a dimmer—so you can use the light to illuminate glassware and decorative objects with a soft, dramatic glow—and a heavy glass top which lets you set down glasses and the like without fear of scratching the translucent Plexiglas beneath. This feature also lets you put large, unmounted transparencies on semipermanent display between the glass and sheet-acrylic layers.

Notice that neither the glass nor Plexiglas top is provided with finger holes. These can be drilled at both ends if desired. Our feeling, however, was to keep the box inside dust free by eliminating any holes, and using a large suction cup (or tipping the table slightly) whenever it's necessary to remove the glass to change a bulb.

**building the table**

Start by laying out all parts on a 4x8-ft. sheet of plywood. Using a portable saw or sabre saw, cut out the parts, making certain that they're slightly oversize. Then recut the pieces to exact size on your table or radial saw using a plywood blade to assure a smooth cut. At this stage, you should have four endpieces, each 21 5/16-in. wide and 18-in. high. You can also rip the sidepieces to a width of 9¼-in.

Rip the edge strips of solid material of the same species as the plywood used. (On the table shown, we used birch cabinet-grade plywood, so edge strips are of solid birch.) Make each of these edge strips about ⅛ in. thick (this dimension is not critical); then glue to all exposed edges. Next set your tablesaw blade to 28° and bevel one edge of a 1-in.-wide piece of solid stock. This will be used to trim one edge of the side pieces.

Now glue all edge strips to the table ends and sides. During this step, a few well-placed brads will keep the pieces from shifting about during the gluing and clamping operation. If desired, solid edge strips can be eliminated and matching flexible wood tape can be applied using contact cement.

When the glue has dried, use a block plane to

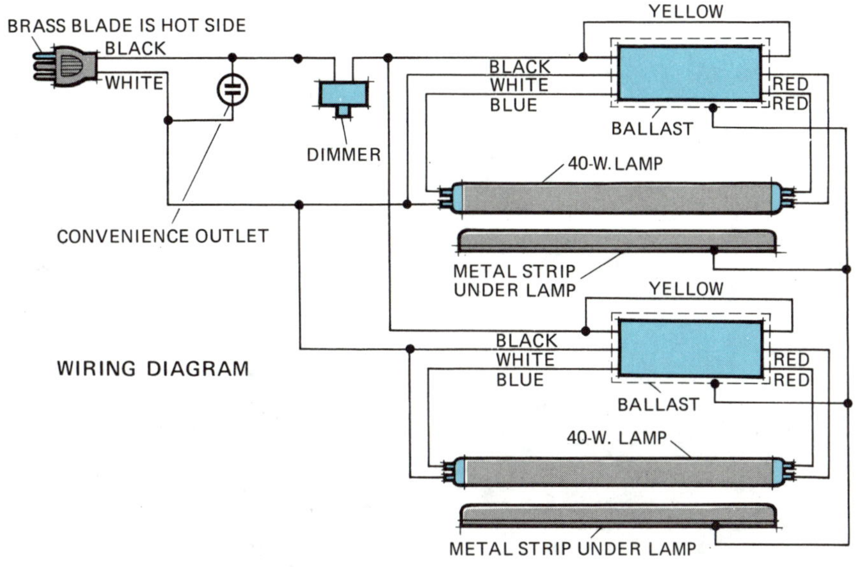


WIRING DIAGRAM

remove any excess material and sand the strips perfectly smooth.

**cord rewind mechanism**

To get power to the table, we have installed a line on a cord rewind mechanism. The table's hollow end sections are made with a spacer around the perimeter as shown. One end contains the rewind mechanism. To assure alignment when gluing up the ends, use dowels as we did. Dowel locating pins make aligning the dowels easier. Notice that the inner end pieces are attached to the slanted side sections before the ends are assembled. By using lagscrews and glue, you are assured of a very strong, tight joint. Make certain that you install washers beneath lagscrew heads.

Make the bottom panel next. Locate and cut the openings as shown; miter the sides and cut the grooves for the reflector.

Before closing in the end containing the rewind mechanism, pass the cord through the opening. To prevent the cord from retracting into the compartment, either install the plug or tie a temporary knot.

The plug used must be either a polarized or grounded type. A polarized plug has one wide and one narrow blade. Be sure to connect the black wire from the dimmer (and transformer) to the brass side of the plug.

If a grounded-type plug should be used, you can follow the same procedure but ignore the green terminal of the plug.

**about the light**

In order for rapid-start fluorescent tubes to function, they must be placed near a metallic surface. In conventional fixtures, this is accomplished by the metal reflector. Here, because the system is of wood, a metal strip must be placed under the tubes. You can do this with a piece of flat aluminum under the tubes. Or run a strip of electrical conducting tape from one end of each tube to the other. Do not, however, allow the tape to come in contact with the tube pins. If aluminum strip is used, run a piece of wire from it to the transformer base.

Wire the convenience outlet to the hot side of the line before it enters the switch to permit it to function independently. Be sure to solder leads to reel terminals.

To insure a perfectly level table, a set of levelers should be installed under the corners. These, and the rewind mechanism, are available from J.C. Armor Co., Box 290, Deer Park, N.Y. 11729. The rewind mechanism is priced at about $9.50, while a set of four leveling jacks is around $1.75. Both are postpaid.

The sheet acrylic used beneath the glass top is white translucent Plexiglas (No. 2447). The dimming system is by Lutron, Coopersburg, Pa. 18036, and available at well-stocked electrical supply houses. The excellent lighting is provided by Vita-Lite fluorescent tubes manufactured by Duro-Lite Co. These, too, are at better electrical houses.

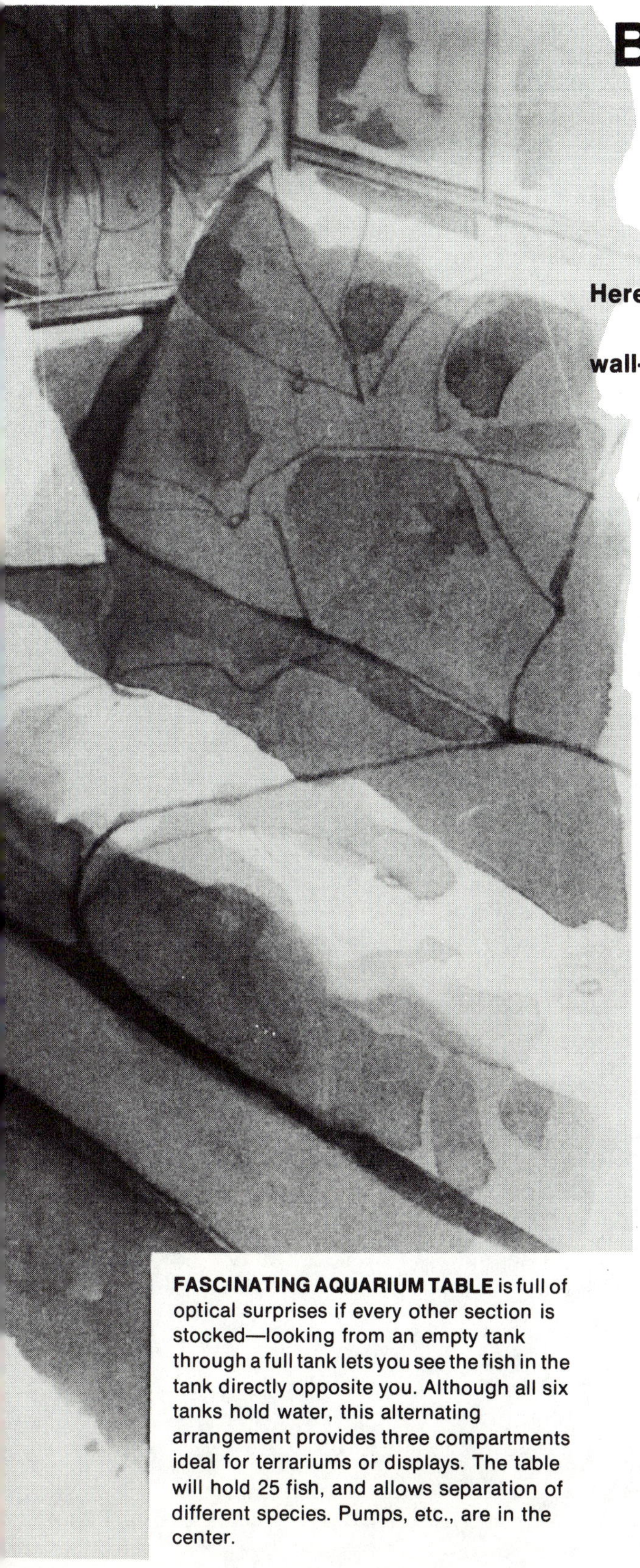

# Build a coffee-table aquarium

By LEONARD SABAL

**Here's a one-of-a-kind project that you'll have fun doing and talking about. There's also a wall-mounted aquarium, if you prefer, that creates a beautiful seascape**

IF YOU'VE ALWAYS wanted a conversation piece for your living room or study, this coffee table or wall-mounted aquarium is the answer. It is, indeed, unique and you can be sure that you'll have your friends talking about it the first time you invite them in for an evening. I designed and built the table, and, although it appears difficult to build, it isn't.

As you see on these pages, the table is divided into six separate compartments, each of which is sealed and completely independent of the others. The dry center well is also sealed and is an ideal location for the air pump, regulating valves and light fixture.

While the six sections can be used as separate aquariums, you can intially use three compartments to stock a generous number of tropical fish and set up the others as miniature gardens, terrariums or even model and trophy display cases.

The table is far less difficult to construct than it might appear. This is due in part to three factors: the absence of a reinforcing frame, use of a sealant that's also a bonding compound, and a totally symmetrical design.

Conventional aquariums are constructed of a slate bottom and glass sides, carefully fitted in a stainless-steel frame, and then sealed at all seams.

A relatively new type of sealant, however,

**FASCINATING AQUARIUM TABLE** is full of optical surprises if every other section is stocked—looking from an empty tank through a full tank lets you see the fish in the tank directly opposite you. Although all six tanks hold water, this alternating arrangement provides three compartments ideal for terrariums or displays. The table will hold 25 fish, and allows separation of different species. Pumps, etc., are in the center.

SEE ALSO
**Family rooms . . . Game tables . . .**
**Hobby centers . . . Plexiglass projects**

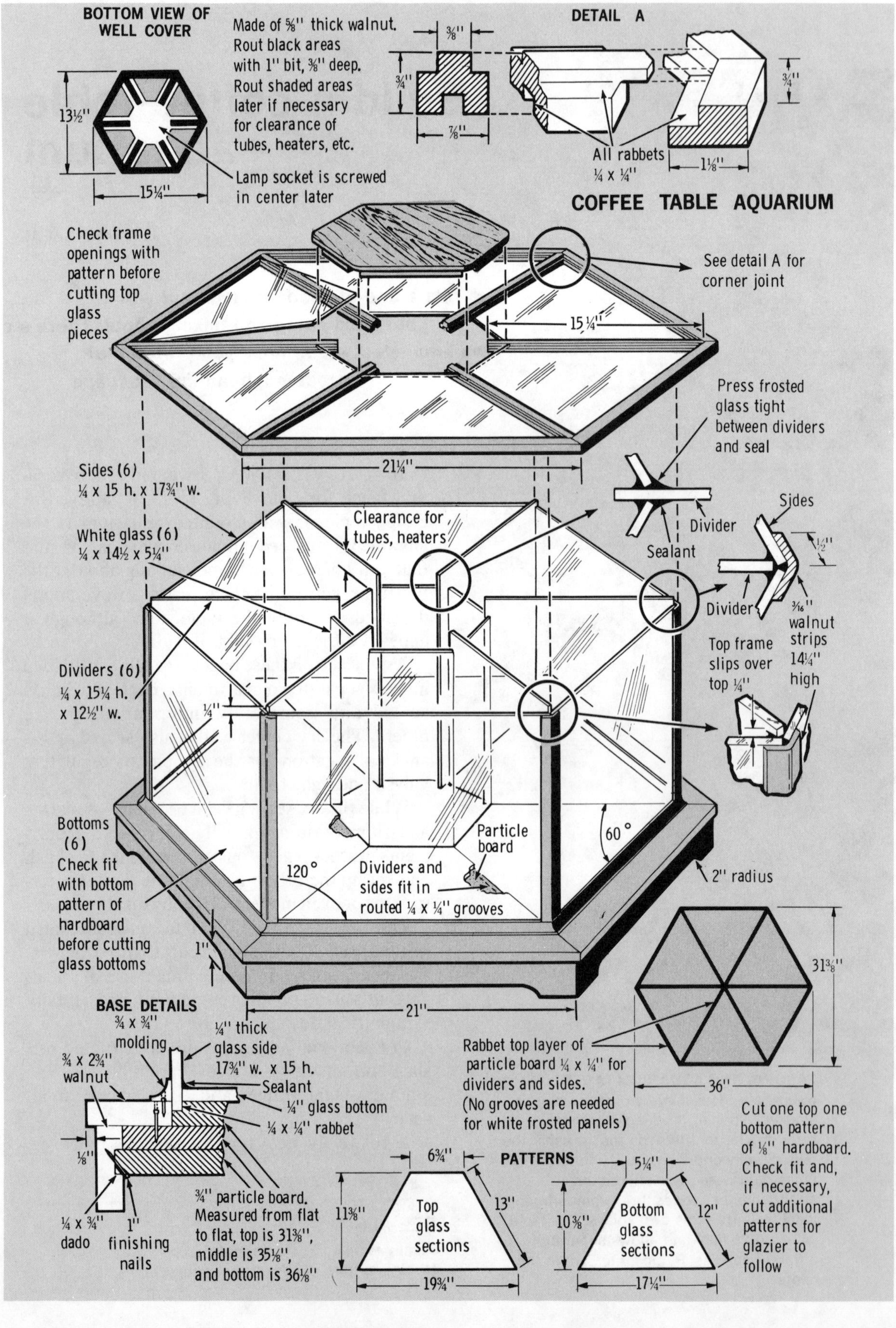
BOTTOM VIEW OF WELL COVER
Made of ⅝'' thick walnut. Rout black areas with 1'' bit, ⅜'' deep. Rout shaded areas later if necessary for clearance of tubes, heaters, etc.
13½''
15¼''
Lamp socket is screwed in center later
DETAIL A
⅜''
¾''
⅞''
All rabbets ¼ x ¼''
1⅛''
¾''
COFFEE TABLE AQUARIUM
Check frame openings with pattern before cutting top glass pieces
See detail A for corner joint
15¼''
Press frosted glass tight between dividers and seal
21¼''
Sides (6) ¼ x 15 h. x 17¾'' w.
Divider
Sealant
Sides
½''
Clearance for tubes, heaters
White glass (6) ¼ x 14½ x 5¼''
Divider
3/16'' walnut strips 14¼'' high
Top frame slips over top ¼''
Dividers (6) ¼ x 15¼ h. x 12½'' w.
¼''
Bottoms (6) Check fit with bottom pattern of hardboard before cutting glass bottoms
Particle board
60°
120°
Dividers and sides fit in routed ¼ x ¼'' grooves
2'' radius
1''
31⅜''
21''
36''
BASE DETAILS
¾ x ¾'' molding
¼'' thick glass side 17¾'' w. x 15 h.
¾ x 2¾'' walnut
Sealant
¼'' glass bottom
¼ x ¼'' rabbet
⅛''
¼ x ¾'' dado
1'' finishing nails
¾'' particle board. Measured from flat to flat, top is 31⅜'', middle is 35⅛'', and bottom is 36⅛''
Rabbet top layer of particle board ¼ x ¼'' for dividers and sides. (No grooves are needed for white frosted panels)
Cut one top one bottom pattern of ⅛'' hardboard. Check fit and, if necessary, cut additional patterns for glazier to follow
PATTERNS
6¾''
11⅜''
13''
Top glass sections
19¾''
5¼''
10⅜''
12''
Bottom glass sections
17¼''

DETAILS OF WELL CONSTRUCTION

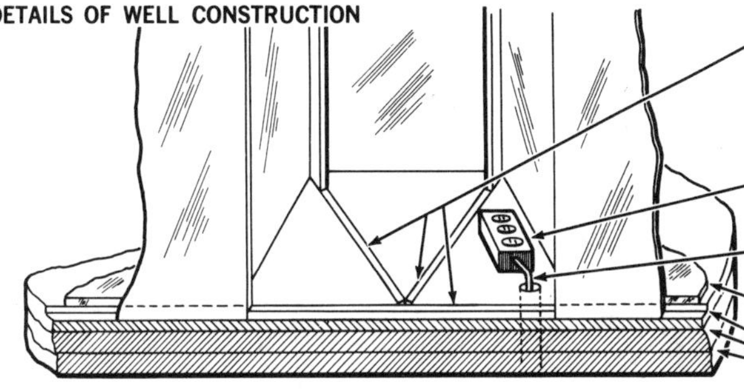


TUBING AND POWER DETAILS

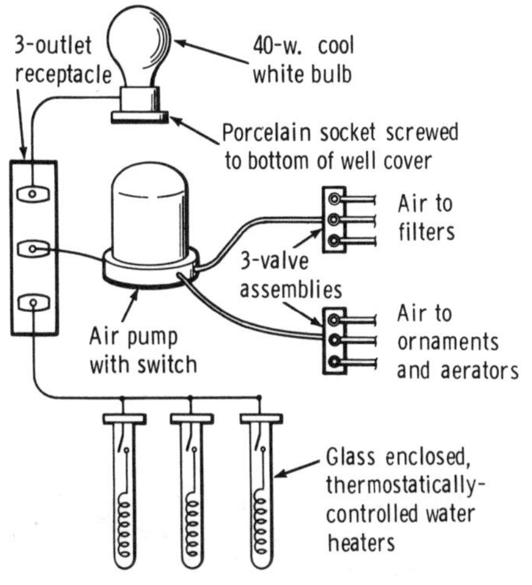


makes it possible to bond glass directly to glass—without the steel frame—to produce strong, clean and leak-proof joints. Made by Dow Corning, the nontoxic sealant is basically a silicone rubber compound available in black, white and clear, and is called, fittingly enough, Silicone Rubber Aquarium Sealant. Because I wanted to de-emphasize the joints, I chose the clear material.

The symmetrical design of the table, however, is what makes the unit relatively easy to construct. For this reason, the six sides, dividers and inner sides of white frosted glass can be cut to their respective sizes at the same time. In theory, all bottom panels should be identical, as should the top pieces, but because woodworking and glass-cutting tolerances can vary quite easily, I strongly recommend cutting these pieces to fit. Other pieces can be off a bit since the design allows you to compensate for marginal errors.

Actual construction of the table will be tackled in three stages. First, you'll assemble the lower half of the base; that is, the bottom two layers of particle board and the lower ring of ¾ x 2¾-in. strips of walnut. Then you'll assemble the tank on the top layer of particle board and attach this to the lower part of the base. Finally, after testing the tank, you'll add the tabletop frame, glass and well cover.

**detailed construction sequence**

Glue and nail together the pieces for the lower part of the base, then cut the top layer of particle board to size (remember that 60° and 120° angles are used throughout). Rout the ¼ x ¼-in. grooves to the pattern shown (use a circular saw and jig if no router is available).

Fit the dividers and outside glass panels in the grooves and tape them together temporarily. Press a panel of white frosted glass between two dividers, clean the glass around this joint and seal the seams between the white panel and the dividers, *on the inside of the dry well only*. Prop the frosted panels so they will remain tight against the dividers and allow the sealant to dry overnight.

Measure and cut ¼ x ¼-in. wood strips to fill the grooves running inside the well from divider to divider. Then remove the glass sides and place the hardboard pattern for the glass bottom in each section. It should fit each opening within a 1/16-in. margin. If the error is greater than 1/16 in., cut additional patterns for the glazier to follow.

When all bottom glass panels fit properly, remove them one at a time and make certain that glass and board are free of wood chips, drops of sealant, and such. Anything sandwiched between the two can cause the glass to crack later.

Now seal the bottom panels in place, beginning at an outer corner and running a continuous bead of sealant along the divider, frosted panel and the opposite divider. Then run another bead from the inner corners up along the seam of the frosted panel and the divider. Again, it's important to thoroughly clean all areas to be sealed.

Reposition the six outside panels on the

grooved layer of particle board and check the corner joints between the sides and dividers before taping the sides securely in place. Then seal *all inside seams* between dividers, sides and bottoms. The outer seams and corners are sealed *after* the tank is set on the lower part of the base.

Let all sealed joints dry overnight before carefully positioning the tank on the base. Now cut and miter the top footing of ¾ x 2¾-in. walnut so that it fits snugly against the tank and overlaps the lower part of the base the same all around.

Glue and nail one section of the footing in place, then slide the tank away and apply sealant to the bottom outside joint. Slide the tank back up against the nailed section. Now apply sealant to the adjoining bottom seam, position the re-

***continued from previous page***

HOW OPENING IS FRAMED IN WALL

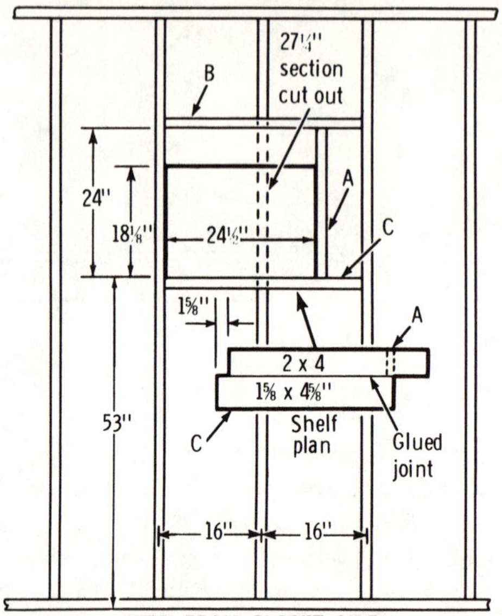


VIEW FROM CLOSET SIDE

**LIVING PICTURE AQUARIUM**

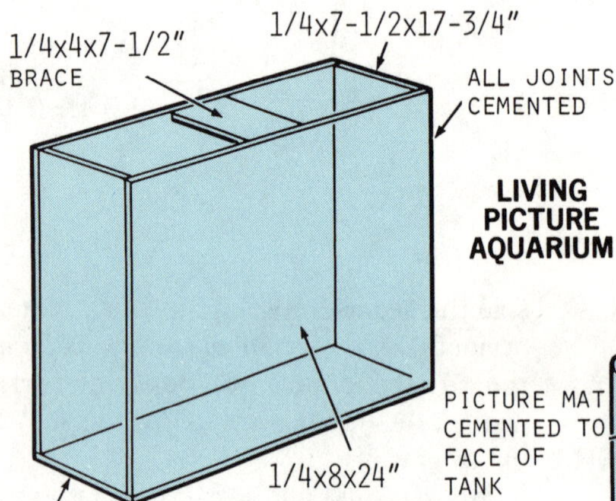


TANK CONSTRUCTION

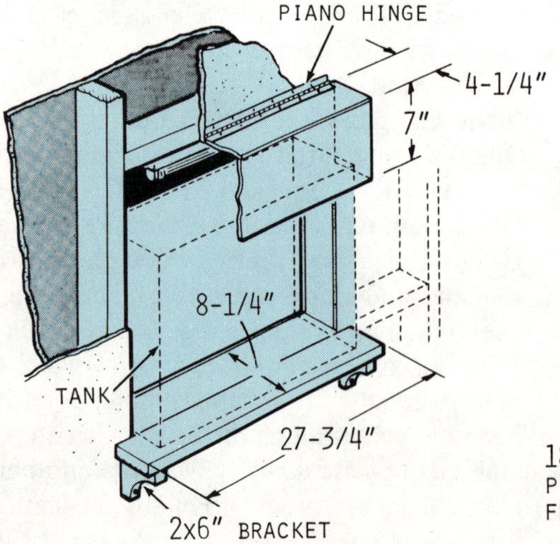


SECTION THROUGH WALL

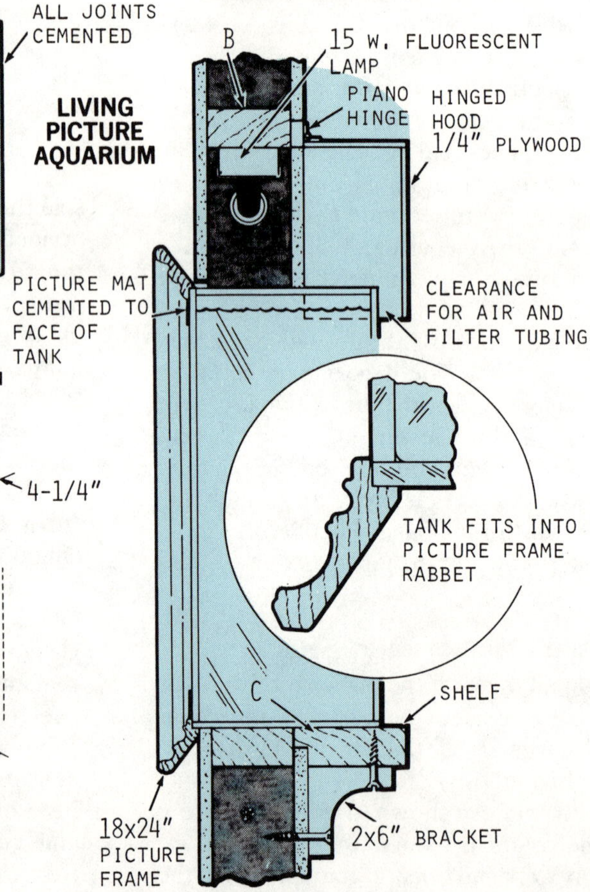

**SPELLBINDING IN-A-WALL TANK** creates a beautiful live seascape to decorate your home and delight your guests. The tank sits on a shelf in a wall opening and is framed by regular picture molding. Made of Plexiglas, the tank has a capacity of 10 gal., and accommodates 12 fish. It requires access from the rear, but the idea also could be used for a see-through room divider or a handsome bookcase.

spective section of footing and nail this in place. Continue in this manner until all six sides are surrounded by the footing and then add the decorative curved molding to the footing.

Now remove the tape from the sides (one section at a time), fill the outside corner with sealant, add a little extra and press on the strip of matching walnut molding. Then firmly tape the strip tightly against the corner.

Remove the tape from the next corner joint, seal the outside seams, press on the walnut strip and retape. When all strips have been applied, wrap two or three turns of tape around the entire tank and let it dry undisturbed at least 24 hours.

You'll no doubt be in a hurry to fill the tank with water, but wait the full 24 hours and then move the tank to a flat spot, such as a patio or garage, where a drain and hose are available. Slowly fill each section of the tank with 4 to 6 inches of water, adding only an inch or so to each section before going on to the next section. This procedure is important as it distributes the pressure evenly among the tank sections.

**guard against leaks**

Turn off the water and examine the tanks for leaks. Mark any that are found with a grease pencil, drain the tank, cut away the sealant around the leak and reseal. Allow this tank to dry thoroughly before refilling. If you were careful with the initial sealing, however, you won't find any leaks. Just remember that the trick is to press a *continuous, unbroken bead* of sealant from corner to corner.

After this initial test, continue to add more water until the tanks are filled to within an inch of the top. Let the tanks remain under test and prepare the top frame and well cover. Fit these on the table, check the top glass pattern in each opening, and have the top pieces cut by a glazier. You can attach the frame to the dividers with sealant, but the top panels simply slip in and out of the frame for easy cleaning and access. Just be sure to dowel the spokes of the top frame to the outer members. An alternative to increase the strength of the frame is to screw metal plates underneath the frame joints.

The pump used in the table is a quiet vibrator model that will easily take care of all six tanks, including ornaments. It's available from Canal Electric, 310 Canal St., New York, N.Y. Heaters, filters and ornaments are available at local aquarium shops.

**"living picture" aquarium**

An entirely different type of sealant is used for this Plexiglas tank. Called MC-25, it's a watery solvent that dries optically clear, yet is strong enough to eliminate the need for a separate metal frame. Thus, if you haven't a suitable wall with a closet at the rear, you can still build such a tank into a see-through room divider, bookcase or even a bar. Just make sure you have access for feeding and cleaning. Industrial Plastics, 324 Canal St., New York, N.Y., supplies the Plexiglas parts for this tank, cut to size, with 2 oz. of MC-25.

**FURNITURE SET** is a two-weekend project. Table and stools are standard and better grade fir. Legs, supports are utility grade.

# Build a coffee table for your patio

By HARRY WICKS

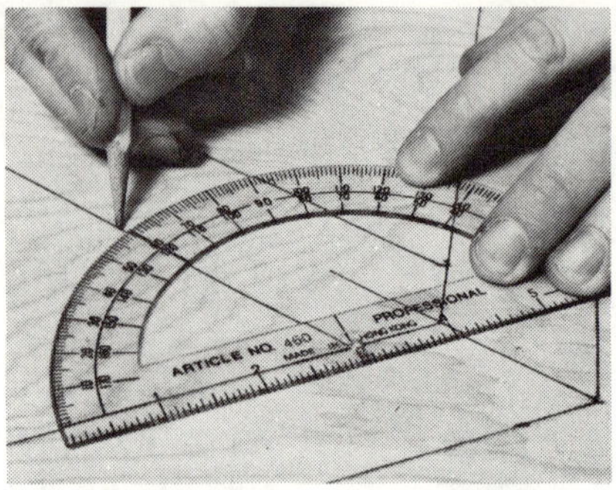


1. **START TABLE** by laying out design on 4 x 4 plywood sheet resting on sawhorses. Use a protractor.

2. **MAKE A** small accurate marking/cutting jig of plywood and a short 2 x 2 strip to speed layout and cutting.

5. **CUT AND FIT** tabletop sections that go between the dividers. Make sure all top pieces are placed best side down.

6. **CUT SUPPORT** pieces and test for a tight fit. Run the longest support at right angles to longest divider.

10. **FASTEN THE STOOL** edges using glue and nails. Repeat the procedure for the remaining stools.

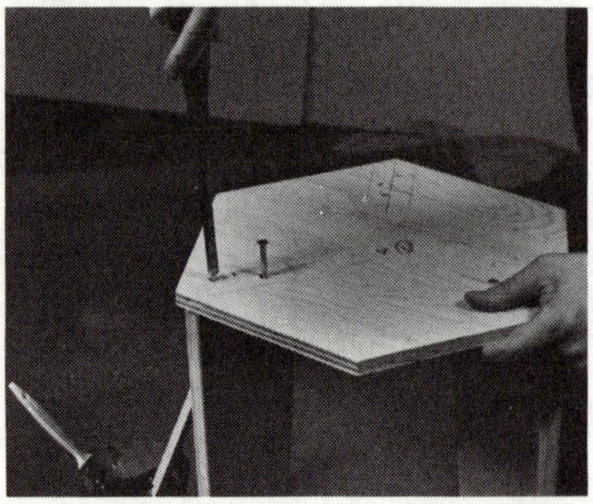

11. **CUT PLYWOOD** seat bottoms and tapered legs, and glue and screw the plywood to legs. Countersink screw heads.

■ YOU'LL ENJOY your patio or deck far more if you outfit it with this attractive coffee table set, developed with the aid of Western Wood Products Assn.

For appearance, we used a standard or better grade of fir on the table and stool tops. To keep costs down, we used utility grade fir for the table and stool legs and other out-of-sight pieces.

Except for the leg braces (J in the drawing, page 818), all angles are 60°. To insure accuracy, use a sharp point on your pencil to mark all cuts and make certain your saw blade is on the waste side of the line when you cut.

To give you a working surface for both drafting and assembly, lay a 4x4-ft. piece of plywood on a pair of sawhorses. Lay out the tabletop outline on the plywood and draw in the parts that form the top. You then can take the dimensions and angles for the various pieces from the drawing on the plywood panel. To facilitate assembly, do it right on the plywood. Install each piece of wood with its best surface down.

Start by cutting the six table edges (A in the illustration) and beveling their ends. Use your combination square to locate the nail holes for both ends and keep nail locations aligned on all edge pieces. Predrill nail holes with a ⅛-in. drill bit, then line up the edge parts on the plywood

**2A. TRIM OFF** corner of jig at 60° and it can be held firmly against workpiece when cutting with saw.

**3. USING PLYWOOD** pattern, cut and miter six table edges. Predrill nail holes and nail table rim pieces together.

**4. CUT AND BEVEL** divider strips to fit. One spans the top; other four meet in middle. Predrill for nails.

**7. MEASURE SUPPORTS** for at least two screws per section. Drill holes and screw supports to dividers.

**8. TO LAY OUT** stools, flop plywood panel and draw pattern for stool top (page 832) on back of plywood panel.

**9. CUT ALL** stool edges to length and bevel. Predrill nail holes before joining edges to form the stool rim.

**12. FLOP LEG** assembly and test fit inside stool rim. If plywood fit is not snug, temporarily toenail in place.

**13. WITH STOOL UPRIGHT,** spread glue on plywood and bottom half of edge pieces, and insert stool top pieces.

**14. GLUE IS** probably sufficient, but for strength drill and nail through each stool side into nearest top piece.

pattern and glue them together to form the table rim. When all parts are joined, countersink all nail heads slightly below the surface.

Next, cut the divider strips (B, C and D) to fit. Notice that one strip spans the entire top, running from one point to the point opposite. The other four strips meet in the middle. Bore pilot holes, and nail and glue at the center and through the outside edge points.

Rough-cut the tabletop sections (K, L, M, N, O) that fit between the dividers. Set the outside piece (K) flush against the table edge and leave a 3/16- to ¼-in. gap between the inner pieces. Number sets by the triangular section of the top

**MATERIALS LIST—PATIO TABLE**

| Key | Pcs. | Size and description (use) |
|---|---|---|
| A | 6 | 1½ × 2½ × 24" (table edge) |
| B,C,D | 5 | 1½ × 1½" × to fit (divider strips) |
| E,F,G | 5 | ¾ × 5½" × to fit (supports) |
| H | 3 | 1½ × 5½ × 27¾" (legs) |
| I | 6 | 1½ × 1½ × 5½" (cleats) |
| J | 3 | 1½ × 1½" × to fit (leg braces) |
| K | 6 | 1½ × 3½ × 20½" (top) |
| L | 6 | 1½ × 3½ × 16" (top) |
| M | 6 | 1½ × 3½ × 12" (top) |
| N | 6 | 1½ × 3½ × 8" (top) |
| O | 6 | 1½ × 3½ × 4" (top) |

**PATIO STOOLS**

| Key | Pcs. | Size and description (use) |
|---|---|---|
| A | 36 | 1½ × 2½ × 9" (edges) |
| B | 6 | ½" plywood cut to fit (seat bottoms) |
| C | 18 | 1½ × 3½ × 14" (legs) |
| D | 18 | 1½ × 1½" × to fit (leg braces) |
| E | 36 | 1½ × 3½ × 7½ approx. (top) |
| F | 36 | 1½ × 3½ × 3" approx. (top) |

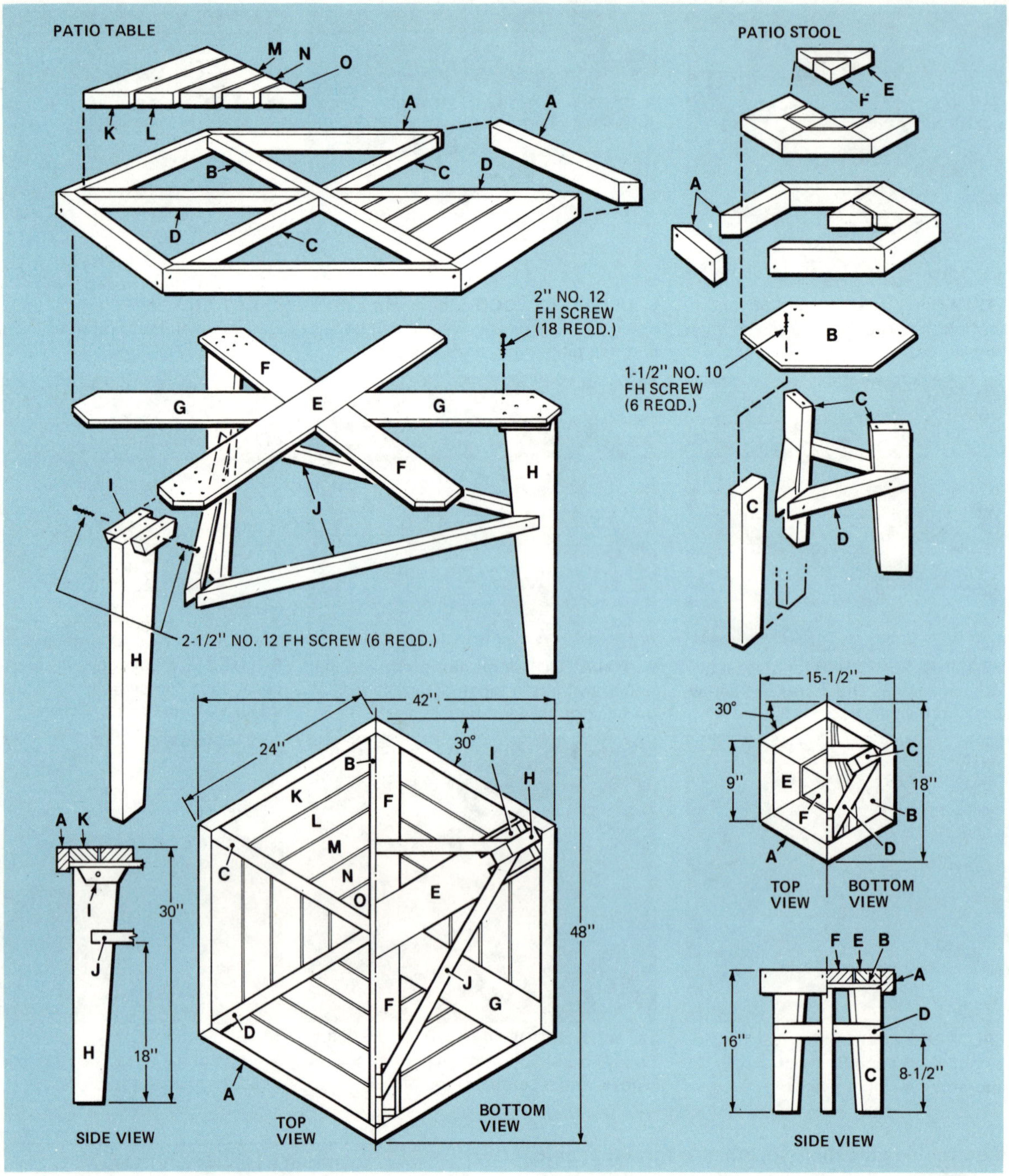


into which they will fit. Mark the tabletop pieces, turn them good side up and miter the ends to fit.

Cut top support pieces (E, F, and G) for a tight fit and position the tapered legs (H) on them. Add the blocks (I). Using at least two screws for each radius section, fasten the supports (E, F and G) to the dividers (B, C and D).

Turn table right side up, spread glue on support pieces and the lower edges of the dividers, and drop all of the mitered tabletop sections (K, L, M, N, O) into place. When top is dry, invert table on sawhorses, trim leg braces (J) to 30° angles, and position them on the legs 18 in. up from the floor. Nail and glue braces to inside edges of the legs.

Flop the piece of plywood and use the back side to draw a pattern for the stool tops. Cut the parts for all six stools at one time. Lightly label each part with a pencil and make up a separate stack for each stool.

Fill all nail holes and defects with a matching wood putty. Give the table and stools a good sanding with a belt sander, dust and finish with two coats of exterior-grade varnish.

**YOU GET A WORM** every time without having to dig when you use a double-ended bait can like that I made from a coffee can. I removed both metal lids and replaced them with plastic lids. Since worms go to the bottom of any container, you just invert the can, remove one plastic lid and pick a worm from the top of the soil.—*Edward J. Kashmer, Osceola, IN.*

**TO RAISE THE SPEED** of my 9-in. metalworking lathe from 1270 rpm (slow for small-diameter work, polishing and wood turning) to 3800 rpm, I added an extra 5-in. V-pulley to motor and jackshaft pulleys. The pulley hubs were machined to fit over the projecting stub shafts, bolted to the face of existing pulleys and fitted with a V-belt cut to fit.—*Carl A. Traub, Milwaukee.*

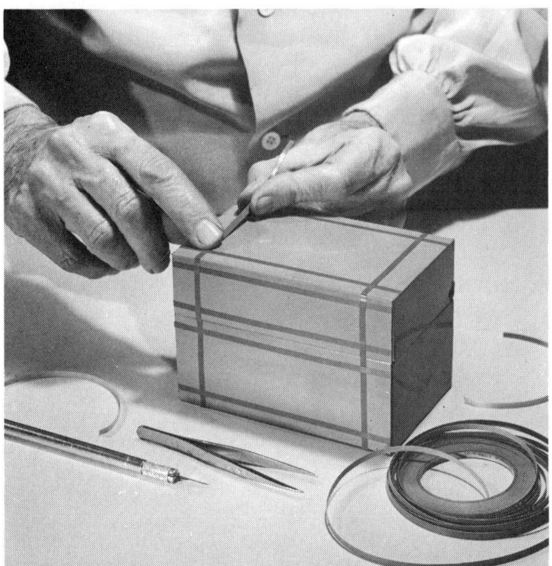

**PIN-STRIPING TAPE,** sold in auto-supply stores, can be used to decorate boxes, picture frames and small objects. The self-adhesive plastic tape is easily applied, can be formed in moderate curves. When a finish is to be used over tape, test its effect first on a scrap.—*Burt Web, Skokie, IL.*

**THE THREADED PORTION** of a bolt, slotted at one end, makes a setscrew for emergency use (it may be less resistant to wear than a hardened one). When sawing the slot, use a scrap of leather to protect threads from vise jaws. Bolt is finally cut to setscrew length.—*Walter E. Burton, Akron, OH.*

**THIS UNIT** is half cold frame, half hotbed. Follow drawings (right) to build either side independently or a custom-sized frame to fit your specific gardening plans

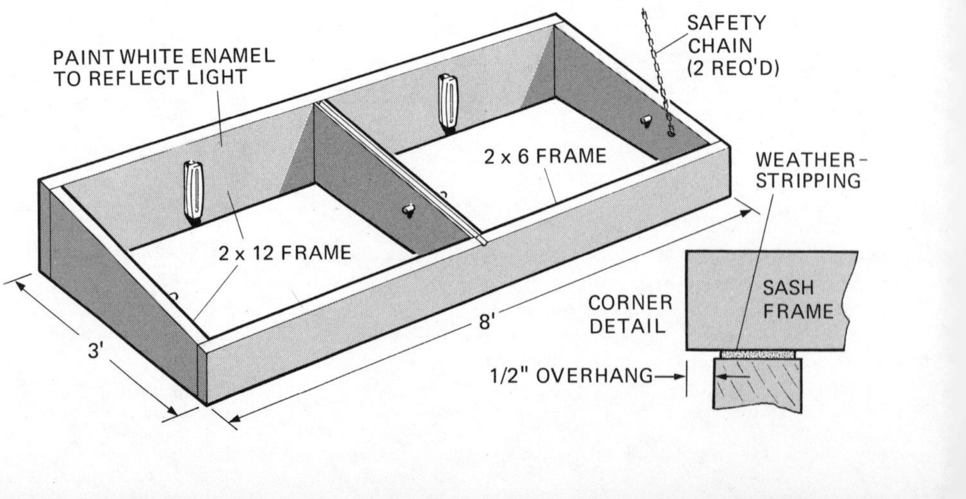

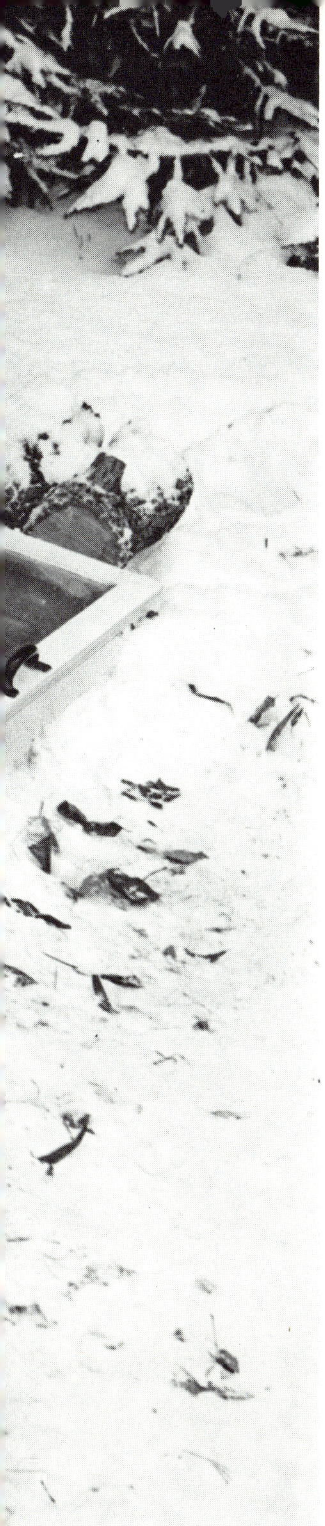

# Get a jump on summer with cold frames

■ THE MOST INEXPERIENCED wood-worker can build a cold frame suitable for the most experienced gardener. And if you like gardening, you'll find that a good cold frame is almost as useful as a small greenhouse, at a fraction of the cost.

The most versatile unit possible is really a combination of cold frame-hotbed. Separate storm sash and a center partition create two different areas. On the left is a cold frame heated by

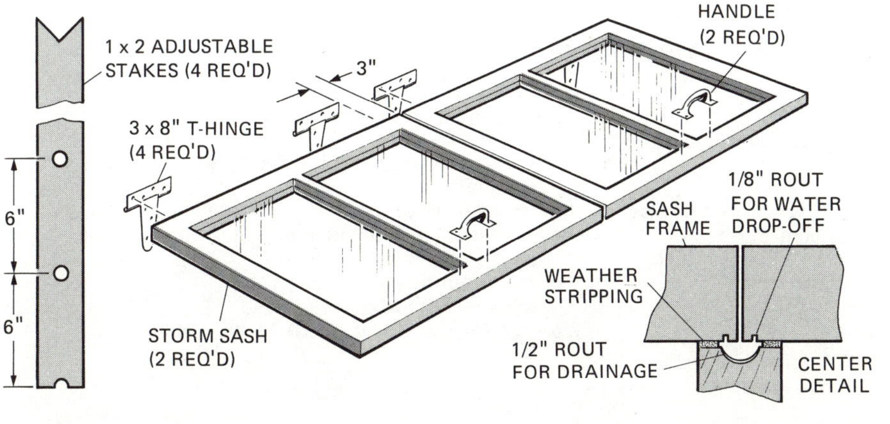

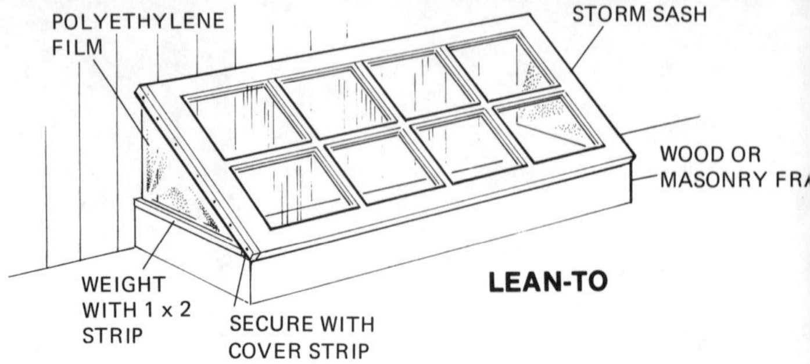


**THIS SIMPLE** cold frame is ideal for the south side of a barn or garage. You can use a wooden or masonry frame at the bottom and plastic sheets along the sides

## ORGANIC HOTBED

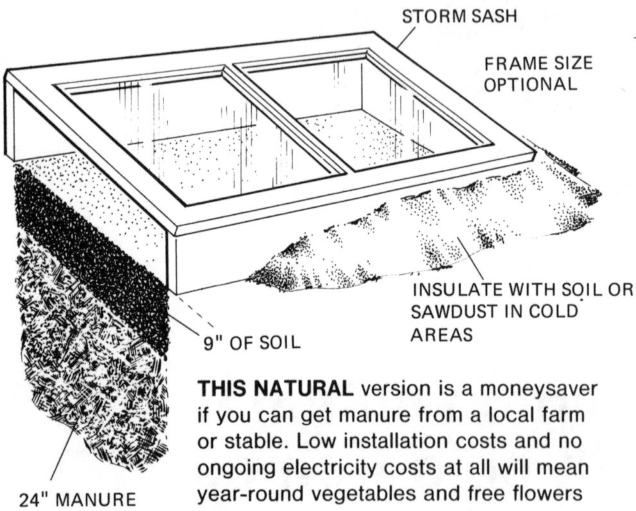


**THIS NATURAL** version is a moneysaver if you can get manure from a local farm or stable. Low installation costs and no ongoing electricity costs at all will mean year-round vegetables and free flowers

## CLEAR FRAME

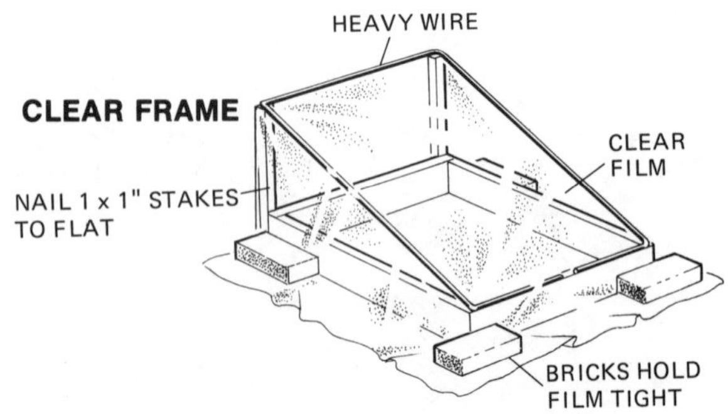


**NO-FRILLS** model here, built with a minimum of time and money invested, will still get you satisfactory results

## ELECTRIC HOTBED

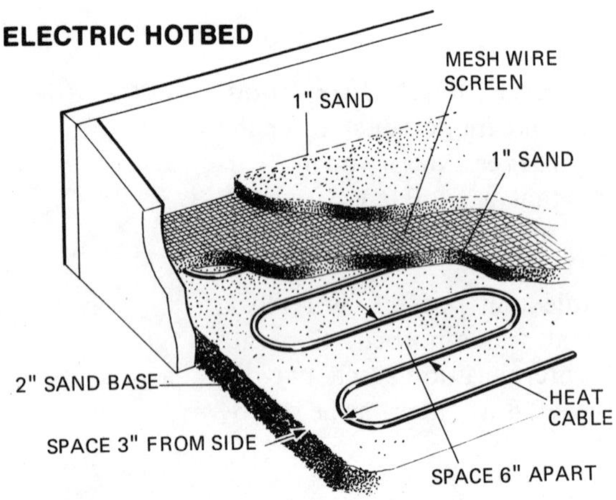


**THIS YEAR-ROUND** frame will do some gardening on its own by automatically controlling temperature level

## RAISED FRAME

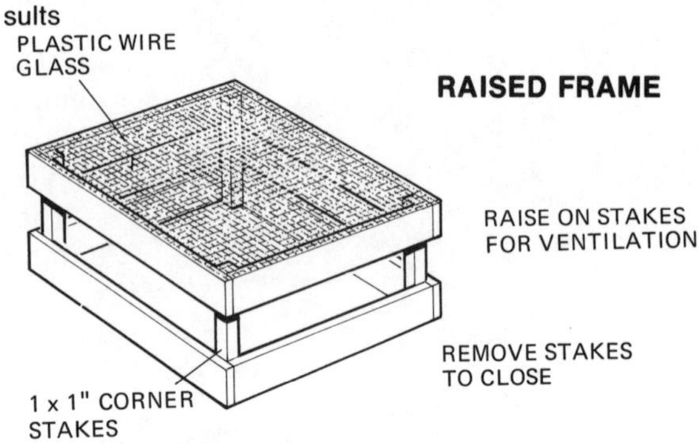


**FOUR CORNER** stakes are used to raise and lower this primitive but functional model. Construction is so simple that it makes a great project for a child

## YEAR-ROUND USES FOR COLD FRAMES

| | |
|---|---|
| **Early spring** | **Hardening-off plants—ease transition for young seedlings from greenhouse to garden.** |
| **Spring and summer** | **Seed sowing.** |
| | **Early start for hardy and half-hardy annuals and perennials.** |
| **Late spring and summer** | **Use sand or peat moss for propagation of cuttings.** |
| **Autumn** | **Seed sowing for dormant winter until early-spring germination.** |
| **Winter** | **Protection for newly started perennials.** |
| | **Growing tender bulbs.** |
| | **Storage for bulbs and plants to be forced.** |

**VINYL DOME KIT ASSEMBLY**

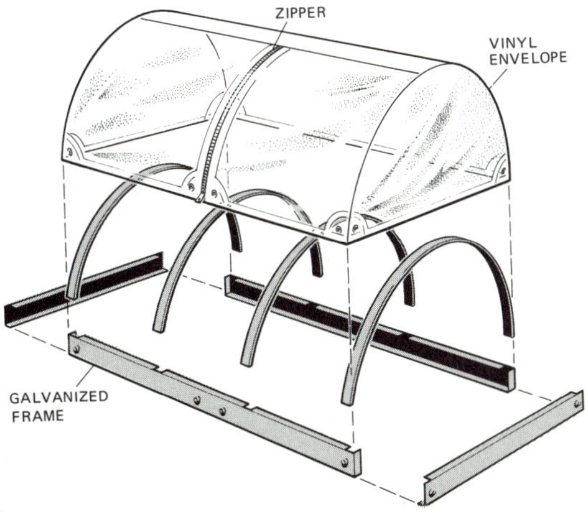

Spring will arrive early at your house with this growth dome from Arrow Industries, 100 Alexander Ave., Pompton Plains, NJ. It provides 12 sq. ft. of heated space under a zippered vinyl envelope. The light-weight galvanized steel frame can be set up in 15 minutes and add 60 days to your growing season. The cost is about $17

**COLD FRAME VARIATIONS**

**TYPES**

**Wooden frame and sash**
**Masonry frame and sash**
**Wooden frame and plastic cover**
**Organic hotbed and conventional frame**
**Electric cable hotbed and conventional frame**
**Kits, growing dome**
**Lean-tos, wooden sash and frame**

**ACCESSORIES**

**Thermometer**
**Electric-heat cable element**
**Lath (snow fencing) for summer sash**
**Safety chains**

the sun's rays. On the right is a year-round hotbed with an auxiliary heat supply. Most garden supply centers sell heat cable in different lengths that can be snaked over a two-inch sand base. The wire has a built-in sensing switch that automatically calls for heat if the in-frame temperature falls below 74°. You can build either side of this frame as an independent unit, or build the double sash size as all cold frame or all hotbed.

**a lot for a little**

Keep construction simple and efficient. Depending on how enterprising you are, you can use scrap wood and used storm sash to help keep the price tag for the complete setup below $100 and as low as $50. A cold frame is simply a slant-sided box with a transparent, hinged lid. Take a total dimension for the storm sash and make the frame ½ in. smaller on all four sides. This gives you a nice overhang to keep rainwater from dripping inside the frame. It also gives you a margin for error. If you're not an experienced woodworker, don't worry; you're not building a finished cabinet and a little enamel paint will make this unit look pretty good. Most garden books recommend cypress or redwood. But you can save some money with fir or any scrap wood on hand. Soak it well with two coats of a preservative like Woodlife and finish with two coats of exterior white enamel. Here are some tips for a successful installation:

- Locate with sash facing south.
- Provide a windbreak on north side.
- Make sure site is well drained.
- Install a thermometer.
- Maintain a temperature range of 40° to 100° F. (85° optimum).
- Keep airtight; use weatherstrip.
- Prevent sash blow-over with safety chains.

We've outlined different cold frames you can build down to the simplest and most temporary varieties. You can even dig a hole and spread plastic across the top secured with a few rocks.

**365 days of summer**

You'll get your investment back from the extra harvest of vegetables and flowers you can start ahead of schedule with a cold frame. Check the seasonal chart for year-round advantages of hotbeds. With either organic or electric versions you can have fresh chrysanthemums on a Thanksgiving table or a centerpiece of poinsettias for Christmas morning. The next stop in year-round gardening is a greenhouse.

# Colonial comb box

By DON SHINER

■ A DECORATOR-INSPIRED piece for homes furnished in early American, this handsome comb box is ideal for a colonial kitchen, hall, bedroom or foyer.

Maple, pine, cherry or birch can be used to make the box and the frame for the mirror. The unit shown, however, is made of golden sumac, which, with its unusual grain, makes it appear centuries old.

The drawing below contains all the information necessary to complete the box. Just be certain to cut both of the scalloped sides identically by using a suitable pattern or template of hardboard or heavy paper to transfer the outline to the wood.

You can use glue, brads and glue, or dowels and glue to join the parts. The latter appears most authentic.

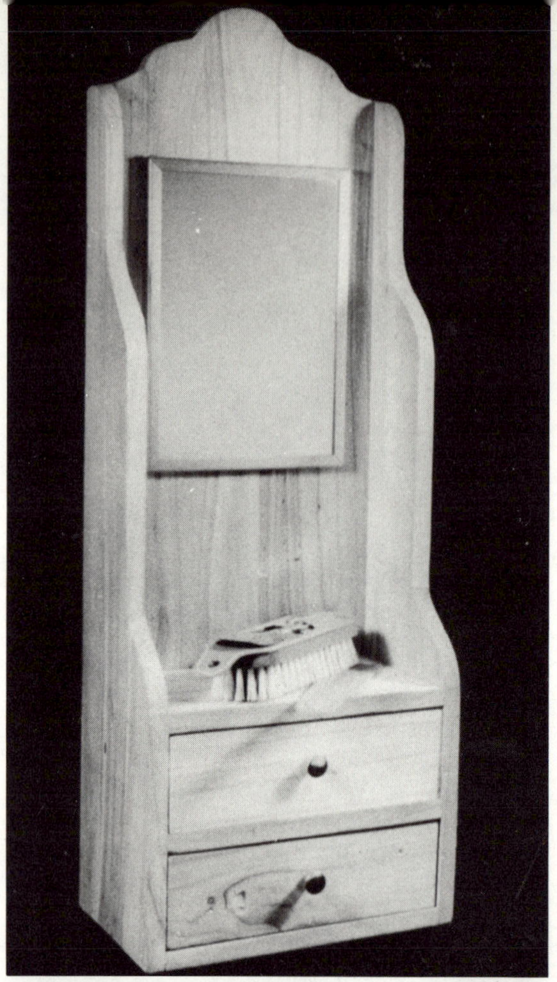

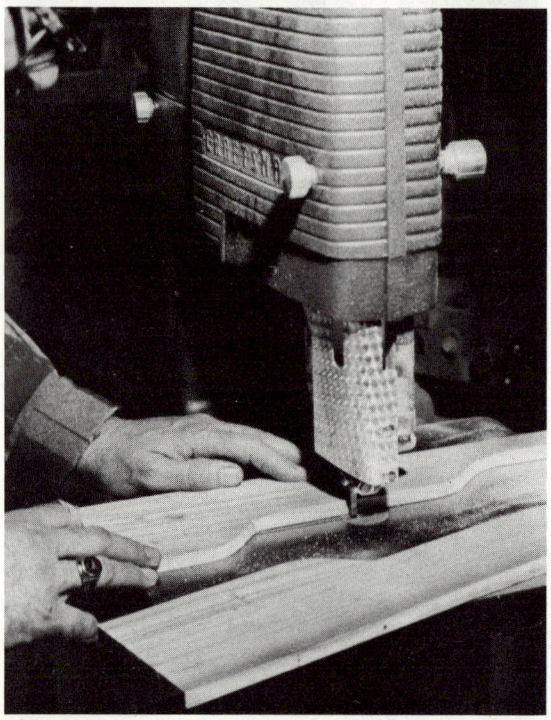

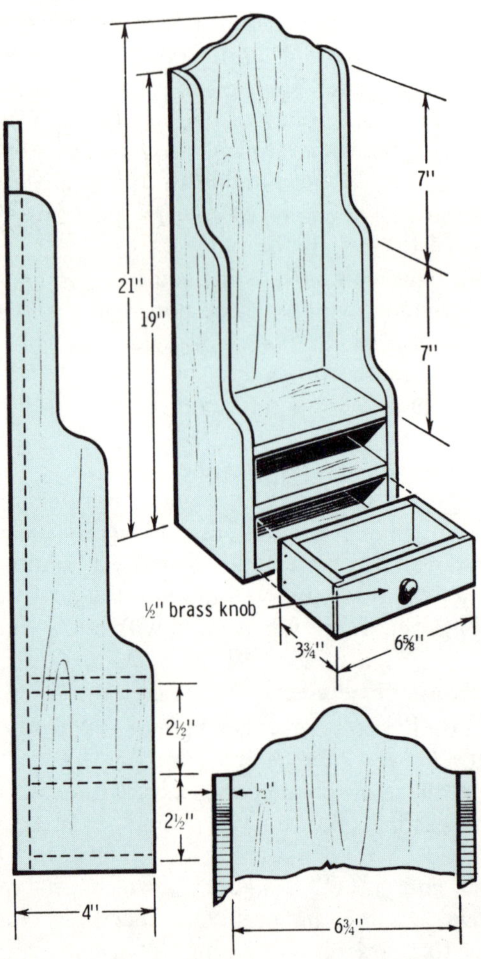


**TRANSFER THE CUTTING** outline to the wood stock, then cut out both sides on either a bandsaw or a jigsaw.

SEE ALSO

**Bandsaws . . . Candle stands . . . Clocks . . . Cupboards, china . . . Dry sinks . . . Gossip benches . . . Pier sets . . . Servers . . . Shaving cabinets**

# Using a combination square

By HARRY WICKS

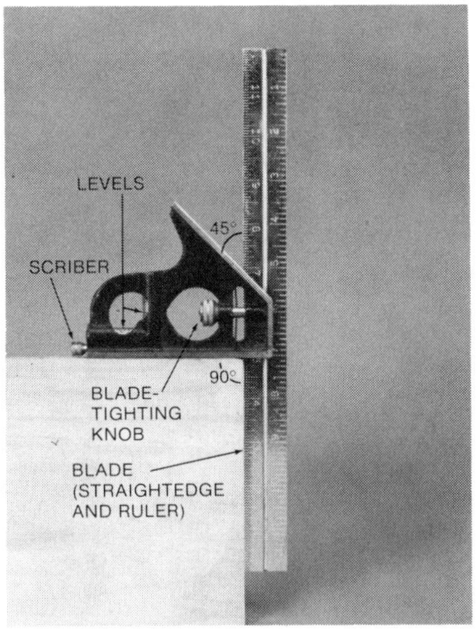


Though a number of special-purpose squares are now available, the combination type is the first you should buy for your toolbox. In fact, because of its versatility, it may even be the only square you'll ever need. Besides giving you instant ability to produce perfectly square 90° angles, as you would with a try square, a combination square will let you:

■ Create 45° angles (see photo below) by butting its 45° shoulder against the workpiece.

■ Use its blade as a ruler or metal straightedge (when making critical cuts with a utility knife).

**VERSATILE combination square performs many functions, including the marking of a miter cut.**

■ Mark accurately because the blade is adjustable. To do it, the tightening knob is loosened, and the blade moved to the desired projection and locked there by retightening the knob. The 90° shoulder is then held firmly against the edge of the workpiece and, with a pencil run alongside the blade's outboard end, drawn along the workpiece to mark the desired width.

■ Draw super-accurate marks, using the scriber that comes in the square's handle—instead of a pencil—to produce a same-width line along its entire length. The scriber is held in its pocket by force fit and is always at hand for such tasks.

**90° SHOULDER is butted against workpiece when a square cut is wanted. Blade is extended to suit board width.**

■ Though I would not recommend using the combination square's spirit levels for checking long work, such as a course of brick, they are useful for quick readings on small jobs. Since the two bubbles are placed at a 90° angle to each other, you can determine accuracy in either a vertical or horizontal plane (plumb and level).

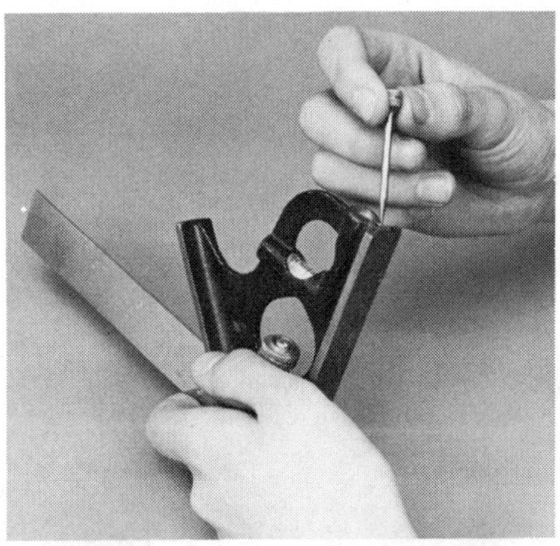

**SCRIBER is neatly tucked into handle. It can be used, along with blade as a guide, to mark accurate lines.**

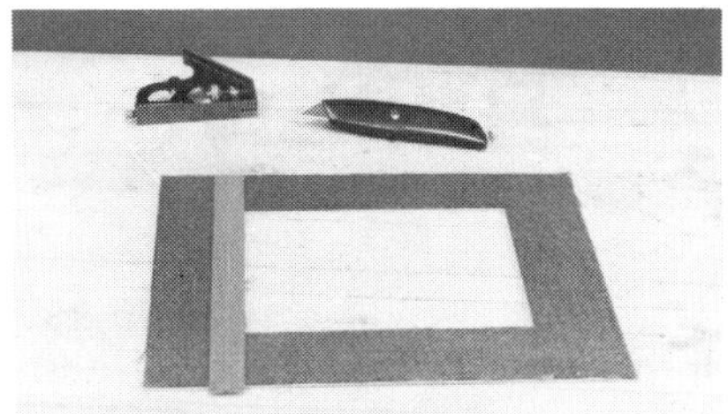

**STILL ANOTHER USE: When removed from the handle, the blade becomes a straightedge for cutting matboard.**

Considering all that the tool can do, the combination square is—for a few bucks—indeed a buy.

The first rule when buying a combination square is to choose only a well-made tool from a reliable manufacturer. Make no mistake about it, there are poorly made versions about—these frequently displayed as leader items with extra-low price tags. Avoid these "bargains"—in the long run you will be glad that you did.

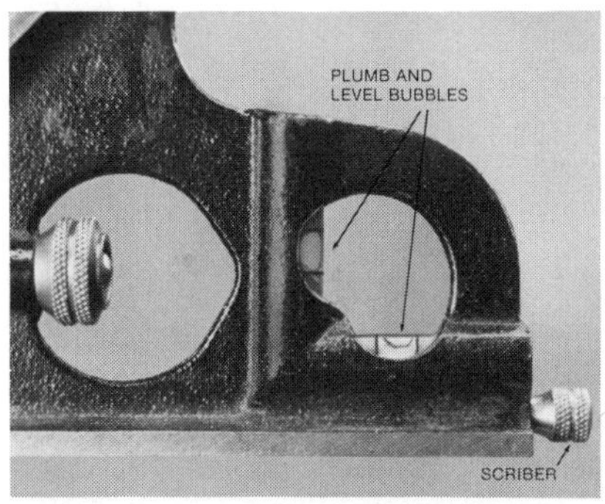


**SPIRIT level bubbles installed at right angle to each other give plumb and level readings for small tasks.**

The combination square needs very little care. Actually, avoiding abusive treatment and minimal cleaning is all that's required. An occasional wiping with a clean, lint-free cloth impregnated with several drops of light machine oil is adequate. If the square has been subjected to excessive amounts of sawdust—such as in a toolbox parked beneath a pair of sawhorses where you've been doing a lot of cutting with a circular saw—remove the blade from the handle and use a compressor to blow dust out of the blade-holding slot. Also, use the cloth to remove any dust accumulations in the blade's groove. Given care, a quality combination square will last for a lifetime.

# Build your own air compressor

**No shop should be without this handy machine. It can be rolled into service to blow, spray and dry. You'll find building one well worth the effort**

**By GARRY SWERDFEGER**

■ AN AIR COMPRESSOR is a practical machine to have in your shop. You can use it often to blow dust off a project you're sanding, as a sprayer and even to speed up the drying time of a finish. Building one is both rewarding and economical.

The compressor shown has an automatic on-off switch set for specified limits, a pressure gauge graduated from 0-160 pounds per square inch (p.s.i.), a check valve to stop air leaking from the tank back through the pump and, for safety, a relief valve set for 100 p.s.i.

SEE ALSO
**Finishes, wood . . . Motors, shop . . . Sanding . . . Workshops**

Start by heating and bending the tank's two front "feet." After drilling holes for the axle, cut axle and install front-wheel assembly as shown. Make and assemble the back caster section.

Bend the conduit for the handle and flatten each end as shown. After drilling the holes in each end, hold the handle at a 45° angle to the mounting stand atop the tank, mark hole locations, drill holes in stand and bolt handle in place.

Next, mount the pump on the stand (with pulley on the right-hand side) using four 5/16 x 3/4-in. bolts. The pulley should clear the side of the stand by about 1 in. and should be about 1/4 in. from the front of the stand. Check the oil level; if necessary, add or change oil (SAE 10).

Remove the adapting flange from the pump inlet, being careful not to damage the gasket. Drill the inlet hole larger and tap it so the air

**HOMEBUILT COMPRESSOR** can be used in the shop or rolled outside. Tank is 10 in. in diameter, 21 in. long.

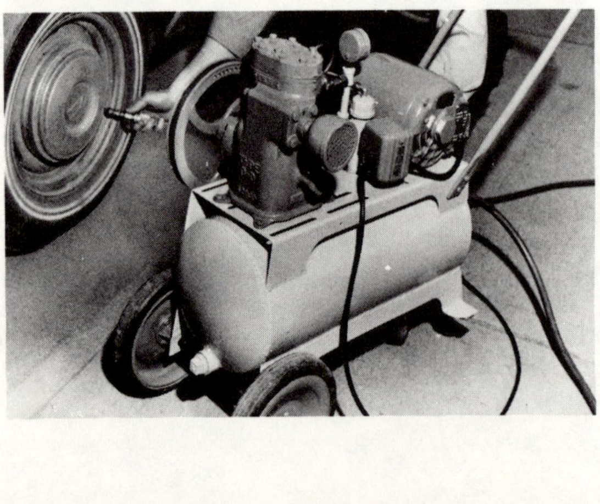

**POWERED BY** a 1/2-hp, 1725-rpm motor, the compressor shuts off automatically when pressure reaches 85 p.s.i.

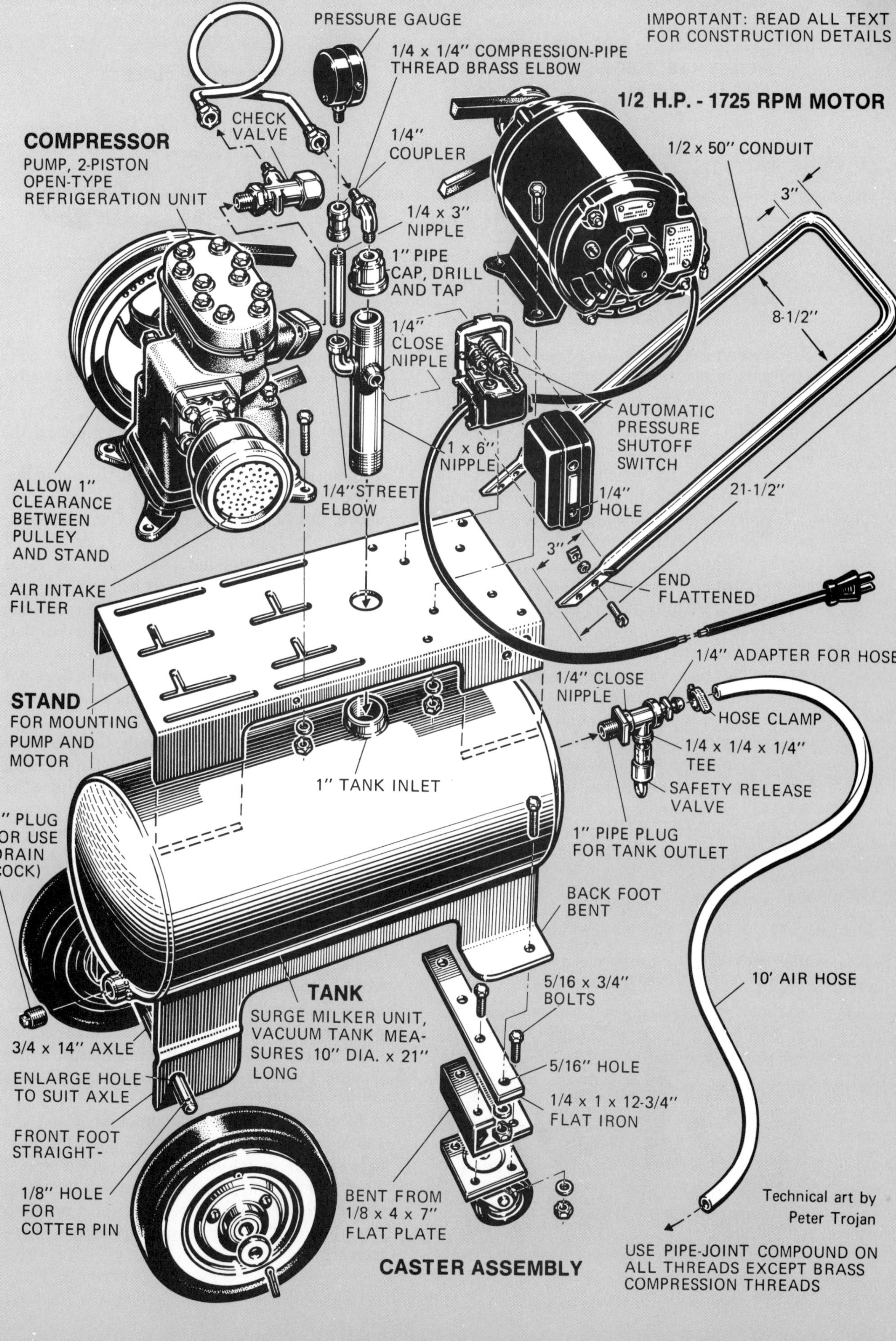


Technical art by
Peter Trojan

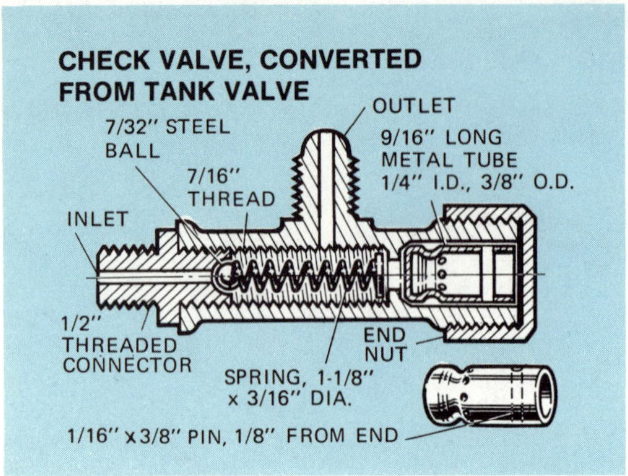


**CHECK VALVE** is made by converting the tank valve from a refrigeration unit. The ball *must* be properly seated.

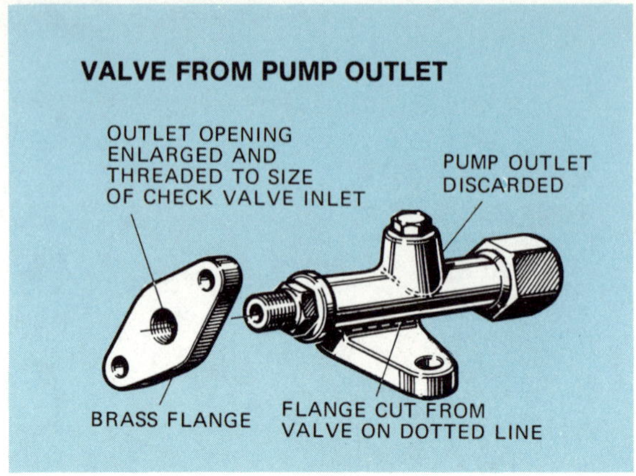


**BRASS VALVE** is removed from the pump outlet; hole is enlarged and tapped to suit connector in end of tank.

intake filter can be threaded into it as shown. If filtering material is not clean, replace it with coarse steel wool. Rebolt adapting flange to pump and thread the air intake filter in position.

Taking care to avoid damaging its gasket, remove the brass valve from the pump outlet and cut the mounting flange from the valve. Drill the center hole larger and tap to the size of the connector threaded into the end of the tank valve. Rebolt the flange to the pump.

Now remove the threaded connector from the front of the tank valve, and the nut from the back. Take out the stem and packing. Solder the hole in the end of the nut (through which the stem extended) closed. Drill at least two ⅛-in. holes $^{3}/_{16}$ in. from one end of the ⅜-in. o.d. metal tube. Cut or file a groove around the tube at these holes to assure ample space for air to pass. Drill two holes, insert the pin from the other end of the tube and rivet the extended ends. This pin will

**ADAPTING FLANGE** on pump inlet is modified and the hole is drilled and tapped to receive air-intake filter.

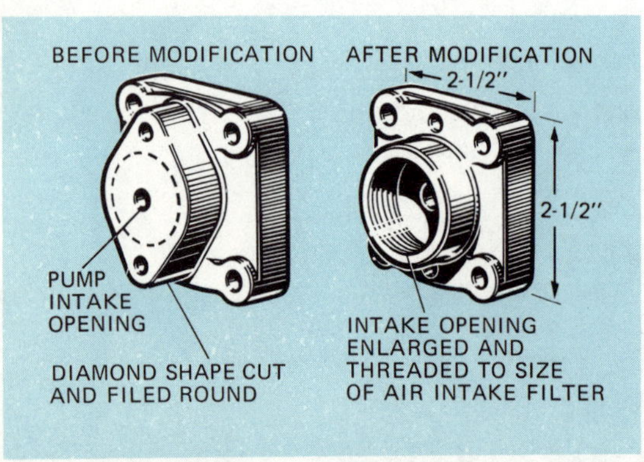


prevent the spring from slipping through the back of the tube.

Using a $^{7}/_{32}$-in. steel ball and fine grinding compound, reseat the end of the connector which threads into the valve. Once finished, thoroughly clean the parts to assure removal of the grinding compound. Assemble the valve using the second $^{7}/_{32}$-in. steel ball.

To test the valve, blow into the inlet and then into the outlet. If air leaks back through the inlet, the ball is improperly seated or the spring is too weak. Check the seat first—the spring does not have to be strong—and thread the valve into the pump.

Install the 1x6-in. nipple into the threaded inlet on top of the tank. Although this will have to be removed, it is *important* to thread the nipple the same number of turns it will be when permanently installed. The pressure gauge and automatic shutoff switch will be connected to this nipple.

Mark the position of this switch on the left-hand side of the nipple, 4 in. from the bottom and with at least 1 in. clearance between switch and motor. Mark position of the gauge connection on front of the nipple, 4 in. from the bottom. Remove the nipple, then drill and tap it for ¼-in. pipe thread. Also drill and tap a hole in the center of the 1-in. pipe cap the same size. Be sure to use pipe-joint compound on all threads except brass compression threads.

After wiping on joint compound, insert the 1x6-in. nipple in the tank inlet. Connect the pressure shutoff switch using a ¼-in. close nipple. Then connect the gauge by threading the street elbow into the tapped hole, a ¼ x 3-in. nipple into the elbow, followed by a ¼-in. coupler and the gauge.

Now thread the 1-in. pipe cap on the top of the 1x6-in. nipple and install the ¼-in. pipe thread x ¼-in. tube compression elbow (compression end of this fitting points to the right-hand side of the tank).

Next, drill and tap a ¼-in. hole centered in a 1-in. pipe plug and install plug in the outlet in the back of the tank. Into this, thread a ¼-in. close nipple, then a ¼ x ¼ x ¼-in. tee. Turn the safety-release valve into the tee outlet pointing downward and turn adapter for the air hose into the tee leg pointing up. Attach hose with a small hose clamp and connect the quick-change coupler to the other end.

**plug the outlet**

The outlet in the front of the tank must be plugged—insert a 1-in. pipe plug or, if you prefer, a drain cock.

Put two ¼-in. flared compression nuts on the 18-in. copper tube, flaring each end of the tube. Attach one end to the check-valve outlet and bend tube into a coil as shown in the photos. (The coil's purpose is to keep the pipe from breaking due to vibration.)

Bolt the motor to the stand about 1 in. behind the pipe in the tank inlet. Carefully align motor pulley with that on the pump. This should allow clearance between the motor and the handle on the compressor so that you can move the motor to tighten the V-belt if necessary.

Wire the switch to the motor and turn it on to see if the motor is turning in the right direction to drive the pump. If not, switch the polarity of the motor windings to reverse the rotation. Put on the V-belt and your compressor is ready for a trial run.

Switch it on and watch the pressure build up. Check all fittings and connections for air leaks. Since you don't know at what pressure the switch will turn off the unit, keep your eye on the gauge. If it does not shut off automatically before pressure reaches 83-85 p.s.i., turn the power off. The safety-relief valve is set for 100 p.s.i., but you should allow for a few pounds pressure between this point and that at which the compressor will stop automatically.

You can now set the switch, increasing or decreasing the pressure to the point where you want the compressor to stop. To increase the pressure, put more tension on the large spring by turning the adjusting nut to the right. To decrease pressure, just turn the nut to the left.

When the switch has been adjusted to stop the compressor automatically at the desired pressure, allow the compressor to build up pressure and stop by itself. Now, slowly let air out of the tank to see at what pressure the unit will restart. The starting mechanism for the switch is controlled by the smaller spring and works on a 1 p.s.i. differential. This, too, can be adjusted by changing tension on the small spring.

Select your accessories and thread them into quick-change adapters. They'll be ready to attach to the quick-change coupler on the air hose.

**MATERIALS LIST—AIR COMPRESSOR**

**Purchased parts**

| Amt. | Description |
|---|---|
| 1 | Refrigeration unit—two-piston, open-type pump (Source: Princess Auto & Machinery Ltd., 600 Panet Rd., Box 1005, Winnepeg 1, Man.) |
| 1 | Surge milker unit vacuum tank, air-intake filter |
| 1 | 1 x 6" galvanized nipple |
| 2 | 1" galvanized plugs |
| 1 | 1" galvanized cap |
| 2 | ¼" galvanized close nipples |
| 1 | ¼ x 3" galvanized nipple |
| 1 | ¼" galvanized street elbow |
| 1 | ¼" galvanized tee |
| 1 | ¼" galvanized coupling |
| 1 | ¼ x 18" copper tubing |
| 1 | ¼" pipe thread x ¼" compression elbow |
| 1 | ¼ x ¼" adapter, pipe to air hose |
| 10' | ¼" air hose |
| 1 | Hose clamp (small) |
| 1 | Quick-change coupler (for coupling accessories to air hose) |
| 1 | Air-line coupling (for connecting quick-change coupler to air hose) |
| 2 | Quick-change coupler adapters (accessories to quick-change coupler) |
| 1 | 0-160 p.s.i. pressure gauge, ¼" threaded |
| 1 | Safety relief valve, ¼" threaded (factory set for 100 p.s.i.) |
| 1 | Automatic shutoff switch (adjustable type used on water-pressure systems, purchased used from pump-repair shop) |
| 1 | V-belt |
| 1 | 3 x ⅝" bore V-pulley |
| 1 | 1725 rpm, ½-hp electric motor, ⅝" shaft |
| | **Salvaged from refrigeration unit** |
| 8 | 5/16 x ¾" bolts |
| 1 | Brass valve from pump outlet |
| 2 | ¼" flared compression nuts (connect copper tubing) |
| 1 | Brass tank valve |
| | **Scrap parts needed to convert tank valve to check valve** |
| 1 | ⅜" o.d. x ¼" i.d. x 9/16" metal tube |
| 1 | 1/16 x 7/16" pin-nial or welding rod |
| 1 | 1⅛ x 3/16" spring |
| 2 | 7/32" steel balls from discarded bearing |
| | **Parts necessary for making compressor portable** |
| 2 | 1.75 x 9½" wheels |
| 1 | 3" caster |
| 1 | ¾ x 14" cold-rolled steel (axle) |
| 2 | ⅛ x 1¼" cotter pins |
| 2 | Flat washers to fit axle |
| 1 | ⅛ x 4 x 7" flat iron |
| 1 | ¼ x 1 x 12¾" flat iron |
| 1 | ½" conduit, length to suit |
| 8 | 5/16 x ¾" bolts, with nuts and lock washers |
| 4 | 3/16 x ¾" stovebolts |

**WHEN THE JOB** calls for a lot of concrete, the ready-mix truck can bring it to your door.

# How to work with concrete

**If you take the time to mix, pour and work concrete by a few simple rules, you can't help but get good results.**

**By LEN HILTS**

■ CONCRETE IS A GOOD MATERIAL for use around your home because it is easy to use, inexpensive, and produces professional-looking results with little difficulty. Use it for walks, driveways, steps, patios, garden borders and similar projects.

To get top-quality results, you need to know a few very basic rules:

1. Do your concrete work when the temperature is between 50 and 80 deg. F. If it is colder than 50, setting and curing time is longer; if it is warmer than 80 to 85 deg., the curing time is too short and you must work hard to slow it down. If you must work during the hotter days, be sure to keep the newly-laid concrete wet and covered for at least five days.

2. Pay strict attention to curing your concrete. Good curing (setting and drying out) takes about 5 days. If the cure is too fast, you may have cracks, weak spots, or other problems.

3. Use only pure water to mix concrete—water that is clean enough to drink. Don't use water containing dirt and don't use sea water. They will affect the setting of the concrete.

4. Mix cement, sand and aggregate with care. Measure each ingredient accurately. This is one time when "a pinch of this and a handful of that" isn't a good way to do the job.

5. Mix everything thoroughly. Mix the dry ingredients before you add the water. Then, after

SEE ALSO
**Asphalt driveways . . . Masonry, painting . . . Paths, garden . . . Patios . . . Retaining walls . . . Steps**

adding the water, mix them thoroughly once more. If the mix isn't thorough, you end up with too much sand in one part and too much cement in another part of the mixture, which makes a slab subject to cracking.

6. Buy good finishing tools, and learn to use them.

**buying concrete**

There are three ways to buy concrete. You can buy the raw ingredients—cement by the sack and sand and gravel by the cubic yard—and mix the concrete yourself. If you are laying much concrete, you'll need to rent a mixer. Hand mixing of concrete in large quantities can be a backbreaking job, and you run the risk of not mixing thoroughly.

The second method is to buy the materials all mixed and ready for the water. It comes by the sack, and each sack contains enough cement, sand and aggregate to make one cubic foot. This is the best way if you are doing a small job such as a short section of sidewalk, a slab for garbage cans, or a step. Jobs of this size can be mixed by hand.

If you are paving a patio slab or a concrete driveway, the easiest way is to order ready-mixed concrete. It is delivered to your home by truck. Before ordering, talk with the ready-mix dealer near you. He'll tell you such things as the minimum amount of concrete you can order, the different types available (air-entrained, for example, for use on surfaces like driveways which are exposed to the weather), the cost per load, and how he can coordinate delivery with your work schedule. He'll also help you estimate the amount of concrete you need. Generally, it's a good idea to order about 10 percent more than you think you need.

**A NOVEL SURFACE** can be obtained by covering fresh concrete with round pebbles. Press these into the concrete before it sets.

**A STIFF BROOM** is a handy cement tool. You can use it to striate the finish to make a non-skid surface, or to expose aggregate.

**estimating your needs**

If yours is a large job, refer to the accompanying table to estimate the amount of concrete you'll need. Concrete is figured in cubic yards. Measure the area you intend to pave and multiply the length by the width to find the number of square feet. Then look in the column under the thickness you intend to use.

Using this chart, you would find that a driveway 25 feet long and 16 feet wide has an area of 400 sq. ft. To pour a slab 6 in. thick, you will need 7.4 cubic yards of concrete.

**formula for mixing**

For most projects around your home for which you mix your own concrete, use a mix consisting of one part Portland cement, 2¼ parts sand, and 3 parts crushed stone ¾ in. in diameter. Common practice calls for 5 gal. of water per sack of cement.

**BEGIN THE FINISHING** by working back and forth across the surface with a long-handled float to level the surface and eliminate irregularities.

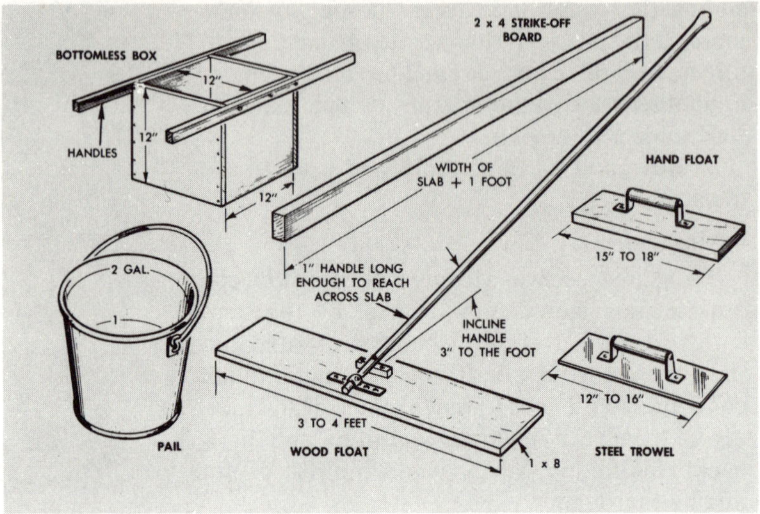


**A COMPLETE SET** of concrete-finishing tools include a bottomless box for measuring, a strike-off board, a long-handled wood float, a smaller hand float, a pail, and a steel trowel. The measuring box is made to hold exactly one cubic foot of material, and the pail should be graduated.

If your pail isn't already graduated, make a measuring pail by filling a pail a quart at a time and marking different water levels on the side. To measure the dry ingredients, make the bottomless box shown in the accompanying drawing, with inside dimensions of 12 x 12 x 12 in.

Measure all ingredients carefully, since the proportions are critical to the mix. A soupy mix, for example, makes a weak concrete. As a general rule, the stiffer the mix, the stronger the concrete.

If you accidentally make your mix too wet, add sand until the mix stiffens.

Keep in mind that when you pour concrete on dry earth or against dry forms, the dry areas suck water from the concrete, causing it to lose moisture rapidly. To avoid this, sprinkle the dry ground and forms lightly with a hose before pouring the concrete.

### making and filling the forms

Concrete is poured into a mold made of boards called a form. For most sidewalks or concrete pads, make the forms of 2x4 lumber. Hold the forms firmly in place by driving stakes into the ground along the outside of the form boards, and nailing the boards to the stakes. The form should be firmly positioned so that it won't move when the weight of the concrete runs against it.

Fill each form completely before moving on to the next one. When the form has been filled, use a strike-off board such as the one shown to level the surface. Make your strike board about a foot longer than the width of the form. To level the newly-poured concrete, saw the strike board back and forth across the form as you work along its length. Fill any low spots after you have completed one pass, then strike the surface a second time.

### finishing the work

When all of the concrete has been poured, begin the finishing operation. First, work a long-handled float such as the one pictured back and forth across the surface to eliminate any irregularities in the surface. For a smaller surface use a smaller float.

After all water has disappeared from the surface and the concrete has begun to harden in its initial set, use a steel trowel to provide the final smooth surface. Press your thumb into the surface and if it just barely makes a dent, the concrete is ready for troweling.

**CUBIC YARDS OF CONCRETE IN SLABS**

| AREA SQ. FT. (LENGTH X WIDTH) | THICKNESS OF SLAB IN INCHES 4" | 5" | 6" | 8" | 12" |
|---|---|---|---|---|---|
| 25 | .31 | .39 | .47 | .60 | .95 CU. YD. |
| 50 | .62 | .77 | .93 | 1.2 | 1.9 CU. YD. |
| 100 | 1.2 | 1.5 | 1.9 | 2.5 | 3.7 CU. YD. |
| 200 | 2.5 | 3.1 | 3.7 | 4.9 | 7.4 CU. YD. |
| 300 | 3.7 | 4.7 | 5.6 | 7.4 | 11.1 CU.YD. |
| 400 | 4.9 | 6.2 | 7.4 | 9.8 | 14.8 CU.YD. |
| 500 | 6.2 | 7.2 | 9.3 | 12.4 | 18.6 CU.YD. |

To trowel properly, sweep the trowel in wide arcs across the work. Finish one section at a time. You'll find that a wood float works as well as steel on plain concrete, but that a steel float is best on air-entrained concrete.

**curing**

Curing is perhaps the most important—and most often neglected—part of the concrete process. During curing, the concrete sets hard, then gradually dries out. It is during curing that the material develops its strength.

To begin the cure, cover the new concrete as soon as you have finished trowling. Use burlap, straw, or a sheet of polyethylene. Spray the burlap or straw lightly, and then spray it regularly for the next five days, keeping it damp at all times. This prevents the moisture in the concrete from escaping too fast, which would produce weak concrete.

Most professionals keep the concrete wet for a minimum of three days in pleasant weather, and a minimum of five days in warm weather. In cooler weather, the natural curing may take as long as 10 days.

If you are working in temperatures of 80 degrees or better, cover the new concrete as soon as you strike it off. Remove small sections of the cover for troweling, but recover each section as soon as it has been troweled. The hot sun will draw water from the concrete very rapidly and cause a weak cure. It is particularly important to keep the cover wet at all times during hot weather—which might mean spraying the cover a number of times a day.

**additional information**

If you pour a driveway or a large patio pad, use welded wire reinforcing, which you can buy from your building supply dealer. For small projects, use a wire mesh with 1x2-in. openings. Fill the form half full, then press the mesh lightly into the concrete, and fill the form the rest of the way.

For larger slabs, use wire reinforcing with a larger mesh. Place the mesh in the forms before beginning to pour the concrete, and support it off the ground with small pieces of scrap lumber. Pour the concrete over it.

When pouring walks, pads, and driveways, and when pouring against a building foundation, keep in mind that concrete expands and contracts when the temperature changes. To eliminate expansion problems, install expansion joints. Plan them for the point where a driveway joins the garage pad, for example, and where it contacts the curbing. Then also put an expansion joint across the width of the driveway every 15 feet or so.

An expansion joint is made by inserting a thick strip of expansion joint material, which you can buy, between sections of the slab. The material compresses as the concrete expands, thus preventing cracking or buckling. It is important to install an expansion strip between the foundation of the house and a new patio pad.

**ANOTHER NOVEL** finish is one made by twisting cans of different sizes into the concrete. Cookie cutters could also be used for this.

**AFTER THE SURFACE** has begun to set, use a stiff bristled broom to roughen or striate it. This makes a non-skid surface, good in wet weather.

# Concrete slabs—pour them yourself

**If you want to put in some time studying the problems and then a fair share of hard work, you can save yourself a bundle and at the same time get a long-lasting professional job**

■ MAKE NO MISTAKE about it, plenty of hard work is involved in pouring concrete yourself. But there is an immediate reward; one you can see in your wallet. For example, recent rates in the New York area for a 4-in. slab, with footings, were about $5.50 per sq. ft. when done by a professional. Do the job yourself and your cost will be closer to $1.50 per sq. ft. But if you don't do the job right, you may have to live with a cracked or heaving slab or drainage problems—that could require breaking up the slab into rubble and starting over. Use the professional

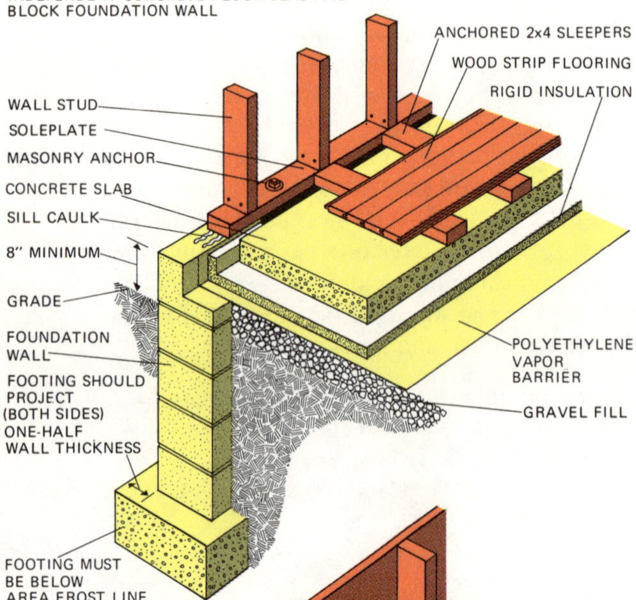

INDEPENDENT CONCRETE FLOOR SLAB AND BLOCK FOUNDATION WALL

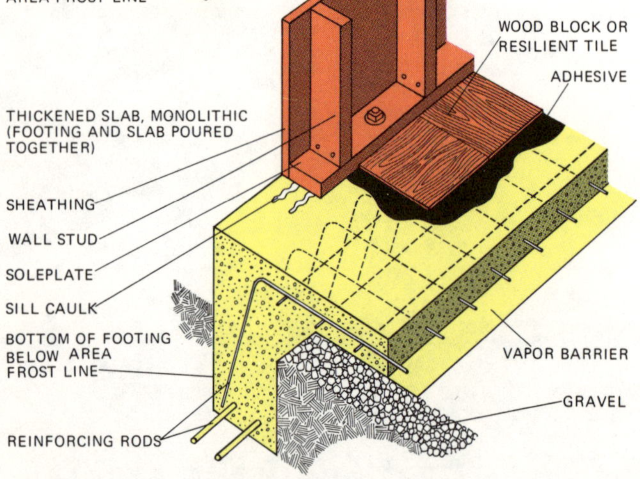

THICKENED SLAB, MONOLITHIC (FOOTING AND SLAB POURED TOGETHER)

**Typical slab construction**

Thickened-edge, monolithic slab-and-footing combinations are recommended for patios, with or without a roof structure or bearing wall above. Independent footings, foundation walls and slabs are the better way when an enclosed structure will be built over the slab; this allows for placing of perimeter insulation and vapor barrier in stages between pours. The bottom of the footing always must be below the area frost line.

Several basic construction rules should be adhered to throughout any job: First, never refill the excavation or trench with dirt if you've dug too deep—pour extra concrete instead. Second, most footings should be a minimum of 12 in. deep, and twice the width of the foundation-wall thickness. For example, for a wall built of 8-in. block, footings should be 16 in. wide, projecting 4 in. to either side of the wall. Third, if the soil is of a low load-bearing capacity, you may find it will be necessary to construct wider and reinforced footings.

"Load bearing capacity" refers to all the weight that will be imposed on each lineal foot of perimeter area (footing area) by the structure above, the live weight it will carry and the snow load on the roof. As all soil has a maximum bearing capacity in tons per sq. ft., it is an important factor in footing design. Imagine standing on a 1-ft.-square piece of plywood on dry beach sand, and then trying the same thing in a marsh—the plywood has to be a lot bigger or you'll sink. Your local building department can provide general information on soil load-bearing capacity in your area. If any question remains about your property in particular, you can have a qualified engineer (P.E.) check it for you.

SEE ALSO
**Asphalt driveways . . . Garden shelters . . . House additions . . . Paths, garden . . . Patios . . . Retaining walls . . . Steps**

know-how on these and the following two pages and your savings will be permanent.

For small jobs you'll find it most economical to buy the sand, aggregate (gravel) and cement and mix them yourself—by hand or with a rented cement mixer. Or you can use a commercially prepared mix sold by the bag. But for the big jobs—a driveway, for example—your best bet is to buy ready-mixed concrete.

The best time to pour is when the temperature is between 40° and 85° F. Cold-weather pouring adds so many complications the homeowner should avoid it. In hot, dry weather, subgrade and forms should be dampened. If it rains on the day you've planned to place concrete, reschedule the job. If you want to color your concrete, use mineral-oxide pigment; it's sold in several colors at most paint and hardware stores. Mix it with sand before combining ingredients. Pigment used should never be more than 10 percent, by weight, of the cement used; otherwise it will weaken the slab. Colored ready-mix concrete is available, but usually only in large quantities.

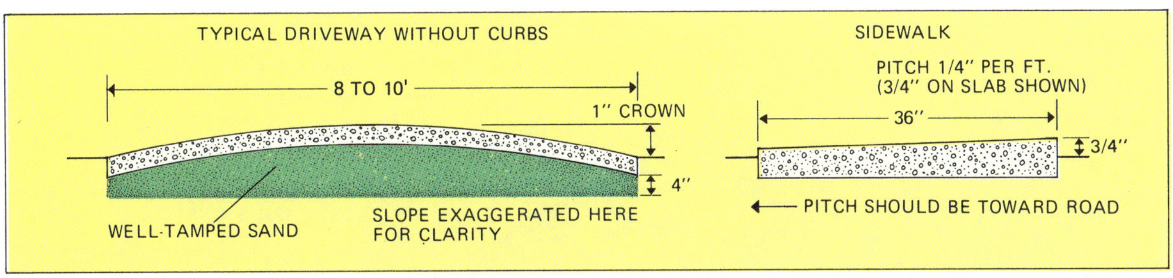


**Typical slabs for driveway and sidewalk**

Each slab shown above is pitched for positive water runoff. A typical driveway (left), 8 to 10 ft. wide, has a 1-in. crown at the center and a pitch of ¼ in. per foot along its length to divert rainwater. A sidewalk from edge to edge is also pitched ¼ in. per foot (right)—its low side should drain toward the street, not onto your property. The driveway slab thickness should be 5 in. minimum. If the driveway is going to be used for heavy loads, you should pour a 6-in. slab and use steel-mesh to act as reinforcing. The typical sidewalk slab would be 4 in. thick.

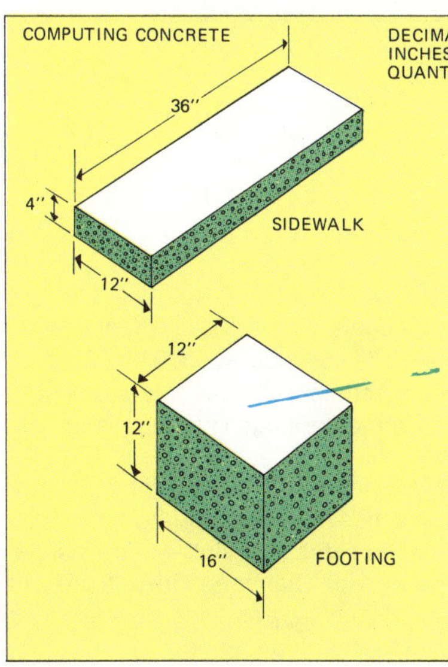


DECIMAL EQUIVALENT OF INCHES (USED TO COMPUTE QUANTITIES)

| | |
|---|---|
| 1" | .08' |
| 2" | .17' |
| 3" | .25' |
| 4" | .33' |
| 5" | .42' |
| 6" | .50' |
| 7" | .58' |
| 8" | .67' |
| 9" | .75' |
| 10" | .83' |
| 11" | .92' |
| 12" | 1.00' |

**Computing quantities**

Ready-mix concrete is sold by the cubic yard; 1 cu. yd. is usually the minimum order. To compute the amount you will need, you must find the cubic footage of the slab to be poured, then convert this figure to cubic yards. Multiply length by width by thickness in feet, then divide by 27. Decimal equivalents of inches make the calculation easier.

Sidewalk slab, 4 x 12 x 36 in.:

$$\frac{0.33 \times 1 \times 3}{27} = 0.037 \text{ cu. yd.}$$

Section of footing, 12 x 12 x 16 in.

$$\frac{1 \times 1 \times 1.33}{27} = 0.049 \text{ cu. yd.}$$

Thus, if your run (lineal footage) of this footing were 20 ft., you would need about 1 cu. yd. of concrete.

It is good practice to add about 5 percent for waste to your estimate—roughly, 1 cu. yd for each 20.

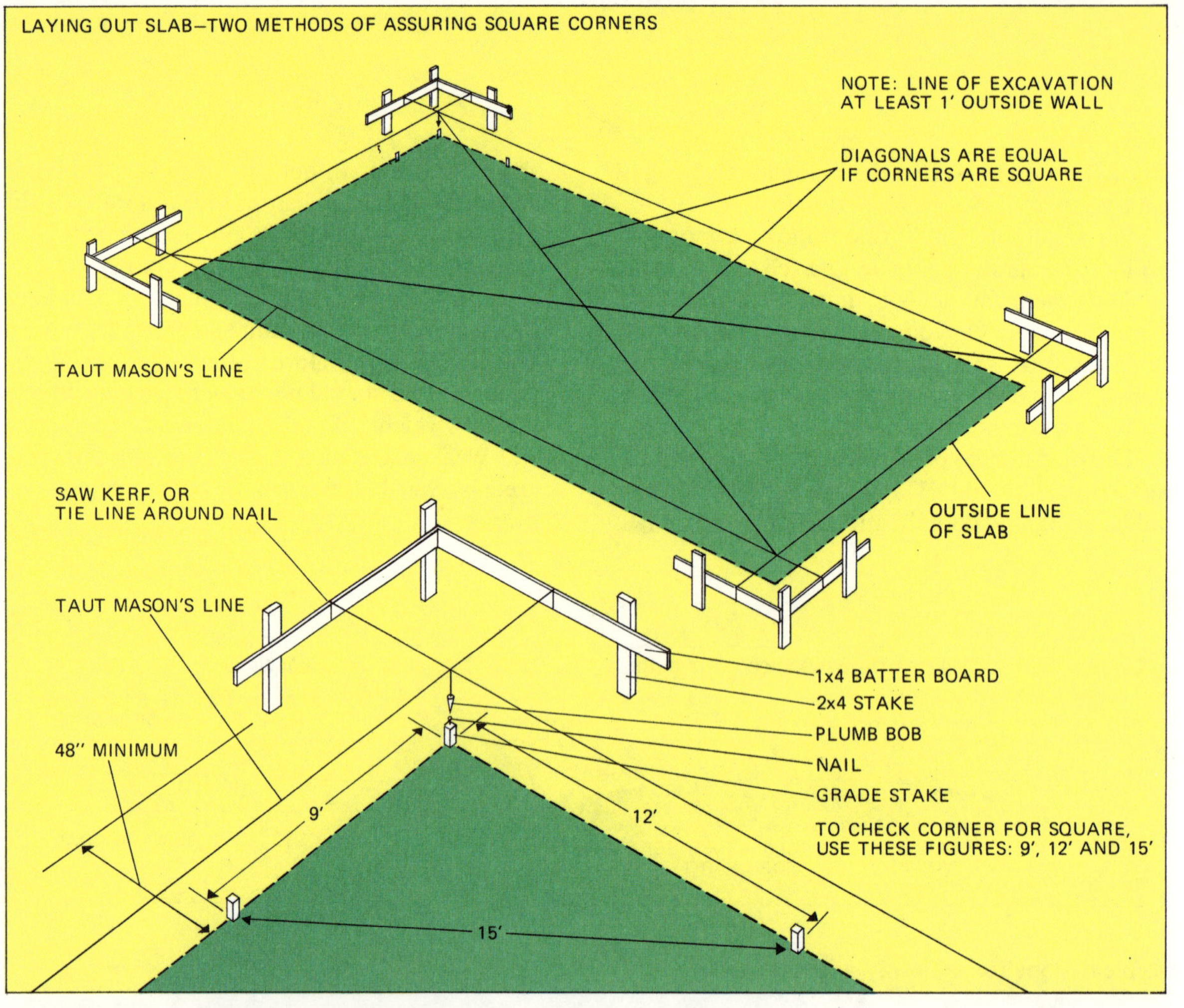


## How to lay out a slab with square corners

To lay a slab, you must locate a grade stake accurately at each of the corners. Each way shown above will give precise, square corners if done properly. Batter boards (on firmly anchored stakes) should be leveled one to the next. Use a plumb bob, or 20d nail or larger, to set the grade nails at the corners. Fix a mason's line to saw kerfs in batter boards or use common nails so the line can be repositioned if it becomes disturbed. Be sure to allow for the form width when you are excavating. Tamp the ground thoroughly, below the footing, before you begin pouring.

## Water use important when mixing and pouring concrete

Water content of concrete is extremely important. For a strong mix, water should not exceed 6 gal. per full sack (94 lb.) of cement. Use clean water only—as a rule of thumb, if you can drink it, you can use it for concrete. Add just enough to make the mix workable. Although too much water makes pouring easy it also keeps cement from adhering to the aggregate. The result of such a pour will be a weak slab.

For most homeowner jobs, a mix ratio of cement to fine aggregate (sand) to coarse aggregate (gravel) of 1, 2 and 3 is best. Ready-mix concrete may not offer you a choice of ratios, and the mix may have to be varied with the size of gravel—measured by the maximum diameter of the pieces of stone—locally available. Coarse aggregate with a maximum size of 2 in. is not recommended for slabs; 1 to 1½ in. is normal.

Mixing your own concrete, when practical, gives you greater control. For a 1:2:3 ratio, a good guideline is that the volume of sand used should be about 2/3 of the volume of coarse aggregate. For a 100-sq.-ft. slab 4 in. thick, you would need 0.64 cu. yd. of sand, 0.95 cu. yd. of gravel and 8.4 sacks of cement. You can figure on using about seven sacks of cement for each cubic yard of concrete at a 1:2:3 ratio.

Whenever possible, concrete should be poured continuously and kept practically level throughout the area being placed. Where the sides of a slab will be visible, smack the forms smartly with a hammer. This will prevent what is called a "honeycomb" appearance, caused by air bubbles, and give neat, good-looking edges.

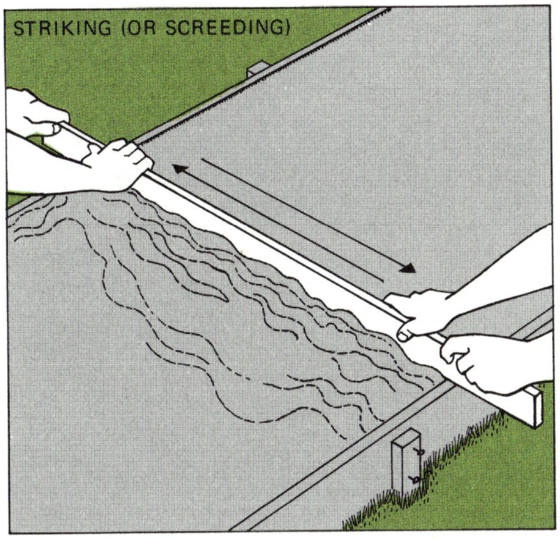


## Surface Finishing

After concrete is poured, it must be struck (trade terms are striking and screeding) immediately by drawing a board back and forth across the surface. Use a side-to-side sawing motion as you advance; press projecting stones (aggregate) below the surface. When concrete built up ahead of the screed makes it difficult to move, shovel the excess away. To crown a driveway, the underside of the strikeboard is cut concave.

An hour after striking off, the surface can be "floated," bringing water to the top and texturing the concrete. Work a wood float in a swirling motion, tajing care not to "saucer" any spot—or it will collect puddles. For a smooth surface, follow the floating with a steel trowel, used in wide, sweeping arcs. Do not trowel until the water sheen has left the surface. Keep in mind that neither floating nor troweling should be overdone—too much water brought up will make the slab weaker. Excess troweling also brings up "fines," small particles that make the surface produce dust.

After floating and troweling (if desired) and removing separators, round off slab edges with an edger and finish cross joints with groover.

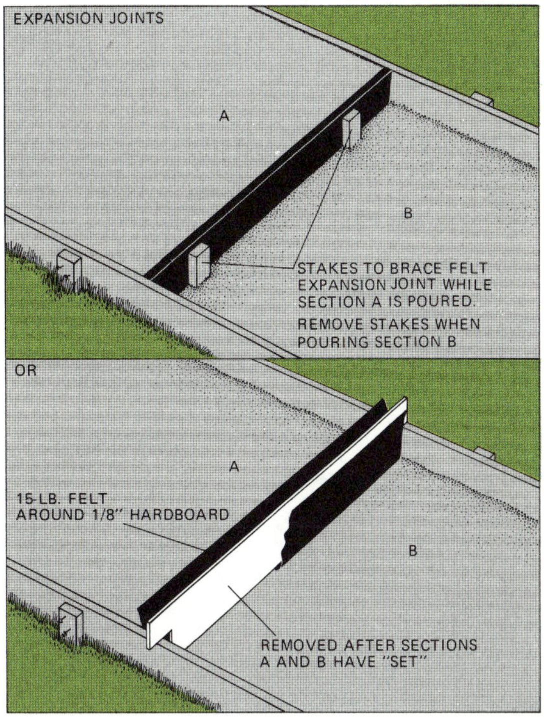


## Expansion joints

Driveways should be divided into 20-ft.-long sections using felt expansion joints (top drawing). Brace the joint as shown while pouring the first section. Remove stakes when enough concrete has been poured in the second section to make the felt immovable. If sidewalks are to have separated slabs, separators should be placed at intervals of 6 ft. You can make separators of ⅛-in. tempered hardboard inserted in folded tarpaper. Place them at right angles to the slab forms, and pour concrete on both sides of each one to keep them straight. When you finish the surface, remove the hardboard but leave the tarpaper in place in the joint. Excess can be trimmed away after concrete has set. False expansion joints—for appearance—can be made with a groover after surface finishing has been done.

## Curing time extends for weeks

Curing of concrete is a chemical process that continues for weeks after pouring. New concrete must be kept damp or the evaporation of water will make hydration (the combination of water with cement and aggregate) incomplete and your slab weak. Cover the surface with burlap, felt or layers of newspaper and keep this covering moist for five to seven days—at least a week in hot, dry weather. Depending on temperature and humidity levels, moisten once or twice a day.

# Cast your own patio slabs

By LEN HILTS

■ DON'T MAKE A BIG DEAL out of pouring a concrete patio pad. Instead, do the work in easy steps which you can spread over a number of days.

The hard way is to prepare the patio area, build the forms, and then order a truckload of ready-mix concrete. When the truck arrives at your curb, you have to have a crew ready with wheelbarrows to haul the whole load to the patio. You have to fill the forms, top them off, and finish them—now. There isn't a moment to lose.

The easy way is to set up your forms as shown here—a network of redwood form boards designed to be a part of the final pad. Once you have these forms set up, you then can use prebagged concrete mixes. You can mix enough concrete to finish a couple of the squares today, and then relax instead of breaking your back. Tomorrow you can do a few more squares at a leisurely pace. If you keep at it, all the concrete will be laid by the end of the week.

The first step in casting this patio is to stake out the pad area. Plan to make the pad 2 in. thick, on top of a base of sand from 2 to 4 in. thick. Excavate to the proper depth, then build the forms out of redwood. The size of the form boards depends on your design. You can use 1 x

SEE ALSO
**Barbecues . . . Benches, deck . . .**
**Carpeting, outdoor . . . Cookout bars . . .**
**Insect traps . . . Paths, garden . . . Patios . . .**
**Privacy screens . . . Yard lighting**

**REDWOOD BOARDS** are used to build a crosshatch of form boards. The boards stay in place and become a part of the final patio design.

**DRY SAND** is used as a base for the concrete. Use at least 2 in. of sand. Place the sand in the forms, then level it, leaving 2 in. for the concrete.

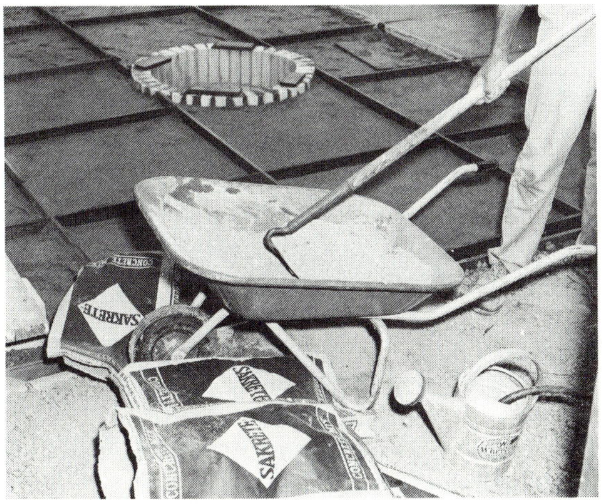


**USE PRE-BAGGED** concrete mix, which you can mix, following the directions on the bag, in a wheelbarrow. Be sure to mix thoroughly.

**FILL EACH SQUARE,** then strike the concrete level with a board. Finally, use a wooden float, as shown here, to finish the square.

4- or 2 x 4-in. boards. Use stakes to hold the boards in place.

With the boards in place, lay in the sand base and level it, allowing space for a 2-in. concrete pad. Note that the concrete used in a 2-in. pad should have a 4000-psi strength rating. Check the bag for a strength rating. Good mixes such as Sakrete have it. Poorer ones offer only 2000-psi ratings, and should be poured to a depth of 4 in.

Once the forms are in place, mix enough concrete to finish a couple of pads at a time. Follow the instructions on the bag and mix thoroughly.

Fill the form to the top of the form boards and use a long board as a striker to level the concrete. Then float the finish, using a wooden cement float, by running the float back and forth across the surface. When water appears on the surface, stop. The job is finished.

Allow the concrete to begin to set, then use an edger (your hardware store has them) to round off the edge along the line where the concrete meets the form boards.

Curing the new patio pads is important. The concrete should be kept damp for at least two days and preferably four or five. Cover each pad after finishing with a plastic sheet, and spray the surface with water before covering. In hot weather especially, lift the cover a couple of times a day during the curing to spray again. The slower and more complete the cure, the stronger the pads will be.

After all of the pads have been cured, you can sharpen the appearance of the new patio by cleaning up the redwood boards. Go over them with a wire brush to get rid of any cement or water stains.

# How to color concrete

**You can make a patio, pool deck or basement floor come alive by coloring it through any one of these four methods: stain, paint, mix-in integrally, or dusting it on**

**By RICHARD DAY**

TIRED OF LOOKING at a great expanse of plain gray concrete around your home? For a few extra dollars your next project can be distinctively colorful. Or you can, at small cost, put color into or onto the concrete you already have.

There is no magic to coloring concrete. You have a choice of four ways to do it: stain, paint, mix color in integrally or dust it on.

If possible, you should color concrete integrally by adding powdered color pigment to the fresh concrete mix. Since the color reaches all the way through the wall or slab, it can't chip or wear off. Integrally colored concrete can be either mix-it-yourself or ready-mix.

The cost of colored ready-mix is only about $3 to $6 per cubic yard more than plain gray ready-mix. Exact cost depends on color and shade. You can save money by using integral coloring only in the top course of a two-course slab casting job. In that case you might have to mix the topping yourself.

Color pigments also can be added to concrete in the mixer, coloring it integrally. The cost of these varies depending on color. Dark red costs the least; blue and green, the most. There are several types of pigments, all fine powders like cement. The best ones, from the standpoint of fade-resistance, are the synthetic mineral oxides. These include chromium oxide (green), iron oxides (buff, beige, maroon, red, brown and black), and cobalt oxide (blue). (For information on where to get a complete line of colors write the Frank D. Davis Co., 3285 East 25th St., Los Angeles, Calif. 90023.)

The two most difficult and expensive colors to achieve are blue and green. Cobalt blue oxide does a good job, but is expensive in the pure form. The only suitable green is chromium oxide. Black is the hardest color to maintain. The slightest efflorescense (bleeding out of soluble salts) causes a white haze.

SEE ALSO

**Asphalt driveways . . . Masonry, painting . . .**
**Paint rollers . . . Painting, exterior . . .**
**Paths, garden . . . Patios . . . Steps**

Color pigment should always be proportioned by weight to assure uniform color from batch to batch. A good way to do this is to weigh it on a postal scale. Proportioning color by volume—the teaspoon way—is a guarantee *against* uniformity.

Always mix coloring powders with dry cement. Add water and other materials to the mixer only after the cement has been uniformly colored. Pigment does not dye the mix. It colors by coating each particle of cement and you must mix until the process is complete. Also, after everything has been added to the mixer drum, the mixing time should be longer than normal for color uniformity. Be careful to keep constant the proportion of water in each batch. Watery batches are likely to turn out lighter in color than normal ones.

Never use more than 10 percent pigment by weight of cement. Full-strength pigments normally create good colors when used at a rate of 7 lbs. per bag of cement. Used at a rate of only 1½ lbs. per bag, they produce pleasant pastels. With carbon black pigment, ½ to 1 lb. per bag of cement is enough to produce a rich black.

White portland cement makes cleaner, brighter colors and, except for black or dark colors, should be used wherever practical in place of normal gray portland cement. White cement costs about twice as much as gray cement.

The weight of color added is always based on the weight of cement. Amounts of sand and gravel don't count. However, the color of the sand and coarse aggregate influences the appearance of a color. Use white silica sand in light pastel mixes if you want to avoid sandy undertones.

The surest way to tell what a color will be like is to make a few samples with varying amounts of pigment. Let them cure, then compare. An easy way of doing this is to cast samples in 1-in. lengths cut from 3-in.-dia. plastic pipe. Slit the sections down one side so they can be loosened

easily and use them as forms. After your samples set up, remove the forms and pop them into a warm oven. Let dry for a few hours. If the finished job is to be waxed or sealed, do this to your samples before judging them.

Coloring agents to avoid in concrete are weak iron oxides and those containing high percentages of calcium sulphate, such as Prussian blue, chrome yellow, chrome green, lampblack and boneblack. Carbon black may be used to color concrete, though it's tough to handle.

To lay an economical two-course slab, make the first, or bottom, course with your normal mix. Strike it off ½ to 1 in. below the slab's top. Then pour a ½ to 1 in. layer of colored concrete topping before the base course has a chance to harden. The saving in materials normally will be worth the extra labor required to build a two-course slab. Your two courses will bond into a single monolithic structure.

Avoid overtroweling of colored concrete slabs. One or two floatings with a wood float are

**SIFT DUST-ON** color through your fingers to cover evenly the just-floated concrete slab surface.

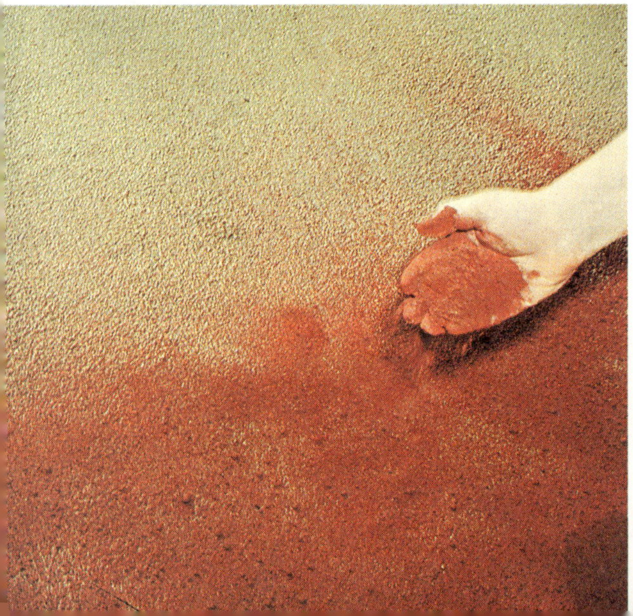

**IMMEDIATELY FLOAT** color into the surface with a wood or metal float, being sure to get even color.

sufficient if followed by a light steel-troweling. If a rougher surface is wanted, float with an aluminum or magnesium float but do not trowel.

Ample curing is essential for colored concrete. Cure for six days by keeping the concrete continuously wet with a soaker hose or polyethylene blanket covering and dump sand on it to insure continuous tight contact. Bubbles leave a spotty surface color. A wet sand covering can be used directly if it's clean enough.

**The dust-on coloring method** is a great money-saver, but it requires careful finishing for uniform coloring. Only the top 1/8 to 1/4 in. of the slab is colored, but that's the only part you see.

Dust-on material is a mixture of color pigment (the same as that used for integral coloring), white portland cement and sand. Your best bet is to buy the mixture in ready-to-use 100-lb. bags. Most manufacturers recommend use of 40 to 50 lbs. of coloring per 100 sq. ft. of concrete. Commercial dust-ons include *Colorcron,* by Master Builders, and *Colorundum,* by A. C. Horn Div., Dewey & Almy Chemical Co.

If you mix your own dust-on, mix enough for the whole job at one time. If you don't, color variations may creep in. Weigh out two parts of gray, preferably white, cement and add two to three parts of dry, screened sand and one part synthetic mineral oxide pigment of the desired color. Figure about 6 lbs. of pigment for each 100 sq. ft. of colored surface. Mix the ingredients dry until all color-streaking has disappeared. Then your dust-on is ready.

### water content should be low

Concrete for dust-on coloring should be low in water content to prevent bleeding. It also should be air-entrained, since this helps prevent bleeding, too. If you use ready-mix, order it with six bags of cement per cu. yd., a maximum of 6 gals. of water per bag of cement and 6 percent entrained air.

Place, strike off and darby the concrete as usual, then wait until all free water has evaporated from the surface. If it lingers, try squeegeeing it off by dragging a garden hose over the surface. Then float. Floating brings up just enough water to combine with the coloring material, also removes any ridges and depressions that might collect pigment and cause color-streaking. Since slab edges often dry up before the center, you may need to color them first.

Right after floating, bend low over the slab with handfuls of dusting mixture and sift pigment evenly onto the slab. Work at getting an even

**ROLL SEVERAL** coats of latex on a porch floor in a single day after scale has been removed from surface.

spread over the entire slab. The first dust-on application should use up about two-thirds of the total amount of material.

After the dry material absorbs water from the fresh concrete, it's ready for floating. Float just enough to spread the coloring evenly into the surface. All tooled edges and joints should be run before and after dust-on applications. Right after the first color-floating, dust on the rest of the mixture and float again. Take care to get a uniform color.

Follow the final color-floating immediately with steel-troweling. For a fully dense and smooth texture, give it a second steel-troweling after waiting for the concrete to increase its set. A fine, soft-bristle broom may be drawn over the surface to produce a roughened texture for good traction under foot. Indoor surfaces may get a third troweling for real smoothness. If smoothness isn't wanted, skip all troweling and leave the surface with a float finish, wood or metal. A metal float leaves a smoother surface.

After they are completely cured in a few weeks, integrally-colored and dust-on-colored interior concrete slabs may be given two or more coats of concrete floor wax the same color as your pigment. Take care to avoid staining the floor before it can be waxed. If you must use the floor, lay scuffproof building paper over it to protect the surface.

**Existing concrete** must either be painted or stained. If you paint a slab, use a paint designed for floors. Paint also offers the widest possible choice of colors.

The best method of coloring existing concrete slabs is by staining. Stains are especially popular on tennis courts, pool decks, patios and basement floors. A few really good concrete stains, both organic and inorganic, are available. When used according to directions, they last many years. A nine-year life is claimed for one type when used in a mild climate. Some stained-in colors tend to be weak, but can be strengthened

**COLOR CONCRETE** (dust-on and integral mixing) by using weighing method of mixing, not by volume.

considerably by waxing (best indoors) or coating with a polyvinyl chloride resin color toner (best outdoors). With wax, occasional rewaxing is necessary, depending on foot traffic.

Before it's stained, concrete must be clean and free of oil, grease, wax, soap and paint. To remove wax and surface grease, pour *hot* water on the slab, sprinkle on trisodium phosphate and scrub hard with a stiff brush.

Read the directions before applying stain. Don't stain concrete less than six weeks old. Some stains require an acid-etch before application, others don't.

Most stains are applied in two coats. Although the coverage varies with surface porosity, a gallon of stain is usually enough to two-coat 200 sq. ft. of concrete. Per-coat coverage of wax is 600 to 900 sq. ft. per gallon.

An inorganic stain is usually applied in two coats with a 4-in. paintbrush. Take care to avoid overlapping of brush strokes into an area that has dried. Stain that collects in low spots makes them darker than surrounding concrete. Keep it well brushed out. There should be from four hours to five days between coats. Timing depends on the concrete, drying conditions and stain. The finish coat is mopped and scrubbed to remove the residue and bring out the true stain color. It often takes several days for concrete to reach its ultimate color.

Don't apply inorganic stains over integrally colored concrete. Also, inorganic stains are most effective on new concrete. Avoid using them at all on slabs of varying ages. The colors may differ.

Some popular stains are Kemiko *Concrete Stain* and *Col-r-tone Finish,* Cabot *Cement Floor Stain,* Rez *Color-Tones, Flor-Dye* by Truscon Laboratories, *Color-Rox* by Tamms Industries and Thompson *Color Waterseal.*

Kemiko stains are inorganic. These stains are not affected by alkali in the concrete. Instead they react with calcium present in concrete to form their color. With them the most success is achieved in staining concrete less than 20 years old and in decent condition. Inorganic stains don't hide patches and other imperfections. A coating of toner does the trick, however, giving a uniform opaque matte finish. Kemiko's *Col-r-tone* toner can be used outdoors or indoors for a flat, nonskid surface.

Cabot and Rez stains are organic oil stains, much like those for wood. They cost less and hide imperfections well, but may not wear as well as inorganic stains. Ordinary oil stains for wood also work well on concrete. But first knock out surface alkalinity by soaking with solution of two to three pounds of zinc sulphate per gallon of water. Spread it over the surface, let it set for two days, then thoroughly wash with water to remove crystals that have formed. After thorough drying, the oil stain can be applied. Concrete can thus be made to look like wood, especially if it has been cast against rough-textured wood forms.

All stains eventually dissipate. Waxing will brighten the color when they do, but don't use a wax without a stain under it. You won't like the results.

Try staining a small out-of-the-way area first. If it works well, start staining at the back door and work around to the front.

### paint can color concrete

Properly applied, paint can be a good way of getting color onto concrete. Eventually it will either wear off or (outdoors) chalk. For long wear, the catalytic coatings are best. Used outdoors, though, they chalk heavily. Chlorinated rubber paint takes wear well and is excellent for slabs. Floor-type oil-base and latex paints are easiest to use but tend to lift off wherever car tires rest on them. Thus, avoid latex paints for garage and driveway slabs. Portland cement paints are fine for walls, but wear off floors too easily. The drawback to using them on walls is that curing is needed for several days.

Concrete must be several months old before painting. Some paints require that concrete be acid-etched first, especially if it's smooth-troweled. Chlorinated rubber floor paint will adhere, even to a glazed surface, without an acid-etch.

Loose, scaling paint should be removed by scraping and wire-brushing. Oil-base paints are best applied in three coats, the first containing equal amounts of thinner and paint. The second coat should contain a little thinner. The final coat may be applied full strength.

THE SURFACE of the driveway should be free of dust and dirt so the new material will adhere properly. Sweep, then wash with a hose.

SPALLED SURFACES are ugly, and once spalling has begun, rapid deterioration of the concrete takes place. New materials enable you to fix these areas.

# How to patch walks and driveways

**Now you can patch cracked walks, patios, driveways and basement walls, then apply a new concrete surface to hide the patches. It's easy and relatively inexpensive**

**By LEN HILTS**

THERE WAS A TIME when the only way to repair a badly cracked walk or driveway was to get out the cold chisel, spend long hours cutting away the sides of the cracks, and then pack the widened cracks with cement mix. These patches seldom were very durable, in spite of all the work you put into them, and when you finished, the driveway looked like one of Grandma's patchwork quilts.

Now, however, thanks to a new kind of concrete product, you can repair cracked concrete without all that chiseling, and then give the walk or driveway an attractive new surface which not only hides the cracks but also provides protection against salt and other chemicals which eat away at concrete surfaces.

Called Megamix, the new product is manufactured by the marketers of Sakrete. You purchase it in packages which contain two separate ingredients—a liquid called Megasil and a powder called Megatite. To prepare the product for use, you mix the powder and the liquid according to the directions, and then add water.

To repair cracks, you make a thick, putty-like mixture. Then for resurfacing, you make a thinner mixture which can be applied with a long-handled paint roller.

Megamix offers a beautiful solution to the old problem of spalling, when the surface of the concrete crumbles and breaks up. Spalling is often caused by using salt or other chemicals to keep the walk or driveway free of ice. Because it can be applied in coats as thin as 1/16-in., Megamix can be brushed over the entire surface, filling in the spalled areas. You end up with a smooth surface that makes your walk or driveway look brand new.

Megamix comes in both white and gray, so you can match existing concrete. The cost of a resurfacing coat is 12 to 14 cents a square foot. If you had to replace a cracked and broken driveway, the cost would be more than $5.00 a square foot when you include the cost of removing the old concrete.

Megamix is the latest in a line of products brought out by various manufacturers in the concrete industry aimed at solving the problem

SEE ALSO
**Asphalt driveways . . . Paths, garden . . . Patios . . . Retaining walls . . . Steps**

**NEW PRODUCTS** like Megamix were designed to allow you to apply thin surface coats to old concrete. The new surface protects the concrete from salt.

**A STIFF-BRISTLED** broom is the best tool to use in cleaning a concrete surface before resurfacing. Sweep away all powdered cement and dirt.

**A GARDEN HOSE** can be used to clean the old surface. In addition, it is used to dampen the old surface before the patching material is applied.

**SWEEP AWAY** any excess water after wetting down the old surface, since patching and surfacing material should not be applied if there is standing water.

of applying thin new surfaces to existing concrete. Until these products appeared, it was difficult to pour a durable surface less than 2 in. thick. Cracks had to be chiseled open wide enough to accommodate mixes containing fairly large aggregates.

The new products, many of them latex/cement formulations, all permit you to lay a thin coat containing no aggregate, and to feather the edges of the patch.

### how to patch cracks

If you have cracks or patches of broken concrete in a walk or driveway, the first step is to clean out all loose or cracked material. Use a hammer and cold chisel to chip away broken pieces. Sweep the crack with a stiff-bristled broom to dig out all dust and sand, since loose material will prevent proper adhesion of the patching material.

One good way to get the cracks clean is to use the high pressure setting on your garden hose to wash them clean.

If you intend to resurface the concrete as well as patching the cracks, sweep and wash the whole surface. You may have blotches of oil on a driveway; these should be removed by scrubbing them with a strong detergent-and-water mixture. The best scrubbing tool is a long-handled, stiff-bristled broom. Pour the detergent

**A THIN MIXTURE** of patching material is poured on the driveway. When mixing these products, follow the directions carefully for best results.

**USE A ROLLER** of the type used to apply paint to spread the surfacing material evenly on the surface of the driveway. Don't roll it out; just spread it.

mixture on any oily patches and give it time to dissolve the oil before you begin to scrub. Finally, rinse the area thoroughly, using the garden hose.

Now mix the patching material according to the instructions on the package. Follow the directions carefully. Most of the new formulations dry quickly, so mix only as much as you can apply in less than 30 minutes. Stir the mixture frequently as you work.

The concrete should be damp when you apply the patching mixture. If it has dried since you washed it down, spray it again, but don't have standing water in the cracks when you finish. Sweep the excess water out if necessary. Use a trowel to pack the patching mixture into the cracks, making the surface of the crack level with the surface of the surrounding concrete. Megamix expands slightly as it dries.

### resurfacing

Once the cracks are filled, you can resurface the entire walk or driveway immediately, or you can wait until another day if you choose. Make sure the concrete surface is damp, then mix the material as directed. Ten lbs. of Megamix will coat 8 sq. ft. to a thickness of ⅛-in.

Pour the mixture on the surface and spread it with a paint roller. Don't attempt to roll the mixture out, as you would paint. Just spread it evenly. To make a neat job, be careful to keep the edges straight. Start at one end of the walk or driveway and work toward the other end.

*Caution:* Megamix and other patching formulations may be harmful to the skin, so wash any material off any part of the body immediately. Also, mix the material in a well-ventilated area.

### curing

Like all concrete products, these new ones must be cured after application. Megamix, for example, should be covered with a plastic sheet within an hour of application, and should be kept moist for about two days. In hot weather, you may have to apply a fine spray from the garden hose several times a day to keep it moist.

After two days, you can put the walk or driveway into normal use. The new surface will bond tightly to the old, will not powder or flake, and will provide good protection for the concrete under it.

You can use these products to patch concrete patios and to seal cracks in basement walls and floors. They are particularly useful when you decide to lay tile on a concrete basement floor, since you can use them to level low spots in the floor and to provide a smooth surface for the tile. When filling a low spot like this, use as much of the patching material as needed, feathering the edges of the patch smoothly into the surrounding floor area.

Note, however, that if you are laying a new walk or driveway, a good air-entrained mix of regular concrete should be used. These new products were not designed for pouring large concrete pads. However, once you have the new pad poured and cured, you can apply a surface of Megamix as a protective coating to prevent spalling as a result of the action of strong chemicals and salt.

**Motor needs oil**

*I have an old secondhand sewing machine and am sure that at some point grease was forced into the oilers where it hardened. I'm also quite sure the bearings are dry. The nearest service center is miles away. Is there any way I can oil the bearings?—O.L., Minn.*

Your service center can give you much better advice than I can at such long range. I suggest that you get in touch with it by phone or letter, giving detailed information including serial number. Or you can detach the motor and send it to the service center, along with a letter of explanation. Be sure to mark the wiring with numbered tabs so that, later, you can rewire the motor correctly.

If circumstances make this impractical, you'll have to try to get lubricant to the bearings temporarily. Old sewing-machine motors have wick-lubricated sleeve bearings and it is possible the lubricant has hardened. Usually there's a small oil hole at the top of the felt retainer. Insert a straight pin into the hole and press down as far as possible. Work with care so that you do not damage the wicking or other parts. Place a single drop of *light* oil (not crankcase oil) in each retainer. Then snip off the point of the pin, insert the blunt end of the pin in the hole already made in the felt and work the pin down as far as it will go. In time the oil should soften the hardened lubricant and reach the bearing. But don't operate the motor until the shaft turns freely. Your best bet, however, is to ask your service center for advice.

**Closet condensation**

*Walls in a clothes closet in one bedroom of my home, especially one outside wall, are sometimes wet and dripping near the ceiling. What causes this, and what can I do to prevent it?—Mrs. I. McClusker, Racine, Wis.*

Walls are at a lower temperature than the air with which they are in contact. This causes the moisture in the air to condense on the colder surface, particularly on the outside walls, as you say. Often a cure can be effected simply by leaving the closet door or doors open. Just leaving the closet light on will sometimes do it.

For a better cure; you can insulate the outside wall by nailing furring strips horizontally on 16-in. centers, packing either blanket-type or polystyrene insulation between the strips, and then covering the wall with plasterboard. Seal the corners with Swedish putty.

Some homeowners install a wall outlet in the closet and use an electric strip heater to solve this problem.

**Rejuvenating old paintbrushes**

*I have three old paintbrushes, including a very good one with long bristles, that have hardened due to sheer neglect. Is there any hope now of making them usable again? Can you outline the process?—B.A., Del.*

If the bristles are not bent due to their standing on end for a prolonged period, place them in individual cans, pour in sufficient wash-off paint remover to cover the bristles and let them stand for an hour or more. Then remove the brushes, wash off the remover, place them on several thicknesses of newspaper and scrub one way—away from the ferrule—with a wire brush. Put brushes back in the remover for about the same time. Repeat the scrubbing and the immersion in remover; eventually you'll soften all the paint and you can comb out the remainder with a special brush "comb" available from your paint dealer.

The procedure is certainly hard on the bristles but it's the only way I've found reasonably successful.

**Unilever faucet leaks**

*My single-lever sink faucet leaks at a point just below the neck, but only when it's turned on for hot or cold water—there's no leak when it's turned off. Can you tell me what is wrong and how to fix it?—W.W., Mo.*

Your faucet seems to be of the type that has two rubber-ring seals called O-rings (or packing) which fit in grooves cut in the sleeve formed at the end on the neck. These seals become worn in time, but you can get replacements from your plumber, hardware store or the manufacturer. Instructions that came with the faucet will tell you how to disassemble it to replace the seals, or your plumber will do this for a nominal charge.

**Linseed-oil finish**

*I've just bought a used sewing machine in a walnut cabinet, so dark the wood is hardly visible. I want to refinish in a lighter color. I'm told to rub on linseed oil in stages to a gloss. Can you advise how to proceed?—C.Y., Va.*

If you use linseed oil you may end up with a darker finish than you now have. I'd sand to the bare wood, using a cabinet scraper if necessary to make sure all the old finish has been removed, and then spray-coat with a water-white lacquer over a sanding sealer. This will give you about as near a natural wood color as you can possibly get with ordinary finishing materials. Your paint dealer will rent you a sprayer and supply the necessary finishing materials.

**The best jobs are often those of an interested beginner who cares enough to pay close attention to details**

**THE EASIEST** reinforcement to install is steel block mesh set right in the mortar. The ends of the mesh strips should be overlapped for greatest strength.

# How to lay concrete blocks

**By RICHARD DAY**

YOU'RE NOT A MASON, so why try to lay blocks like one? Especially when you can get better results by taking advantage of your amateur status.

A professional mason spends years mastering the skills of his trade. Once he has acquired the necessary experience, he can lay blocks quickly with a machine-like efficiency that seems almost effortless. On the first job, though, the professional method is actually much more difficult than a straightforward amateur approach.

The following nonprofessional method of laying concrete blocks is designed for an unskilled man working alone. All you need is the desire to do a good job and a few specialized tools.

The first tool to buy is a mason's trowel. This is used to pick up and place mortar. The blade is about 10 in. long and 5 in. across.

Mason's trowels come in two shapes—Boston and Philadelphia. For block laying, you'll probably prefer the Philadelphia, because its straighter edges are better for picking up straight beads of mortar.

Incidentally, professionals use the wooden trowel handle for tapping blocks into position. When amateurs try this, they usually end up spattering mortar all over. Better to resist the temptation to "do it like a pro" and position the blocks by tapping lightly with a hammer.

The hammer you use will depend on the job. A regular mason's hammer has a square head at one end and a chisel edge on the other. It's used for cutting the blocks to size, making holes or chipping the edges to special shapes. If your project doesn't include any of this type of work, you can get along very well without it.

You can't get along without an accurate level, for the whole success of the project depends upon how carefully it is leveled. As in the case of the hammer, however, it doesn't have to be a mason's level. A true mason's level is 4 ft. long, with the extra length for use as a straightedge. As an amateur, you can get along fine with a good

SEE ALSO
**Basement waterproofing . . . Garden shelters . . . Gazebos . . . House additions . . . Insulation . . . Remodeling . . . Retaining walls . . . Steps**

**DRY LAYOUT** of blocks on the footing is a good precaution. Use scraps of ⅜-in. plywood as spacers.

**SMALL CONCRETE MIXER** makes it possible to mix a fresh batch of mortar while you are using up the first.

**BOTTOM COURSE** is laid on full mortar bed which has been furrowed with a trowel point. Note the guide line.

**CORNER BLOCKS** are laid to interlock. These govern position of all other blocks, so level them both ways.

2-ft carpenter's level.

You'll also need a jointing tool in order to produce smooth, tight mortar joints. For rounded joints, the tool to use is a ⅝-in. round bar or pipe that's curved at the ends to prevent gouging. For V-joints, use a ½-in.-sq. bar with curved ends. The ends can be used for tooling short vertical joints. A good jointing tool should be at least 22 in. long to span irregularities. The main reason for tooling mortar joints incidentally, is to compact them and make them more weather-resistant. Just as important, though, is the fact that this finishes off the joints and produces a better looking wall.

Other useful items are a nylon mason's line (the amateur can use a strong fishline) and a pair of line blocks. The blocks hook over the ends of the wall to anchor the line.

A small concrete mixer is also highly desirable, since it produces better, more workable mortar than you can get by mixing with a hoe or shovel. The 5-gal.-bucket type is ideal. If you can't rent one, they sell for about $50 to $100.

So much for the equipment. Now you're ready to plan the job. The most important thing here is to use modular dimensions, if possible. This will avoid hours of tedious cutting and fitting. Concrete blocks are made to fit 8-in. modules, so if you design the wall to fit them, using full and half blocks, you'll do yourself a favor. Draw a rough-dimensioned sketch to be sure you've got everything straight and you're ready to install the footing.

A good footing is twice as wide as the wall. It should be cast on unexcavated earth, not on backfill. The bottom of the footing must be below the frost line in your area and at least 12 in. deep.

Build your footing of quality concrete containing six bags of portland cement per cubic yard and not more than six gallons of water per bag of cement. Ready-mix can be ordered to these specs. If the job is small, use packaged concrete mix. Don't overwater. Place it stiff.

Strike off the footing level to the proper grade. Floating it once will make the surface as smooth as you need it. Cover with wet soil or sand and let the footing cure for six days. Then clean off all of

**LONG FACE** of each corner block must be lined up and plumb with the blocks below. Tap lightly into place.

**CHECK THE HEIGHT** by measuring from the footing to top of corner. If block has settled, remove and re-lay.

**LINE BLOCK** holds line flush with top of corner. Move to the next course when the blocks will stand pull.

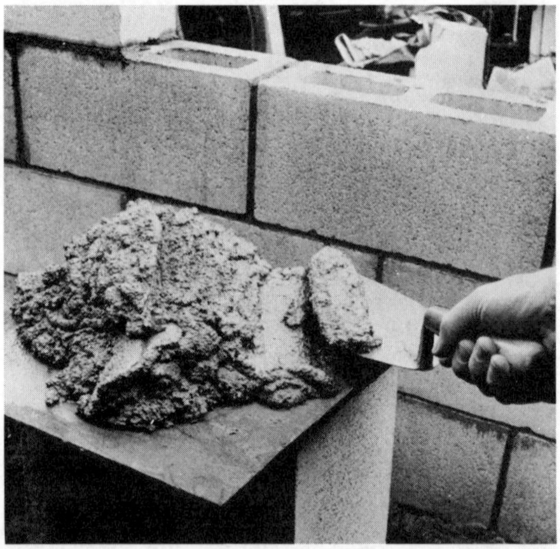

**GOOD MORTAR BOARD** is an 18-in square piece of plywood. Support it on a pair of upended block legs.

**RIBBONS OF MORTAR** on ends of each intermediate block fill vertical joints. For best bond, slap them on.

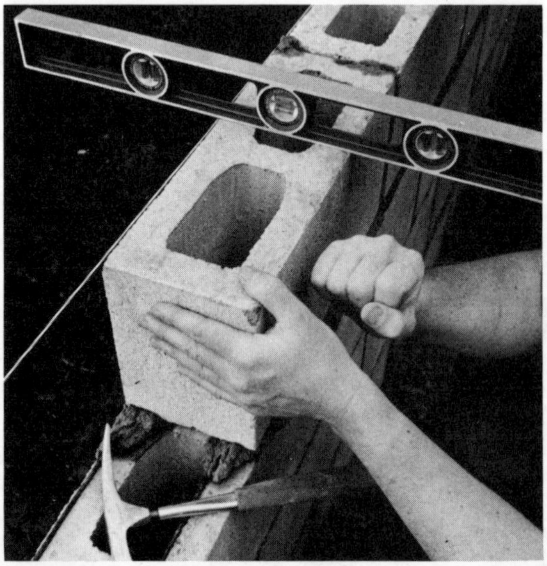

**INTERMEDIATE BLOCKS** should be laid to align with the guide line and leveled across to square them.

**CONTROL JOINT** is needed in walls more than 20 ft. long. Grout transfers lateral load. Joint is raked, caulked.

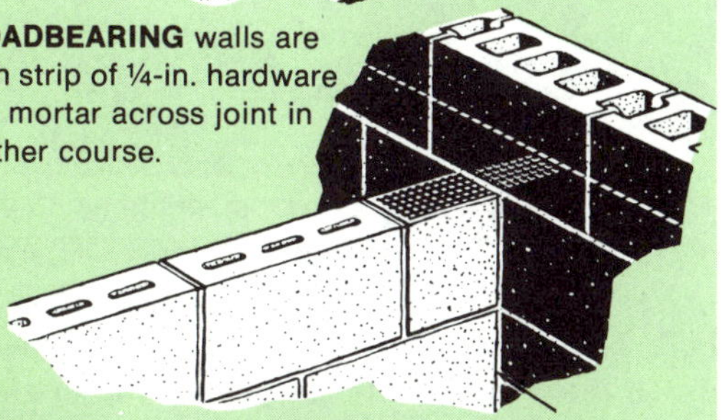
**NONLOADBEARING** walls are tied with strip of ¼-in. hardware cloth in mortar across joint in every other course.

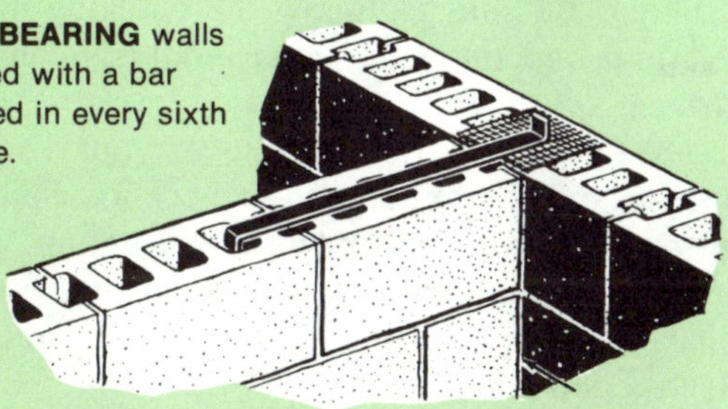
**LOADBEARING** walls are tied with a bar grouted in every sixth course.

the sand or soil and you're all set to start laying block.

The strength of your wall will depend largely on the strength of the mortar. Also important is the "bond" of the mortar—how tightly it holds to the blocks once it has set. Your best bet is to buy a packaged mortar mix (Sakrete, for instance).

Mortar should be mixed as wet as you can get it and still have it workable. Workable mortar is buttery, yet sticky. It clings to the trowel, even holds to vertical end-joint surfaces.

A good way to judge if your mortar is the right consistency for block-laying is to see that the blocks hold to the right height while you're laying them. If they sink, add more mix to dry out the mortar. If they have to be pounded down, add more water to the mortar and re-mix. It's important to measure everything, though, so you will be sure of getting the proper mix next time.

If you have to mix the mortar by hand, spread the dry materials on a flat concrete surface or in a mortar box and add about three quarters of the water. Mix these with a hoe until the mortar is uniformly damp, then add the remaining water a little at a time while you continue mixing. Let batch stand for five minutes. Before use, remix the mortar thoroughly without adding water. Mortar not used within 2½ hours should be discarded. Within that time you can mix in more water with the trowel.

The procedure to follow when laying the

**TO LAY LAST** block in each course, butter the ends with mortar and lower it carefully down into the slot.

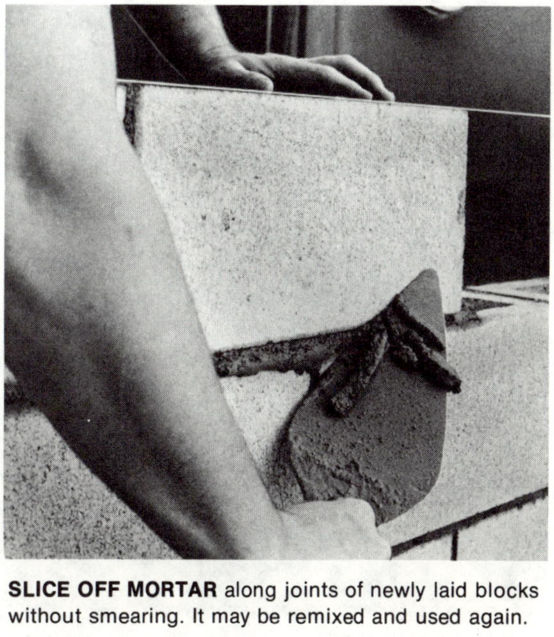
**SLICE OFF MORTAR** along joints of newly laid blocks without smearing. It may be remixed and used again.

**TO KEEP** mortar fresh, slice through it occasionally with the trowel and add more water if it is necessary.

**TOOL JOINTS** when mortar is thumbprint-hard by working the jointing tool back and forth along each joint.

blocks is detailed in the accompanying photos. However, one thing that can't be overstressed is the importance of control joints in any block wall more than 20 ft. long. As shown in the drawing a control joint is a continuous vertical joint from top to bottom which lets the wall change dimension slightly without cracking.

You can use either special control-joint blocks or regular blocks with provision for transferring lateral loads across the joint, as shown in the drawing. Lay up the joint with mortar. Then, before the mortar gets too hard, rake it out to a depth of ¾ in. and fill the joint with an elastic caulking. Be sure to follow the caulking manufacturer's recommendations about priming the surface.

One final precaution: Whatever your project happens to be, make sure you check local building codes before you begin construction. Besides, your building officials are familiar with local conditions, and they often can help you get off to a good start.

**ANCHOR BOLTS** or other fixtures can be installed in the wall by grouting. Just place a piece of mesh across the core beneath to prevent grout from dropping to the bottom of the wall, then fill the core with concrete or mortar and set the bolt in this. To avoid the possibility of the bolt working loose, it should either have a large head or be bent to a right angle. Use ½-in. bolts for most such applications.

**TO REINFORCE WALL** laterally, use strips of steel block mesh, below left. For vertical reinforcement, cast reinforcing bars with bent ends into the footing and grout cores around bars as in center and lower right photos.

**TOOL VERTICAL** joints with end of jointing tool. Remove burrs by rubbing across joint with a wire brush.

**MORTAR DEPOSITS** on face of wall can be rubbed away with a piece of broken block after mortar hardens.

## A THUMBNAIL GUIDE TO CONCRETE BLOCKS

The workhorse of concrete blocks is the standard 8x8x16-in. block, commonly known as an 8-in block because it makes a wall 8 in. wide. You can also buy 6-in. block, which is primarily for nonloadbearing walls, and 4-in block for even slimmer nonloadbearing walls. For big jobs, like foundations and heavy retaining walls, there are 10 and 12-in blocks.

Block measurements always describe the area a block will take up when laid in the wall. Actually, the block measures ⅜ in. less on a side to allow for a ⅜ in. mortar joint. To estimate the number of blocks required for a job, figure the wall area in square feet, subtract the area of openings and multiply by $1^1/_9$. For example, a 90-sq.-ft wall would require 100 blocks. Half blocks used at ends and corners are counted as halves, not whole units.

Most blocks have two or three cores. The two-core type, which offers somewhat better insulating qualities, is popular in the West. Both are available in standard and lightweight types, the latter containing cinders, shale or slag for aggregates. A standard block weighs from 40 to 50 lbs., a lightweight only 25 to 30 lbs.

Many blockmakers are doing away with special corner blocks, and are making all their structural blocks with square ends.

Among the glamour types are: split block (made by breaking an oversize block into two pieces so the resulting faces resemble rough stonemasonry); slump block (like adobe brick in appearance); grille or screen block (for garden walls) and sculptured block (to create a three-dimensional affect). Like all blocks, they can be painted with latex or portland-cement paint. Some makers even sell blocks ready-colored with mortar to match.

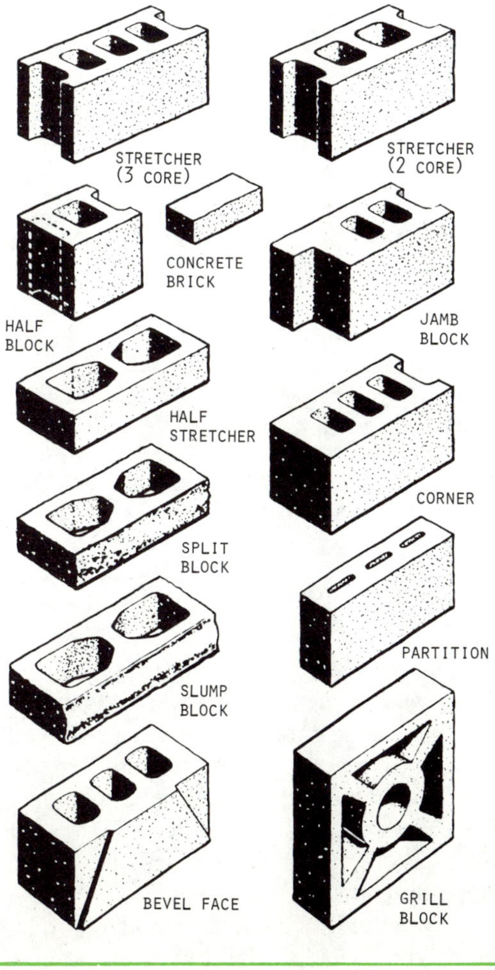

# A champ's design for a home gym

By MIKE MCCLINTOCK

WHEN ARE YOU going to get in shape? Every year millions of Americans solemnly vow to remove excess inches from their bodies. Half an hour is reserved each evening for sit-ups, push-ups and jogging, but somehow, after a few short days of aching muscles, the resolution fades. Well, here's how to get (and keep) a shape-up habit.

We went to Bruce Jenner, world record holder and Olympic gold medalist in the decathlon, for expert advice on keeping the whole family in shape—and having fun while doing it.

"One reason I was able to keep training day in and day out was that I really enjoyed it. Even though I'm retired from competition, I still work out every day."

The room we planned with Bruce is small and simple enough to be a reasonable renovation project. Once you set it up, your family will enjoy using it every day.

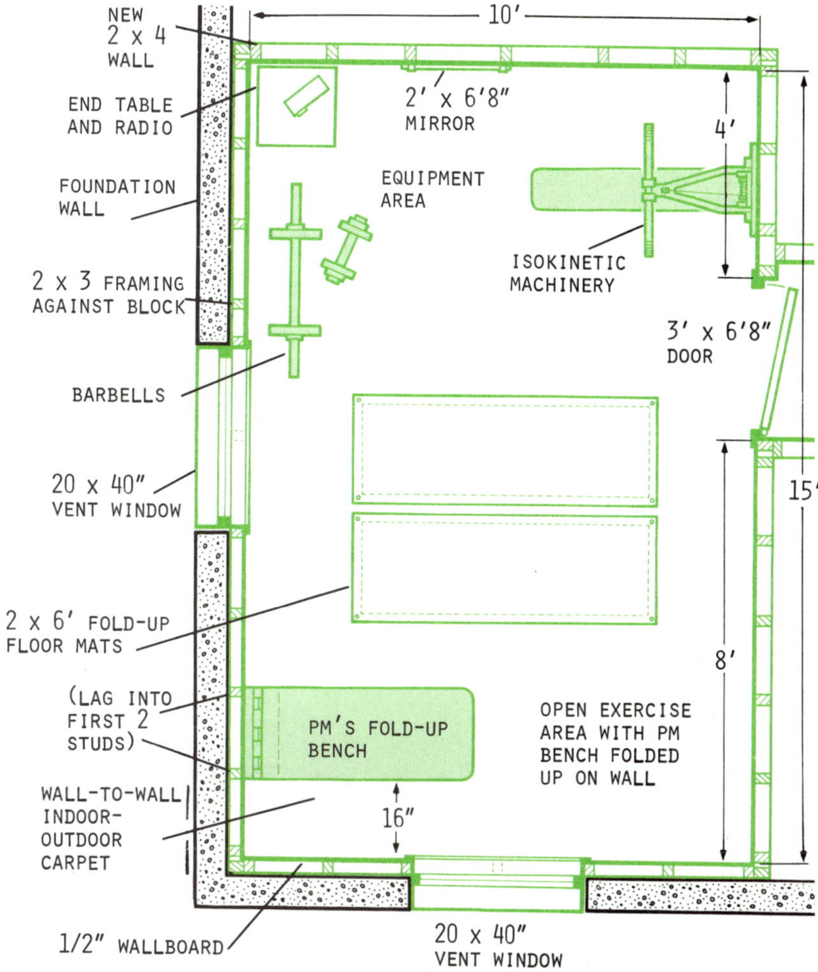


**SHAPE-UP ROOM PLAN**

**OUR PLAN** (10x15 ft.) is small enough to fit into a corner of your basement, but big enough to hold the features recommended by Bruce. Among them are a padded floor (we used indoor/outdoor carpeting), and exercise bench, isokinetic machines, barbells, a mirror and a radio. If possible, choose a room with a ceiling that is high enough for lifting the weights

**A LOW** basement ceiling (typical in many new homes) does not rule out weightlifting. Even if you are as tall as Bruce (6-foot-2 and 190 lbs.), you can adapt the way he did by lifting from a sitting position. For general conditioning, he advises a lot of bar motion covering many exercises, with a low weight total on the bar. Don't strain muscles by trying a few big lifts

**THE HEAVY-DUTY** wall attachment (near right) lets you fold the bench up and out of the way. A 1-in. foam pad (far right) is wrapped with a layer of Naugahyde to make a comfortable, long-lasting and attractive top for the bench

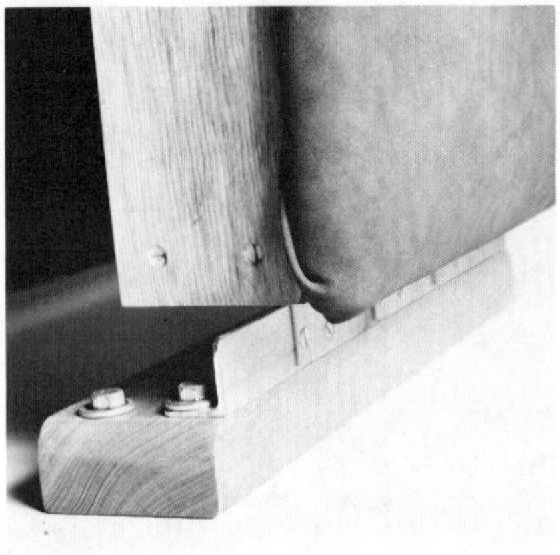

## FOLD-UP EXERCISE BENCH

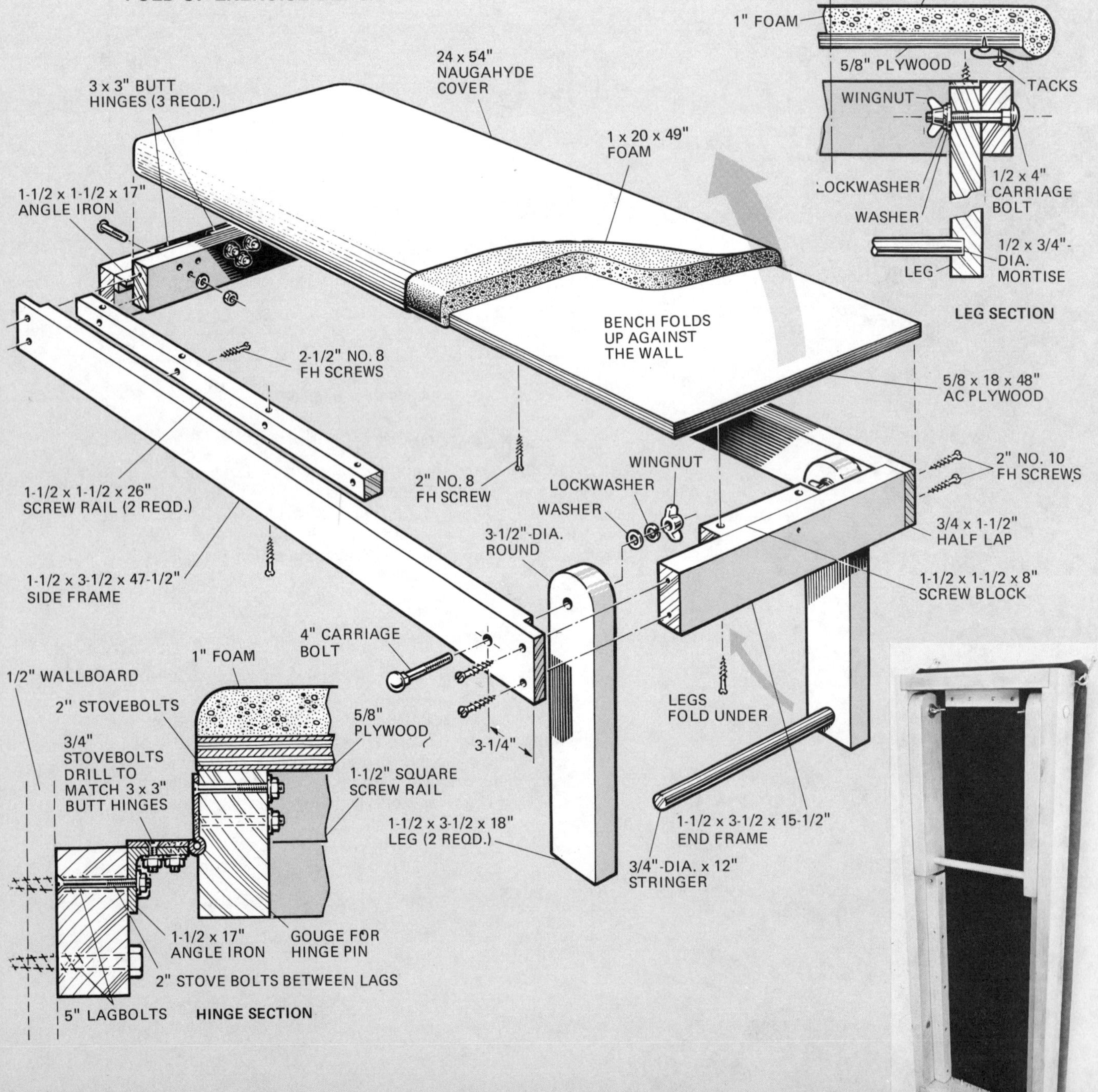

**STAYING IN SHAPE**

**OVERHEAD** presses can be made from a sitting position. A barbell set (like the one that we purchased from Sears for use in these photos—about $40) is a valuable workout tool. You should start with a low weight total and gradually work your way up

**SQUAT LIFTS** strengthen a lot of muscles simultaneously. Standing, load the bar on your shoulders and balance it with your hands. Bend your knees (head and shoulders erect) until you touch the bench seat. Then return to a standing position

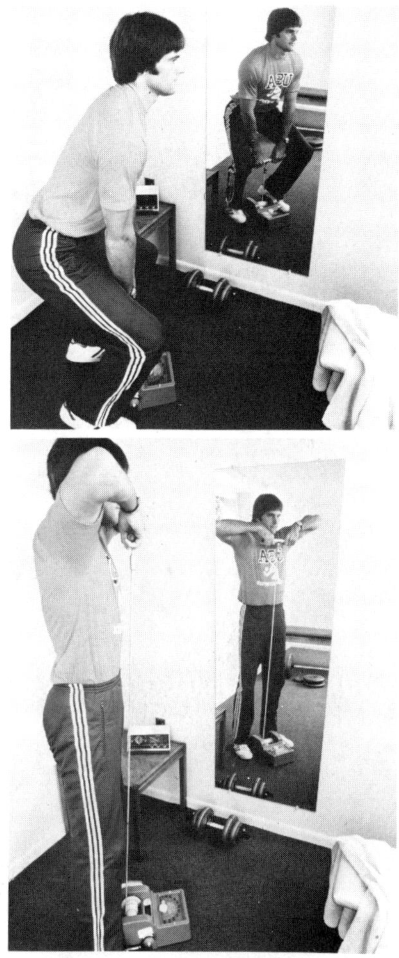

**SPECIALIZED GYM** equipment is not essential, but isokinetic devices (like the one shown above) are good for all ages. Bruce suggested the mirror and radio. They'll make your room more attractive and more fun so you will want to spend more time there

About the biggest mistake you can make is to set up a crushing schedule of exercises and jump right into them. Your body (and your mind) isn't ready for the shock.

Tip No. 1: Start your shape-up program with a *short* series of *simple* exercises. Bruce says consistency is the key to getting in shape. "Just walking up and down the stairs 5 or 10 times is good for you—as long as you do it every night. Granted, it'll take you a few months to see results if that's all you do, but even a simple routine *will* get you in shape.

You can sneak yourself into a shape-up program by making an exercise out of some routine you do daily. Whether it's picking up mail or cooking dinner, you can find a minute to jog 50 steps in place or lift a frying pan over your head 10 times. It may sound silly, but if you do it regularly you'll start feeling and looking better. So don't start with 50 sit-ups—your stomach won't like it.

Although Bruce went through specific exercises for each of the 10 decathlon events, he also trained for general conditioning and stamina.

Tip No. 2: Bruce told us that "for general conditioning, do *more* of something *easy*, rather than a *little* of something *tough*." You'll be more likely to stick to your exercises if you can do

**SIT-UPS ARE** a crucial part of staying in shape. Bruce says, "Sit-ups are really essential. They strengthen your stomach and your lower back." For the best results, you should hook your feet underneath the bar and bend your knees

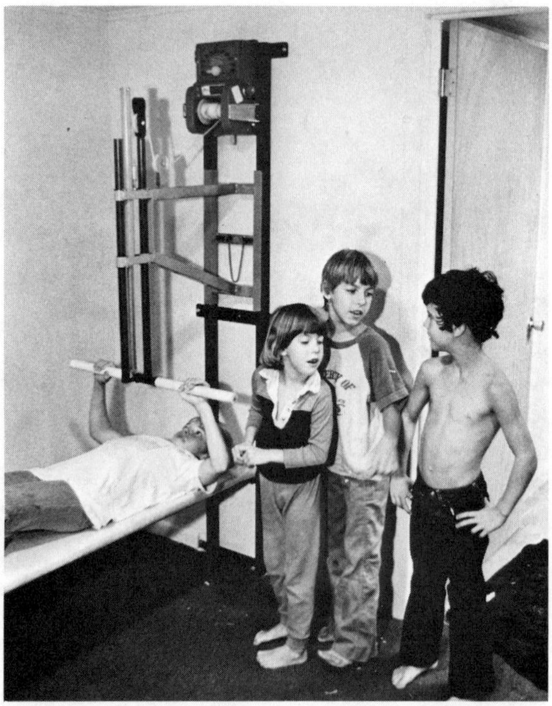

**EVEN CHILDREN** will want to use your new exercise room. It's never too early for them to learn the importance of exercise for good health. We found that they wanted to give all of the equipment a try

them at home. If you rely on jogging to keep in shape, a few weeks of bad winter weather can put a crimp in your conditioning.

You don't need a lot of building experience to set up your own exercise room. Our plan (10x15 ft.) is easy to build and will fit nicely into a corner of your basement (see page 183 for construction details). Here are guidelines Bruce gave us on how to set up your room and enjoy it.

- Keep it at a comfortable temperature. It should have some ventilation, but doesn't need special heating or airconditioning.
- The floor should be resilient—working out on a concrete floor will be hard on your feet. Our plan calls for indoor/outdoor carpeting to cushion your feet and make the room look attractive. Bruce told us, "A padded floor is fine as long as it's firm—you shouldn't sink into it."
- You should have an exercise bench. You can use it for bench presses, sit-ups, squat-lifts and other exercises. Our bench is simple and inexpensive to build. The whole assembly is hinged to a wall so you can fold it out of the way. You can leave the legs tucked up and fold the bench down to the floor for inclined sit-ups.
- A barbell set is a good investment. For overall conditioning, Bruce says, "The idea here is not to lift a lot of weight, but to carry some weight through a range of motion. That's a lot more interesting than repetitive bench presses." Don't try for a big lift right off. Always warm up with some jogging in place or calisthenics.
- For family fitness, *isokinetic* exercises are ideal. We tried one isokinetic device (Mini-Gym, made by Mini-Gym, Inc., Box 266, Independence, MO 64051). You tension your muscles by pulling on a counter-weighted rope. The resistance will depend on how hard you pull, so it's just as good for a 10-year-old as for a 50-year-old.
- There are a few "extras." Bruce suggested a radio and mirror. After we mounted a mirror in the room, everybody who went in managed to take a quick look at himself. "One of the most important parts of any exercise program is to see some progress. When nobody's looking, you check those muscles—seeing some results really keeps you at it."

## EXERCISE ROOM CONSTRUCTION

**WE BOXED** in the basement furnace with standard 2x4 walls covered with ½-in. wallboard. You can simplify the job by framing one of the inside walls under a basement girder. This way you can also box the lally column. Cut the 2x4 shoes (wide side on the concrete) to notch around the bottom of the columns

**USE** 2x4s for the new interior walls. Rather than nail on 1x2 strips that can cause leaks, we used 2x3s against the outside walls. Nail studs to a 2x3 shoe on the floor and another 2x3 plate nailed on the flat to the first floor joists. No special tools are needed

**CELLAR VENT** windows can be boxed in with 2x3s. Extend the casing flush to the inside of the new wallboard. Narrow, ½-in.-thick trim and a coat of paint finish the job

**RECESS THE** exposed lines like the wire below. Protect them as shown from nails

**THE "DEADMAN"** (shown below) is simply two pieces of 1x2 stock nailed in a tee and cut about ¾ in. shorter than the height from the floor to the joists. It supports one end of the unwieldly wallboard for the ceiling while you nail the other end

# How to choose a home improvement contractor

**Beware of contractors who promise a 'special' price for one reason or another. Quality remodeling by a first-class contractor can't be offered at a cut rate. Here are some tips on how to choose a reliable contractor and get your money's worth**

By HARRY WICKS

THE FACT that homeowners in all 50 states spent more than $35 billion for home improvements, remodeling and do-it-yourself activities in a recent year is reason enough for the quick-buck boys to make their annual move into the home improvement contracting field. The Better Business Bureau repeatedly warns of schemes that are commonly used by the con artists who hope to lure unwary homeowners into signing contracts without giving them a great deal of thought.

A responsible home improvement contractor will be the first to help you make the necessary choices and decisions to see that you get true value for dollars spent. The fly-by-nighters couldn't care less.

The National Home Improvement Council has a checklist for getting good contractor value:

☐ **Check your needs;** determine which repairs, improvements, and additions are most needed. Establish a priority list of jobs to be done in the order in which you plan to do them. Until the must-do jobs are out of the way, forget about those jobs that are intended to satisfy your personal tastes for luxurious living rather than actual needs.

☐ **Planning your remodeling.** The first step when planning any home improvement is to make a list of exactly what you think you want in the finished job. If you're adding a room, spell out what activities the room will be used for. In some cases, you may have plans for multiple use of the room. A family TV room, for example, can double as a guest bedroom.

SEE ALSO

**Additions, house . . . Attic dormers . . .**
**Basement remodeling . . . Decks . . .**
**Garage remodeling . . . Home improvement . . .**
**House additions . . . Remodeling, exterior . . .**
**Scaffolding . . . Summer houses**

**what is an estimate? a bid?**

There is a marked difference between an estimate and a bid. An estimate is just what the name implies—an educated guess as to what a particular job will cost. A bid, however, is a precise determination of the amount for which a contractor can perform a particular job. For example, suppose you ask a contractor what it would cost to replace your existing front door with a brand new one. He may quickly reply, "About $200." That is a rough estimate. If you then decide to proceed, you would lay out the job exactly, including the specification of materials to be used—door, hardware, and so forth. With such concrete facts in hand, the contractor can then proceed to work up a bid for the exact amount of his contract.

Depending upon the materials that you selected for the job, the bid price in this case might be anywhere from $150 to $250.

*The point is that you should never use an estimate as an ironclad cost-of-project figure.* Keep in mind that an estimate is only a ballpark figure intended to help you to make a sound decision as to whether or not to go ahead with a particular job.

**working with a contractor**

There are several ways to select a contractor—or a number of contractors—to call in for bidding. The most obvious is recommendation by a friend or neighbor who has had work done by a reputable local contractor; one who is completely satisfied with his work performance. This also gives you the opportunity to inspect the work that the contractor did for your friend.

A quick way to find a number of remodeling

contractors in your area is to check the Yellow Pages. But keep in mind that the classified directory only tells you who is available—not who is best.

There are three things you should think about before you select your contractor.

**1. His reputation:** Ideally, the company you choose will have an unblemished record and be respected for its honesty, workmanship, and delivery record. It should be obvious that you would be wise to steer clear of those contractors who leave behind a string of complaining customers and unfinished jobs.

You can get a line on a builder by checking with the local Better Business Bureau and by talking with neighbors and friends in the business community (i.e., real estate brokers, bankers, lawyers).

**2. Credit standing:** Ask your prospective contractor the name and branch of his bank so you can check his company's financial standing. An honest business person will not be insulted; in fact, a reputable dealer will be proud of his good credit standing because it indicates his reliability, stability and solvency.

Though you may be embarrassed to ask the contractor these questions, you shouldn't be. Keep in mind, for instance, that you are well checked out whenever you ask the bank for a home improvement loan.

**3. Work performance:** A reliable contractor will have a list of satisfied customers readily available. Don't be afraid to request this list of names and addresses so that you can inspect his craftsmanship and talk with his customers. If your planned project is a large one, you would be wise to visit at least three similar jobs your prospective contractor has done for others.

Beware of contractors who say that they can't seem to find any customers' names in the immediate area. Be even more wary if they claim that such records are unnecessary and that they don't bother to keep them. Such negative responses should be your cue to dismiss the contractor from further consideration. It's a pretty safe assumption that he's a fast-buck artist on the hustle.

### competitive bidding

In remodeling work, it's best to get competitive bids on jobs in the $500-and-up range. You can, of course, request bids on smaller jobs but many contractors aren't that eager for work in the lower price range these days. Some will decline the invitation because they have more attractive opportunities elsewhere, or because they do not have the time or incentive to work up estimates for small jobs.

In fairness to the contractors bidding on a project, make certain that all of them are bidding on exactly the same job. All bidders should be working up their prices from identical sets of drawings and specifications that clearly spell out how the project is to be constructed and with what materials.

My personal experience in the home improvement and building business has led me to conclude that too often a homeowner merely asks the contractors to give him a price without spelling out details. Then, he is usually overwhelmed by a wide range of prices the various contractors submit. As a result, and the homeowner may not realize it, the lowest bid may be based on the lowest-quality materials available. Similarly, the high bidder may have figured upon using the very best materials which can be substantially higher in cost.

For example, if you are planning a room addition that will have, say, four casement windows, one bidder may choose to install locally-fabricated windows without storms and screens. The bidder on the high end may, from experience, choose a top-of-the-line double or triple glazed window that comes with screening. The latter may cost $60 to $80 per window more than the cheapies—and be worth every penny of it.

The point is that unless all contractors' figures are based upon exact and identical criteria, there is no way you can evaluate competitive bids fairly.

The bottom line is that when all bids are in, you may not necessarily go with the lowest bidder. You may have learned in your pre-bid investigations that the low-bidding outfit never meets promised completion dates—or never seems to completely finish the job.

### get a contract

Though some may justifiably argue that a contract with a home remodeler isn't worth the paper it is printed on, the contractor you choose should present a formal contract for both parties to sign. The job should be fully explained therein, materials clearly spelled out, and dates of completion indicated. Terms of payment should also be detailed. Many contractors split the fee into three payments—the first one is usually up front, at the time of contract signing; the second is after an agreed upon amount of work has been performed, and the final payment after the job is completed and you (the customer) are satisfied.

# A cookout bar—the focus of summer fun

By ROBERT D. BORST

**The whole family can join in the fun of building and using an elegant patio-grill. This one's equipped with storage bins, water, electricity, two grills and a tile surface for lounging or dancing**

MAYBE YOU ALREADY have a portable grill and find it adequate, but when it comes to real outdoor entertaining, southern style, you can't beat a cookout bar like this one.

For one thing it's big enough to let you host a king-size crowd. On its two grills you can play chef like a pro. You can have hamburgers working on one and steaks broiling on the other. The big wide counter gives you room to spread out a buffet. Charcoal and hickory chips are nearby in handy storage bins. Water, electricity and a phone make you independent of the house, and the connecting patio lets you have a ball on its slick tile surface. Two yellow yardlights add a glow and a low cushion-fitted wall provides extra seating.

The chances are you won't build yours exactly like mine. You may just settle for a poured patio and not bother tiling it. Maybe the cookout bar is

SEE ALSO
**Barbecue tables . . . Barbecues . . .
Benches, deck . . . Carpeting, outdoor . . .
Firepits . . . Garden shelters . . . Gazebos . . .
Grills . . . Insect traps . . . Patios . . .
Picnic tables . . . Planters . . . Privacy screens**

**A PLACE** for both dining and dancing, this elegant-looking back-yard patio is just right for the young and old alike. When cleared of the tables and chairs, the tiled area paves the way for teen-age dancers to make summer parties at home a real ball for the younger set. And, of special appeal for the older members of the family, the cookout bar comes equipped with everything except the kitchen sink, though there's running water.

**PATIO EXCAVATION** is made 13 in. deep (upper left) from a level string. Then the area is covered with a layer of fine sand (above, center) and raked smooth to a depth of 9 in. (above, right). After sprinkling with water from hose, sand is tamped (below) to form a firm 8-in. bed for concrete. Footings are dug 18 in. deep inside separate form boards and filled with rock.

all you'll want. You may be happy with just one grill.

Whatever ideas you borrow, construction is basically the same. If you do plan to tile the patio, it's wise to make it a size which will accept a given number of full tiles (not forgetting mortar joints) so you won't have to cut any. I used 6-in. quarry tiles and bedded them in mortar.

The photos on pages 864 and 865 show the steps I followed in building the patio section. This involved leveling off the area, covering it with a 9-in. layer of sand, sprinkling this with

**STEEL RODS** and welded wire fabric are both used to reinforce the concrete slab and guard against possible cracking by freezing and heaving action of the earth.

**FOOTINGS ARE POURED** first and struck off level with a straightedge. Then the forms are removed and strips of expansion felt inserted before pouring the slab.

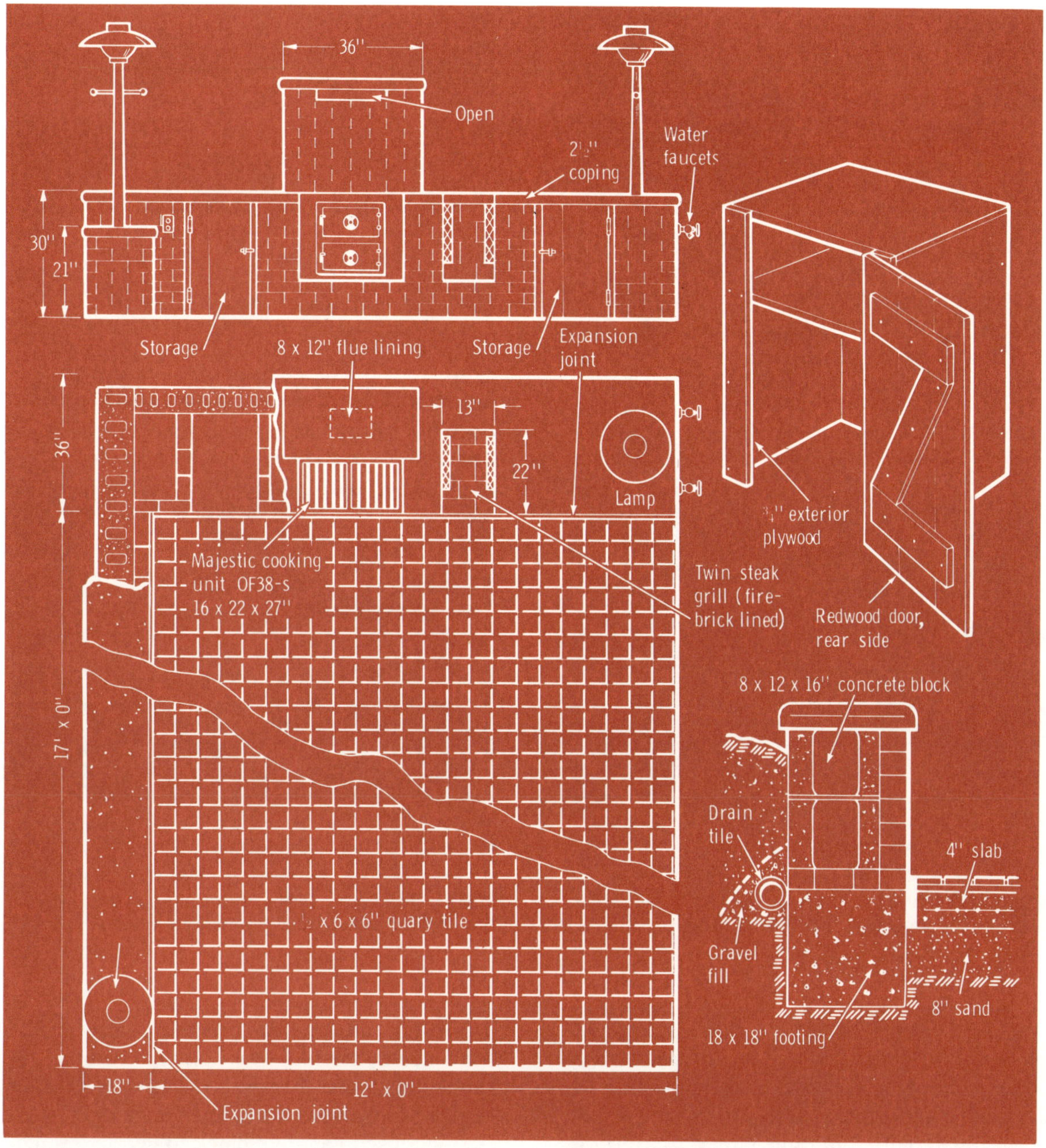


**ROUGHENING THE SURFACE** by raking lightly gives partially set concrete a "tooth" for bonding tile to it with a mortar bed. Tile is grouted in usual manner.

**BUILDING PAPER** or burlap laid over poured slab keeps concrete from drying too fast. Keep the covering moist by spraying it with water once a day for a week.

**CLAY FIELD TILE,** laid in ditch along footing of wall and covered with gravel, drains seepage from the bank.

**COOKOUT BAR IS** built up of blocks and faced with brick after the water and electric lines are in place.

**COMPLETED WALL**, faced with brick, is finally capped with a poured-in-place concrete coping that is 2 in. thick.

**METAL GRILL** establishes height of poured counters. Partially completed open firepit is shown alongside.

water and tamping it to 8 in. This was followed by installing form boards, adding reinforcing wire, pouring the concrete, striking it off level, scratching the surface with a rake and finally covering it with building paper for curing. Scratching the surface is done only if the patio is to be tiled, otherwise you simply trowel the concrete smooth when it begins to set. It will take a week for the concrete to cure properly during which time it should be kept moist with a hose.

You will notice in the photo showing the form boards that separate forms are provided so the footings for the wall and cookout bar can be poured separately from the patio. The footings are actually poured first, then the forms are pulled out and strips of expansion felt are placed against the concrete before the patio is poured. Wiring for the lamp posts and piping for the water should be in place before any concrete is poured.

I built the cookout bar around two metal grills, one made by the Majestic Co., and the other by Donley Brothers, (be sure to have your grills on hand for measurements before you start the project) and used concrete block to lay up a rough structure. Then I faced the block with used bricks bought for a penny each.

Forms for the poured-slab counters are partially supported by two wooden cabinets which provide on-the-spot storage for pots and pans and charcoal. Note that I covered the chimney top with a slab, too, leaving an opening in the brick at the front for the smoke. I later gave the counters and the coping along the top of the wall a coat of latex paint. The pit for the twin-fire grill holds two charcoal baskets which hang on each side to char-broil steaks hung between them. The pit measures 12½ in. wide, 20 in. deep and 32 in. high. The main grill is a complete unit—you simply brick around it.

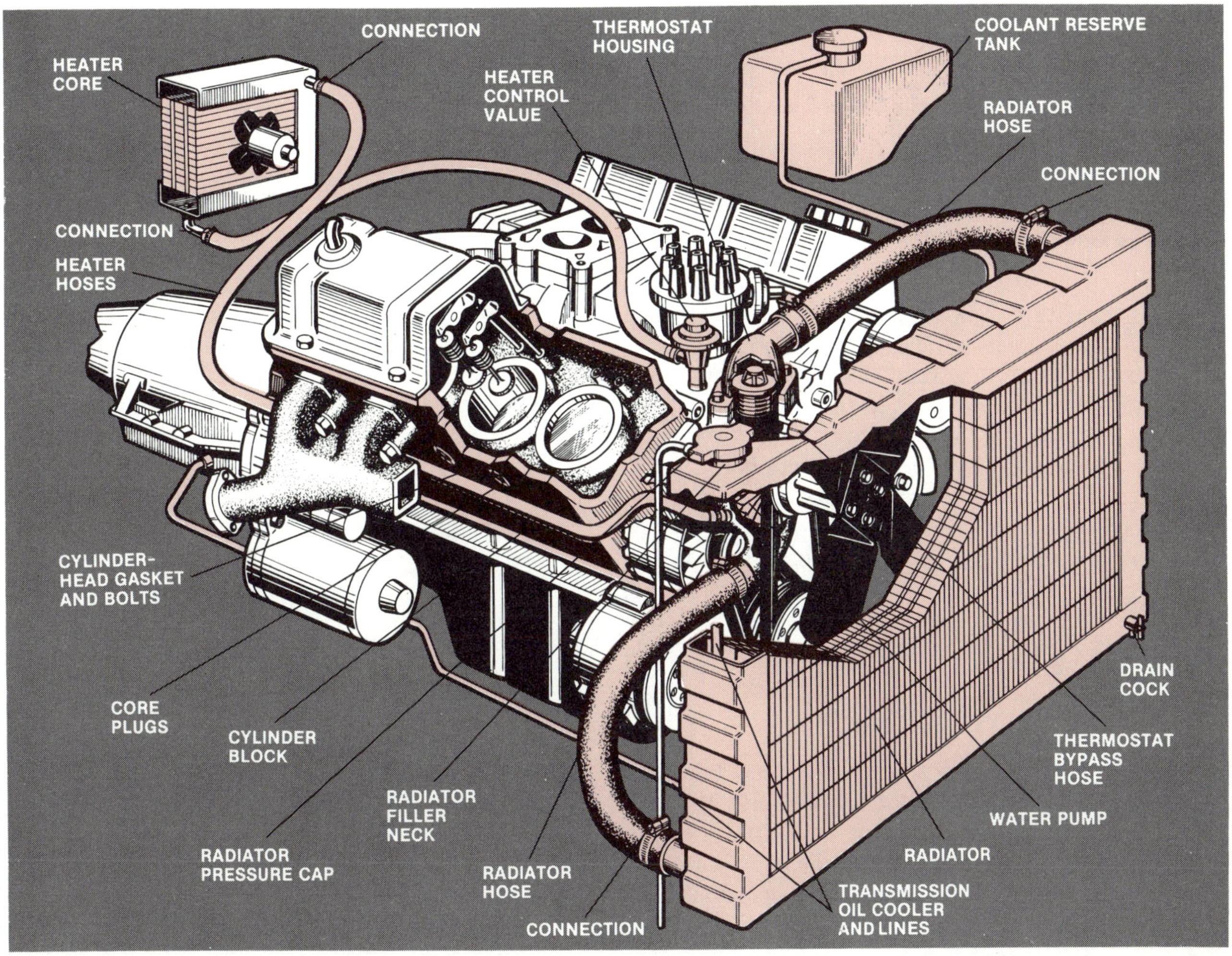


# How to find the cause of engine overheating

■ FREQUENTLY, engine overheating occurs because the owner fails to maintain his car's cooling system. Maintenance requires draining and flushing the system at least once every two years, seeing that components (hoses, drive belt, radiator-pressure cap and thermostat) are operational, and filling the system with ethylene glycol coolant.

| CAUSE | CORRECTION |
|---|---|
| System loses coolant. | Coolant loss is a result of several factors, summarized below. |
| Inadequate ethylene glycol coolant mixture. | Ethylene glycol protects engine against cold weather, also corrosion leading to curtailment of coolant flow, overheating. |
| | Check solution with hydrometer. Protection between −35°F. and −45°F. is considered normal. |
| System loses pressure. | Test radiator-pressure cap; Check loose hose connections. |
| Obstructed radiator. | Clean bugs, debris from fins. |
| Radiator tubes blocked by scale. | If flushing doesn't work, have radiator shop treat radiator chemically. |
| Cooling-system passages blocked by scale. | Flush system; add fresh coolant. |
| Loose drive belt. | Tighten. |
| Inoperative thermal control fluid coupling fan. | Repair. |
| Damaged water pump. | Repair. |
| Lower radiator hose collapses due to weak internal spring. | Replace hose. |
| Defective thermostat stuck in closed position. | Replace thermostat |
| Incorrect ignition timing. | Set timing to spec; test vacuum advance for functioning. |
| Restricted exhaust system. | See that muffler, exhaust system pipes haven't collapsed. |

**Areas of coolant loss**

Check the following areas when coolant is being lost:

| Areas of leakage | Corrective action |
|---|---|
| ☐ Radiator. | Try sealer if leak is small, repair or replace radiator if leak is large. |
| ☐ Radiator drain cock. | Tighten if loose; replace if defective. |
| ☐ Transmission-oil cooler lines | Tighten connections. |
| ☐ Coolant reserve tank and hose. | Repair or replace tank; replace hose. |
| ☐ Hoses (radiator and heater), connections. | Tighten if loose; replace if defective. |
| ☐ Water-pump seal. | Repair. |
| ☐ Water-pump gasket. | Replace. |
| ☐ Radiator pressure cap. | Tighten if loose, replace if defective. |
| ☐ Radiator filler neck. | Reform if distorted; cut off and solder on new filler neck if repair fails. |
| ☐ Thermostat housing gasket. | Replace. |
| ☐ Heater core. | Repair or replace |
| ☐ Heater-water control valve. | Replace. |
| ☐ Cylinder-head gasket. | Replace. |
| ☐ Cylinder-head bolts. | Tighten to specification. |
| ☐ Cylinder-block core plugs. | Replace. |
| ☐ Warped cylinder head or blocked surface. | Resurface. |
| ☐ Cracked cylinder head or block. | Replace. |

SEE ALSO
**Alternators, auto . . .**
**Carburetors, auto . . . Chokes, auto . . .**
**Dieseling, auto . . . Engines, auto . . .**
**Ignition systems, auto . . .**
**Stalling, auto . . . Tune-up, auto**

# How to maintain your car's cooling system

By MORT SCHULTZ

WHAT GOES THROUGH your mind when you see someone standing forlornly next to a car by the side of the road? The hood is up, and a plume of white smoke jets from the engine compartment.

Do you think, "I'm glad I'm not in that fix?"

Or do you think: "That *could* be me if my car's cooling system can't take the strain."

The people downed by cooling-system failure are normally those who take this important system for granted. Although the cooling system has been developed into one of the most reliable units in a car—only 25 years ago it required servicing every six months—it is *not* maintenance-free.

Today's cooling system will maintain efficiency for the life of the car, but only if it gets some basic maintenance periodically. "Periodically" is defined as once every two years.

Periodic service, detailed here, will do the following:

- It helps avoid engine freeze-ups during cold weather.
- It improves total cooling efficiency, assuring that the engine won't overheat.
- It helps prevent corrosion and sludge build-up in the cooling system and engine, which leads to expensive repairs.
- It allows the engine to operate within its most efficient temperature range, which provides the most effective and economical operation.

The sensible maintenance program outlined here is designed to let you avoid unnecessary work while still providing the cooling system with the conditioning it needs to remain viable. Keep in mind that this program is *preventive* maintenance—that is, maintenance which is done to help avert a breakdown. We are not discussing what has to be done if a cooling-system failure occurs—specifically, overheating. Our purpose is to avoid failure.

The sensible cooling-system maintenance program we outline here consists of seven parts, as follows:

- Checking radiator hoses.
- Checking drive belts.
- Cleaning radiator fins.
- Checking the integrity of the radiator pressure cap.
- Checking the thermostat.
- Cleaning the system.
- Filling the system with a high quality coolant which contains rust inhibitor.

Let's discuss each.

SEE ALSO

**Autos, body repair . . . Autos, maintenance . . . Engines, auto . . . Gaskets, auto . . . Leaks, auto . . . Lubrication, auto . . . Tune-up, auto . . . Winterizing, autos**

### hose examination

Examine top and bottom radiator hoses, and two heater hoses. Squeeze each hose over its *entire* length. If the hose feels spongy or exhibits cracks, replace the part. Failure of hoses is the dominant cooling system malfunction leading to roadside breakdowns.

While at it, look for corrosion or rust-colored stains around hose clamps. These signify a coolant leak. If hose clamps are the screw-tightening rather than vise type, tighten clamps and clean off deposits. If the leak reappears or clamps cannot be tightened, the hose or clamp has weakened. Both should be replaced.

The correct way to remove the old hose is the way you find easiest—cutting it off if necessary. Clean connecting surfaces thoroughly with a wire brush.

Coat connections with water-resistant sealing compound. Place new clamps on the ends of the hose, and install the new hose all the way on connections. If the ends of the hose are stiff and aren't easily manipulated, soak them in hot water for a minute or so before connecting them. Slide clamps into position. Tighten.

Be sure to locate clamps at least ⅛ inch from the ends of the hose. If they are placed at the ends, the hose may bulge behind them. That can lead to premature hose failure.

**THE "FEEL"** of a radiator hose will tell you if it has rotted, gotten mushy, and is due for replacement. Retire any that show cracks under pressure, too.

**YOU'LL FEEL** a spring in the lower radiator hose. If it doesn't feel tense, replace the hose. Check the drive belt's condition at the same time.

Don't discount the importance of examining heater hoses. They are part of the cooling system. Coolant flows through them just as it does through radiator hoses. If a heater hose fails, you will lose coolant and overheating will result—just as quickly as when radiator hoses fail.

### checking drive belts

If the drive belt that runs the water pump and cooling fan is damaged or not adjusted properly, cooling will be curtailed. Further, the power steering, alternator and air conditioning, depend on belts.

Examine belts for cracks, frayed spots and glaze on the underside. Glaze on the belt or on the pulley will cause slipping. Belt damage of any kind is cause for its immediate replacement.

Whether the old belt is adequate or a new belt is installed, correct adjustment is necessary. A belt that is adjusted too tight will put strain on water pump, fan pulley, and alternator components, causing early failure. One that isn't tight enough can't drive components efficiently.

The most effective way of testing belt tension is with a professional drive-belt tension gauge, which you can purchase at an automotive supply store. Hook the tool's tang on the belt and press down on the knob until resistance is met. Read the gauge and compare it to manufacturer specification in the service manual. Adjust the belt accordingly.

Without a gauge, you can judge tension by laying a straight-edge between the pulleys and pressing a ruler down on the belt at the midway point. The deflection shouldn't exceed ½ inch.

Newer cars often have a fan clutch that disengages when the engine needs less cooling. The clutch is easy to check. With the engine cold, start the car and let it warm up. As temperature increases, the clutch should engage. With no increase in engine speed, you should see the fan speed up abruptly—often with a distinct click. Otherwise the clutch probably needs repair.

### cleaning radiator fins

In the two years since your last maintenance work, lots of trash—bugs, leaves, and dirt—may have built up around the fins. It can handicap the system seriously. Clean it out with air pressure or a long-handled, soft-bristled brush.

**HOSE CLAMPS** should be at least ⅛ inch from the hose end and the hose seated firmly in place.

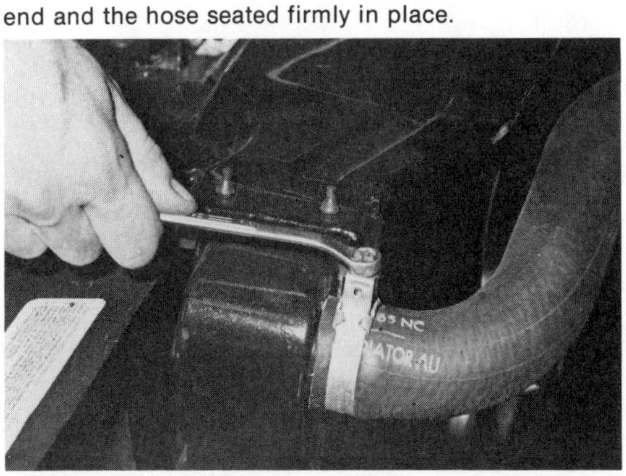

**FOR EXACT** drive-belt tension, a gauge is the only reliable guide. Anything else is second best.

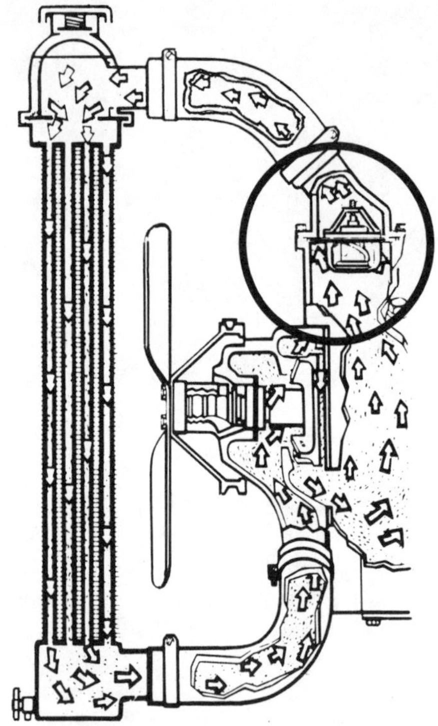

THERMOSTAT (circled) stops or permits coolant circulation according to the engine's need for cooling. Special fan clutches on newer cars have a similar role.

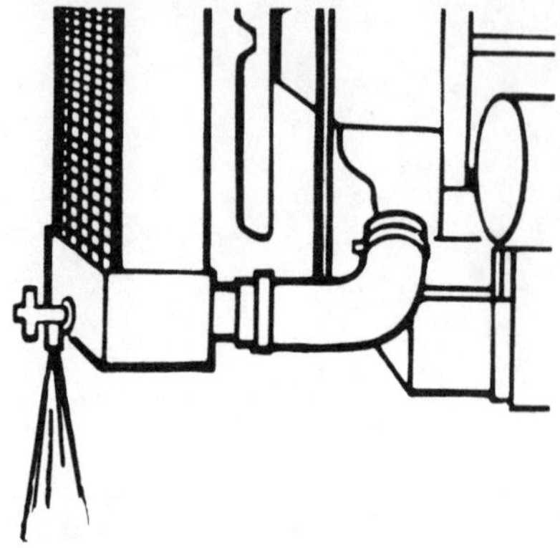

EVERY radiator's lower tank has a drain cock, but you may have to grope to find yours.

If you have compressed air, aim it from the side instead of directly at the fragile fins. The brush is slower, but safer. If dirt is caked on, you may need to wash the radiator surface.

**testing the radiator pressure cap**

Your radiator cap is designed to let go only after coolant reaches a preselected pressure. This function is important. A modern engine runs best with coolant under pressure. That keeps it from boiling at running temperatures above 200° F. So long as it remains liquid, the coolant keeps circulating as it should.

TO DRAIN ALL the coolant, remove drain plugs in the block. This one was difficult to find.

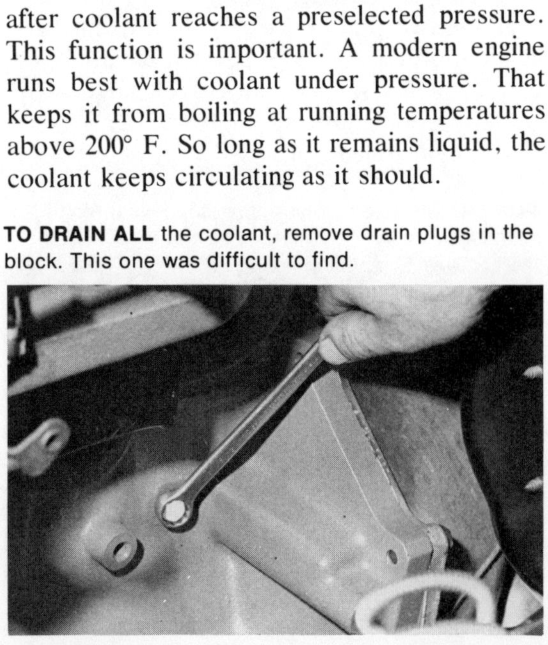

Under 15 pounds of pressure, the boiling point of a typical ethylene glycol mix is raised about 40° F. If it would normally boil at 225° F., a 15-pound cap prevents its boiling until about 265° F. Thus it can keep transferring excess heat from the block to the radiator where it can be rejected to the atmosphere.

Caps are checked with a cooling-system pressure tester—standard equipment at most service stations. The charge is usually nominal.

**checking the thermostat**

The thermostat is another element to check. Its function: It opens to allow circulation to start only when the engine has reached running temperature.

Sooner or later, thermostats fail. Since the cooling system has to be drained for cleaning anyway, this is the time to check the thermostat, too.

Follow these steps:

1. Make sure the engine is cold. Remove the radiator pressure cap.
2. Set the heater control to ON and open the drain cock at the base of the radiator. Let old coolant drain.
3. To ensure complete draining, remove engine drain plugs. V8s usually have two, Sixes, one.
4. After draining, close the cock and reinsert the plugs securely.
5. Remove the thermostat bolts and move the housing aside.
6. Remove and discard the old gasket. And if, in that cold engine, the thermostat wasn't closed, discard it, too.
7. Note the thermostat's temperature rating marked on the housing.

8. Hang the thermostat from a wire in water in a heat-resistant-glass pot (glass, so you can see inside). Add a thermometer and put the pot on the stove.

9. The thermostat valve should open wide before it is 15° above its rating. If it isn't, replace the thermostat.

10. Wire-brush the mating surfaces of the thermostat housing and the engine thoroughly.

11. Reinsert the thermostat, making sure the bolt holes line up.

12. Put a *new* gasket in place, reattach the thermostat housing, and tighten the housing bolts.

**cleaning the system**

If you clean the cooling system with a commercially available fast-flush chemical every two years, you probably won't ever have to have it back-flushed. Back-flushing is pressure-cleaning and requires special equipment. Follow mixing instructions printed on the package.

Occasionally increase engine speed by pressing the accelerator pedal slowly about halfway to the floor. This allows more forceful circulation that will dislodge scale.

At the end of the prescribed time, drain the system by opening the drain cock and removing the drain plugs. The heater should have been kept *on*. Do *not* remove the radiator pressure cap.

But never add cold water or coolant to a hot engine. The block may crack.

**adding antifreeze**

When the discharge from the drain cock looks clear, finish draining. Close the drain cock and drain plugs and let the engine cool down. Then add a reliable brand of ethylene glycol to the cooling system.

Confusing questions are sometimes raised about ethylene glycol. Let's summarize the pertinent points:

- You needn't add anything to ethylene glycol antifreeze. A good brand already includes all the needed additives, including rust inhibitor, to protect the cooling system for two years.
- Don't use straight water as a coolant, even in areas where you need no antifreeze protection. You'll miss the protective additives you should have. And remember that a modern engine—especially one with air conditioning—may often run at a temperature above water's 212° boiling point. Ethylene glycol's boiling point is still higher.
- The proportion of ethylene glycol your system needs depends on how cold your area will get. Instructions are on the antifreeze container (you'll have to know your system's capacity). Drain the system down to leave ample room, then add the antifreeze called for.
- Check the coolant's potency each year before cold weather. Use a hydrometer; it's a good tool to have and needn't be expensive.

All in all, this maintenance program may take only about an hour every two years—little enough considering its importance.

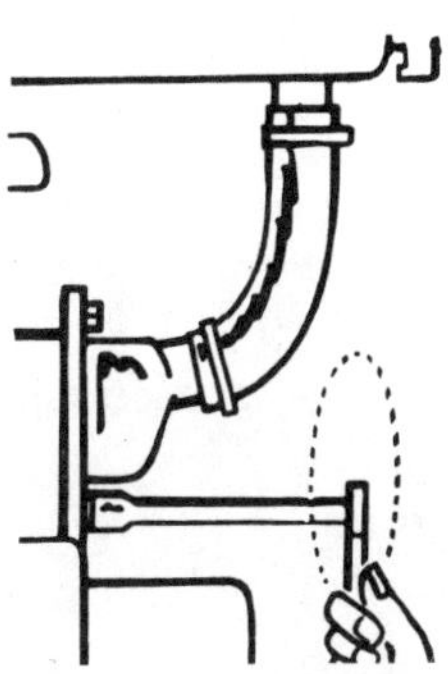

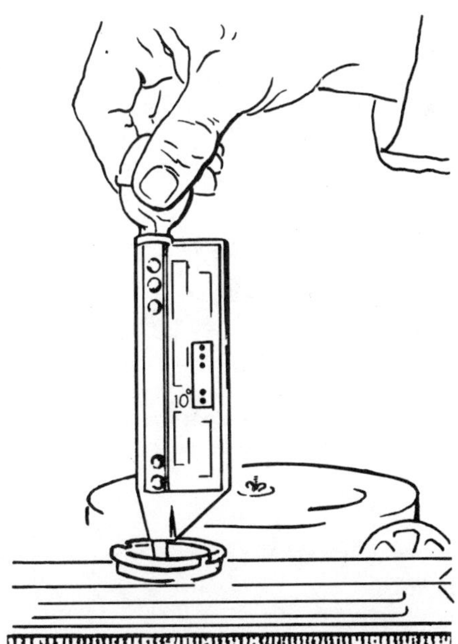

**TO GET AT** the thermostat, first remove the housing bolts (left). Then lift the housing or swing it aside and remove the thermostat itself (center). Don't try to reuse this gasket; throw it away. At the right, a simple and low cost hydrometer does an adequate job monitoring coolant strength.

# Install a coolant recovery system

By BILL HARTFORD

■ IT'S JUST A see-through container that catches overflow from your car radiator. If you have one you take it for granted. If you install it following instructions, you'll wonder how you ever got along without it.

The container is essentially an expansion tank. It is mounted near the radiator and is connected by the radiator overflow hose. It makes a sealed system of your cooling system.

**1. OVERFLOW BOTTLE,** from a kit such as parts stores offer, should be mounted high in engine compartment near the radiator. A spot ahead of the radiator, perhaps inboard of a front fender, is preferred.

SEE ALSO
**Gaskets, auto . . . Leaks, auto . . .**
**Tune-up, auto . . . Winterizing, autos**

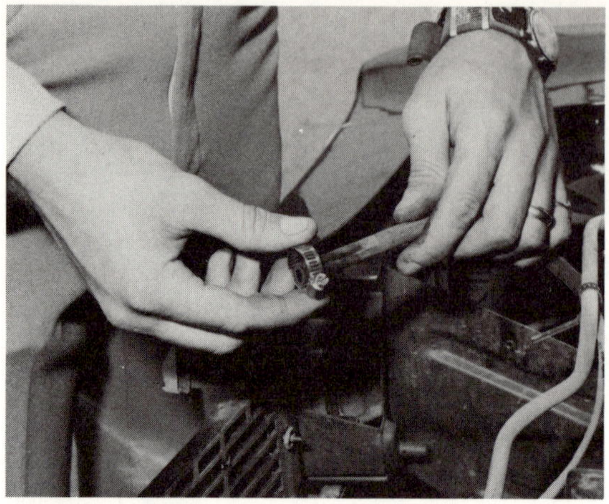

**2. HOSE CLAMPS** should be used at both ends of the radiator overflow hose. That hose usually runs from the radiator neck down alongside the radiator.

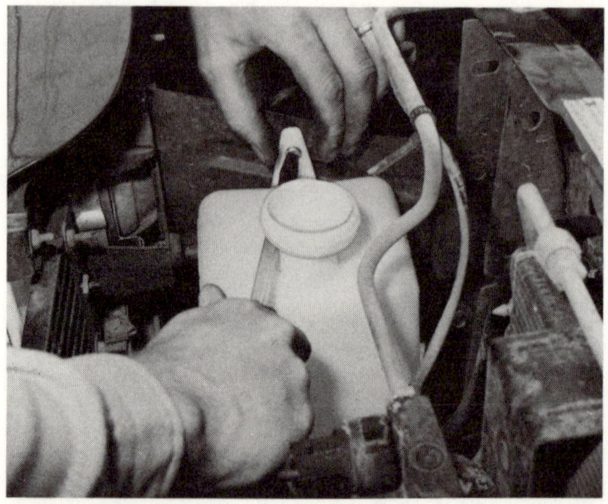

**5. THE OVERFLOW** bottle, hoses in place, is positioned and held with sheet-metal screws. Holes drilled for the screws shouldn't be too big.

As your engine heats up, expansion takes place in the system and coolant is forced into the tank rather than lost on the road. As your engine cools, temperature and pressure are reduced and coolant is drawn back into the radiator from the tank.

Consider the many advantages:

- You can visually check the coolant level. You don't have to remove the radiator cap and peer inside.
- You eliminate the danger of removing the radiator cap to be confronted by a scalding geyser.
- You save costly antifreeze, now at record high prices.
- A sealed system keeps air out of your cooling system, reducing corrosion and bubbling that impairs heat transfer.

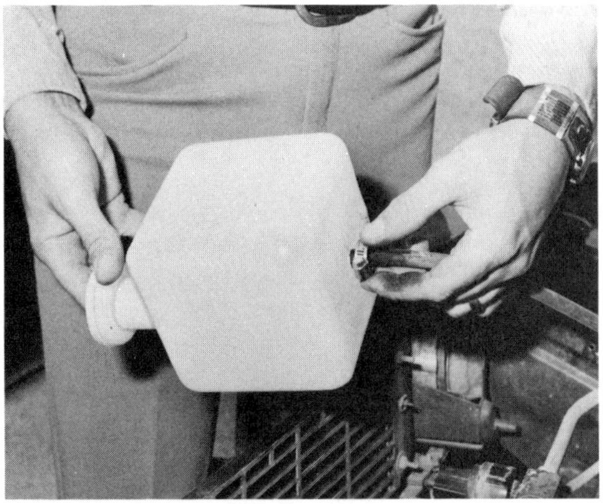

**3. THE OVERFLOW HOSE** goes over a flange on the bottom of the bottle. Slip a clamp over the hose, install it, then slide the clamp into place.

**4. TIGHTEN THE CLAMP** holding the overflow hose in place at the bottom of the bottle as well as the other clamp at the radiator end of the hose.

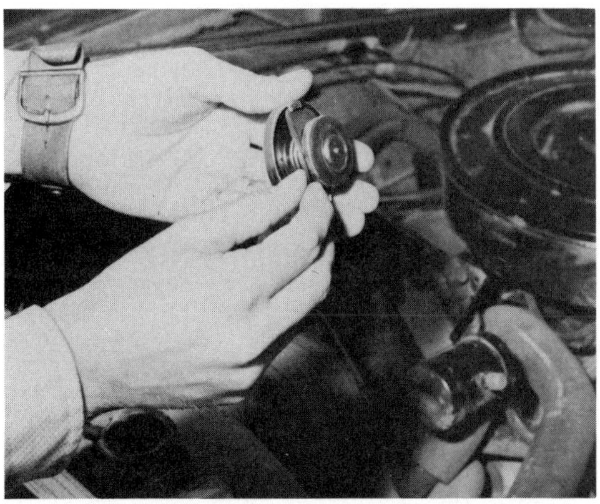

**6. NEW RADIATOR CAP** comes with overflow bottle kit. The cap's rubber seal is necessary in order to seal the cooling system; make sure it's in place.

**7. INSTALL THE CAP** after filling the radiator with a 50/50 mixture of ethylene glycol antifreeze and water. Fill it to the top.

**8. FILL THE OVERFLOW** bottle halfway with antifreeze. Most bottles have "Min" and "Max" marks; a level midway between them is right.

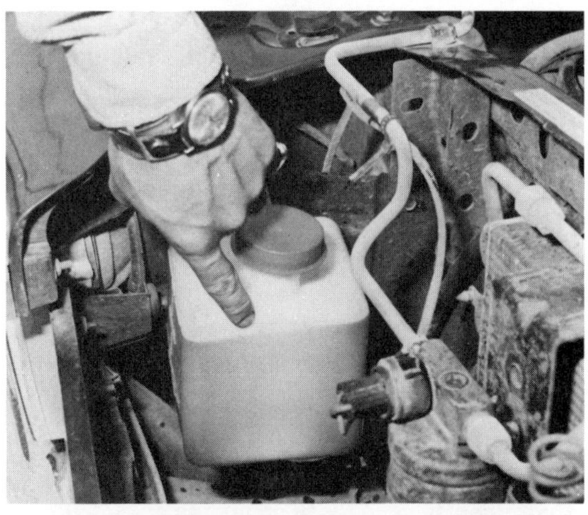

**9. LEVEL WILL RISE** as the engine warms coolant. That's why the "Max" marking leaves some unfilled capacity—for expansion. Don't overfill.

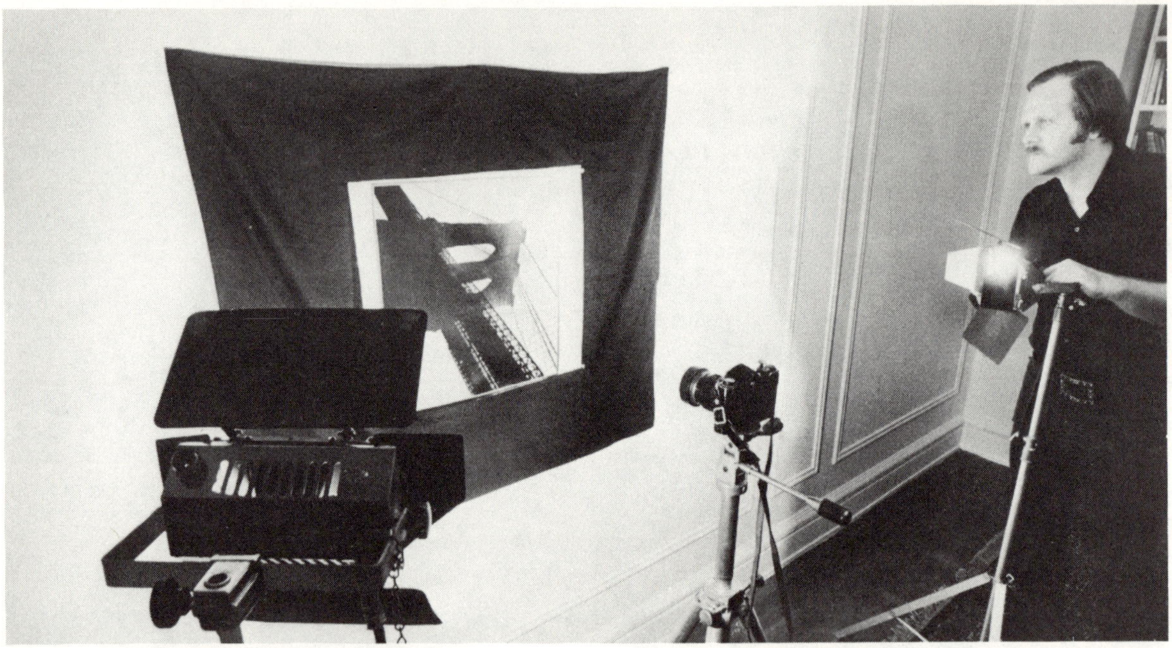

**BASIC COPY SETUP** uses two lights at 45° angle to subject. To prevent glare, lights are *behind* camera, and subject is on black background. Professional lights aren't necessary—you can even make your own units.

# Copy photography —useful and inexpensive

**By DAVE SAGARIN**

■ COPY PHOTOGRAPHY is one of the most useful things you're probably *not* doing with your camera. But once you get into the swing of it, you'll find its uses almost endless. For example:

■ Copy old family photos, so the relatives can have prints even though the negatives have long since disappeared.

■ Improve old faded photos by making copies that improve the contrast and minimize the spots and stains.

■ Add images from postcards to your travel slide shows.

■ Copy maps, artworks, and pictures in books for school or reference purposes.

SEE ALSO

**Camera care . . . Candid photography . . . Cartridges, film . . . Close-up photos . . . Darkrooms . . . Developing, photo . . . Dryers, photo . . . Mountings, photo . . . Photography . . . Prints, photo**

■ When a negative is so badly exposed that it's impossible to make a good, big print of it, make a good small one (which won't be easy, either), retouch it, and make a good copy negative for use in making future prints.

■ Copy multiple-image and other experimental prints that would take you hours to duplicate in the darkroom.

■ Copy on high-contrast or lithographic film to separate images into tone value levels for use in silk-screen and other graphic processes.

You don't need a macro lens, a copy stand, elaborate equipment or unusual films for copy photography either. But you do need to work slowly and carefully.

**what you need**

Work in a large room with a minimum of furniture, traffic and windows. Shoot against a black cloth or cardboard background to minimize flare in the lens.

Fasten your original, with its larger dimension horizontal, to the backdrop. If the original is translucent, back it with heavy white paper, to keep the black background from showing through.

Set your camera on a sturdy tripod just far enough away so that the image of your original doesn't quite fill your view-finder or focusing screen. Your lens is less sharp at its edge, and this loss of sharpness will be more apparent when you copy flat materials.

Make sure your lens is exactly perpendicular to the center of the original. Once that's measured and set, mark centerlines on the backdrop for use in setting up each subsequent copy.

If you're copying something you can't hang on the wall (a book, for instance), use a vertical setup with the camera pointing down from a tripod or copy stand and the original face up on a table. To flatten book pages, use a clean, heavy glass plate with black strips laid on the glass to mask off the copy area.

**what lens to use**

If you have a choice, use your sharpest normal or moderate tele lens. A macro lens is even better, if you have access to one, but it's not absolutely necessary.

For very small originals (roughly speaking, anything less than about 10 times the size of your negative), you will need close-up gear. A macro lens is best, but an enlarging lens mounted on a bellows will do about as good a job for a lot less; just be sure to add exposure to compensate for the fall-off in light due to the bellows's extension (a through-the-lens meter does this automatically).

If you only have your standard lens to use, get a reversing collar (available from Spiratone, Vivitar and others) so you can mount it backwards on your extension tubes or bellows; at very close distances, it's sharper that way. If your camera's lens isn't removable, then you'll have to use supplementary close-up lenses, but avoid them if you can: Putting more glass in front of your lens can only cause additional flare, loss of sharpness and added aberrations.

Whatever lens you use, it should be very clean, and have a big lens shade. As you've probably gathered from my frequent mentions so far, light flaring in the lens is the biggest single enemy of apparent sharpness in the final print.

**lighting and filtration**

The basic lighting setup for most copy work is simple: light at each side of your original with each light set behind the camera lens and aimed at about a 45° angle toward the original's far edge. Check each light individually for glare, and move it further over, if need be, to get rid of a glare. Make sure the light is balanced by pointing your finger at the center of the original—almost touching it. If the shadows your finger casts are equally dark, then the light is balanced.

You don't need professional studio lights like the ones I'm using. You can make a perfectly good unit using a 250-watt photoflood bulb, a clamp and socket unit from the hardware store, and a stand made by setting a six-foot pole in a paper paint bucket filled with plaster.

You can even make your own reflector from about 30 inches of heavy aluminum foil. Fold and flatten a three or four-inch hem along one long edge for stiffening, then wrap the hemmed

**FILTERS CONTROL CONTRAST** in black-and-white copies of color originals. Red filter lightened red car (above right), darkened glass; without filter (below right), car and grass show as similar tones of gray.

**REPRODUCING TEXTURES** of oil paintings, textiles and some other originals requires a main light that skims the original's surface at a shallow angle, to produce surface shadows, plus a soft "fill" at a 45° angle, to open but not erase them.

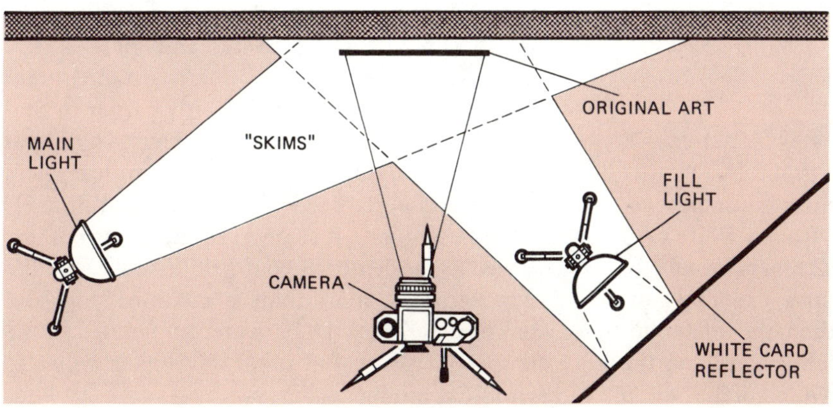

edge around the socket, so the rest of the foil extends past the bulb in a rough cone. Shape it with your finger until it reflects fairly even light onto the wall. Such home-brew reflectors can be better than the spun-aluminum, store-bought ones, since you can easily mold the foil to control light spread and eliminate hot spots.

Filters are also useful in copy work. A filter lightens its own color and darkens its opposite. A yellow filter, for example, could be used to either partially bleach out a yellow stain on an old print, or to increase the contrast of a faded blueprint by darkening the blue background.

In making black-and-white copies of color originals, filters can help maintain contrast between opposite colors that might print as the same shade of gray, as in the example of the red car on the green background in the photos below.

On the other hand, filters can help reproduce the tonal relationships between colors more exactly. Since panchromatic films tend to lighten reds and darken greens, a light, yellow-green No. 11 filter is needed to restore the tonal balance—if you're perfectionist enough to care.

Polarizing filters are often recommended for "cutting glare," and they do help. But it's always better to remove the source of the glare, if you can, by shading the glare spot with a black card, moving a light, or pulling a shade over an offending window. If your original is glossy, or is mounted behind glass, block reflections from its surface by aiming the camera through a hole in a big, black card.

**line and tone originals**

There are two different kinds of originals. *Continuous tone images* that are made up of series of gray values or colors, as in a photo print or painting. But printed texts, drawings, and the like, are *line* originals which carry all their information in one tone against a background of a contrasting tone or color. These require special techniques to give you black-on-white results instead of gray-on-gray.

**adjusting exposure for tone**

For tone originals, I use Kodak Panatomic-X film, for its sharpness and fine grain, but "push" it to 80 ASA to get more contrast. For best results, take your meter reading from a white card or paper that matches the white background of the original you're copying and use two-and-a-half stops more exposure than the meter indicates. If you can't find such a card, or the original's background isn't white, meter off a standard, 18 percent gray card or use an incident meter; with either gray-card or incident metering, use the meter's recommended exposure. For maximum sharpness, close down two or three stops from your lens's maximum aperture, and adjust exposure by changing shutter speeds.

If you're using a filter (never use more than one at once), hold it over the meter when you take your reading. Then, if the original is similar in color to the filter, give the film one half stop less exposure than indicated; if the original and filter are opposite in color, give it one half stop more.

**test roll**

Now you're ready for a test roll. Pick a normal-looking original, and shoot it, bracketing your exposures at half-stop intervals from two stops less than the calculated exposure to two stops more. Process 10 minutes in straight Microdol-X at 75° F. If you have the film done by a custom lab, ask for a one-stop push. Testprint on smooth-surfaced, grade 3 paper, to find which exposure gives the best copy. From there on, use this as the basis for future exposures.

Low-contrast tone originals, like faded photographs or pencil sketches need extra contrast to reproduce well, so treat them not as continuous tone, but as line originals.

Line originals don't require the subtle separation between grays that you need for tone originals. Here there should be just two, unsubtly differentiated tones: pure black and pure white.

For line work, I use either Kodak Panatomic-X or High Contrast Copy films. Of the two, Panatomic-X is the easier to get and use. Rate it at 125 ASA, meter by either the gray-card or incident methods, and use that reading as the basis for your exposure tests. To develop, try Kodak HC-110, in dilution A, for six-and-a-half minutes at 68°, for a two-stop push. This is my choice for low-contrast tone originals, too.

Kodak High Contrast Copy film is made for use in copying line originals and gives a very good high-contrast negative with ultrafine grain and very high resolution. But it's harder to find than Panatomic-X, and it's trickier: Any slight variation in lighting, processing or printing will show up as a marked defect in the final print. If you do use it, rate it at ASA 32, meter the corners as well as the center of your field to make sure the light varies no more than a one-third stop, and develop in Kodak D-19, as recommended in the film's data sheet. But other developers will also work: Experiment.

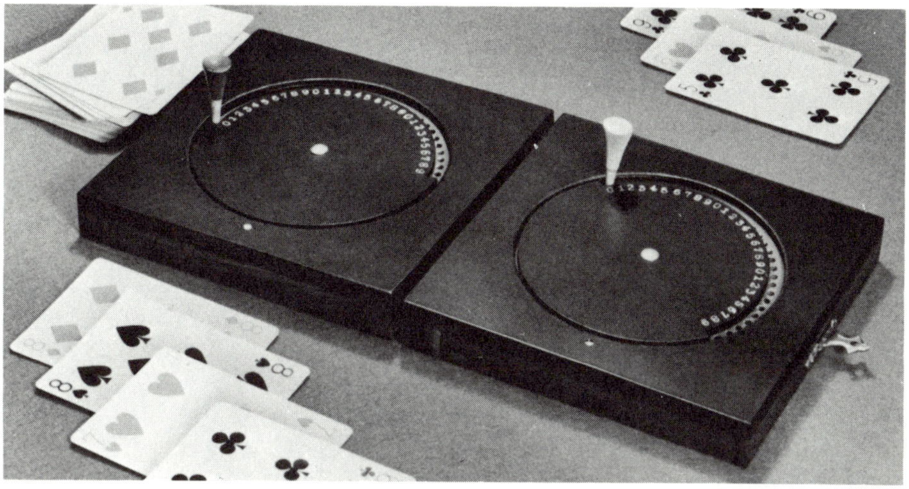

# A cribbage board for your pocket

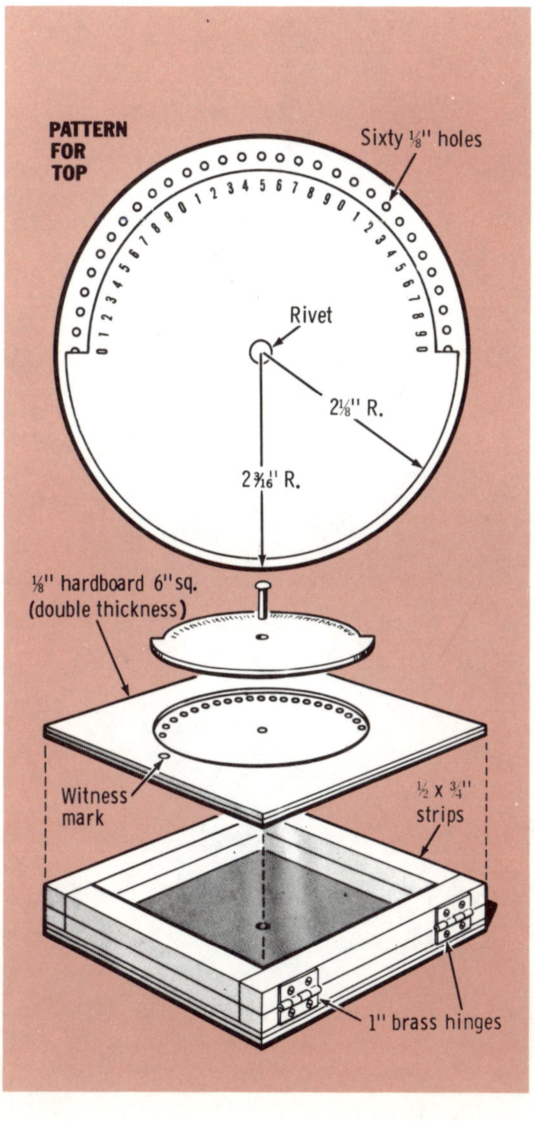


■ PEGGING A 24 HAND will be a cinch with this novel cribbage board on your card table. Just turn the revolving disc until it's against the peg (actually a golf tee) and the chalking up of any score can be done without counting each hole.

As detailed at the right, the board consists of two identical sections that are hinged together to form a pocket-size box in which to carry the pegs and cards. Construction is simple—you just use a protractor to index the holes 6° apart, and then use the holes to position the jig for the number punch.

SEE ALSO

**Air games . . . Backgammon tables . . .**
**Bridge sets . . . Chess sets . . . Family rooms . . .**
**Game tables . . . Pool tables . . .**
**Shuffleboard tables . . . Weekend projects**

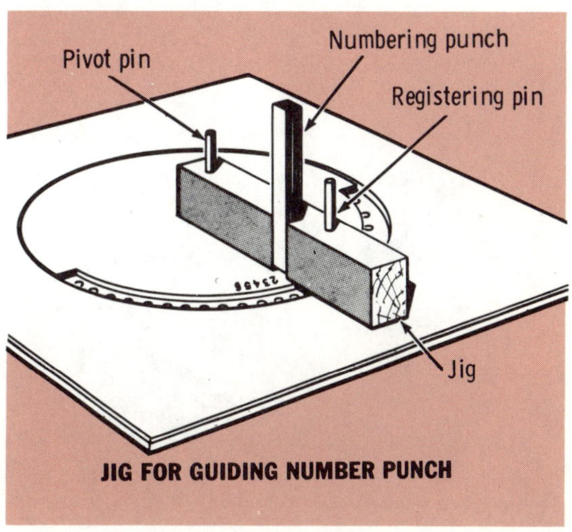


**JIG FOR GUIDING NUMBER PUNCH**

# How to saw firewood on the double

By DOUG NEWMAN

**Depending on the amount of wood you cut for the heating season, the almost-forgotten handsaw may be the way to go. It's a quiet, healthful alternative to the chain saw**

■ ONE- AND TWO-MAN crosscut saws will never replace the chain saw for most of us—even if gasoline goes to $3 a gallon. For some, however, it provides a sensible alternative. The trick is that you should spread out your woodcutting chore over two or three dozen hour-long stints—instead of two or three all-day marathon sessions with a chain saw.

There are several bonuses, not the least of which is that it's more healthful. In an age of paying money to keep in shape, a crosscut saw is a cheap and productive way to get exercise. The saw shouldn't cost you much more than a couple of hours of tennis-court time, or the price of new running shoes. It won't numb your arms or ears with intense vibrations and noise, the way prolonged use of a chain saw will.

The crosscut saw is cheaper and less messy. There's no worry about mixing gasoline and oil. And it will always "start."

If you want to buy a saw, here are some pointers:

■ Two types of basic blades are available—one-man and two-man crosscut saws.

■ A one-man saw is asymmetrical and features a conventional saw handle at the wide end of the blade. An auxiliary handle can be attached to the small end of the blade to allow two people to work the saw. One-man saws, once produced in

SEE ALSO

**Chain saws . . . Fireplaces . . . Firewood . . . Handsaws . . . Log cutting . . . Sawbucks . . . Saws, buck . . . Trees**

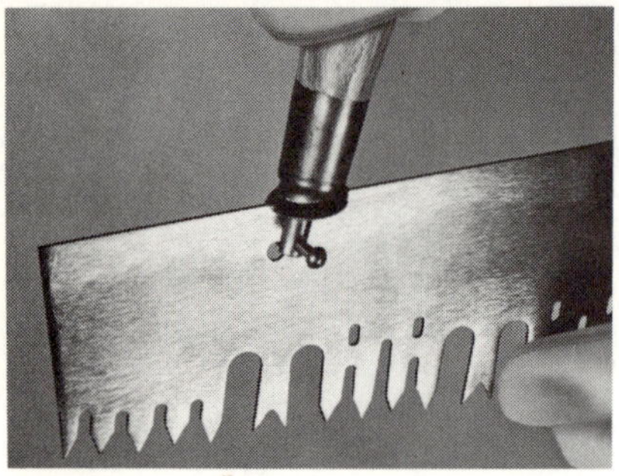

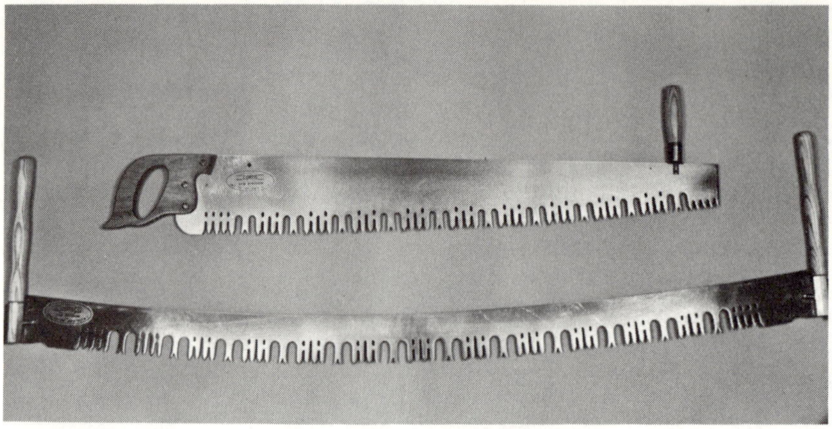

**CROSSCUT SAWS** are available in one- and two-man types. With the addition of an auxiliary handle (above), two men can work a one-man saw.

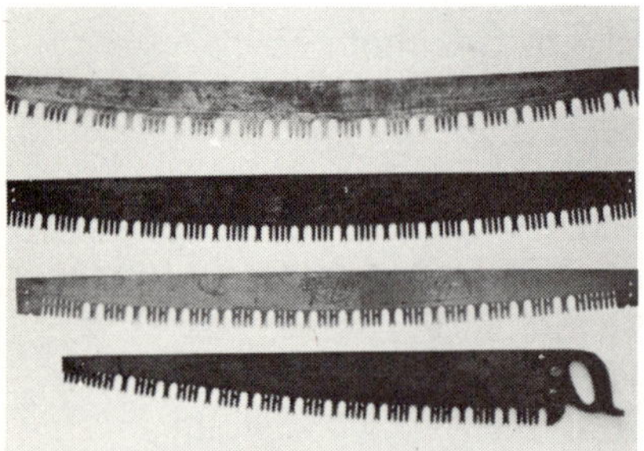

**SAW PATTERNS** vary but fall into two classes: felling and bucking. Felling has curved back, bucking straight.

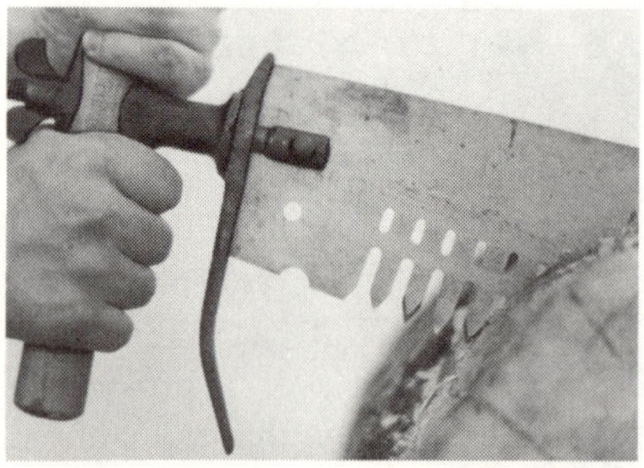

**OLD-STYLE SAW** handles, often seen at flea markets, have rugged guards to prevent jammed fingers.

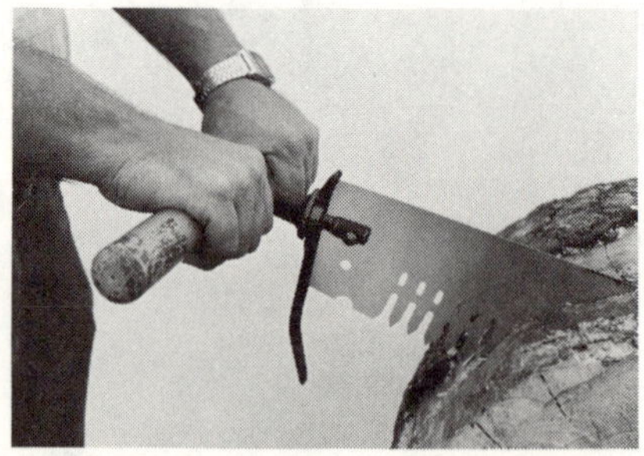

**ANOTHER** desirable feature is adjustable handles that let the grip rotate 90°— handy for avoiding obstacles.

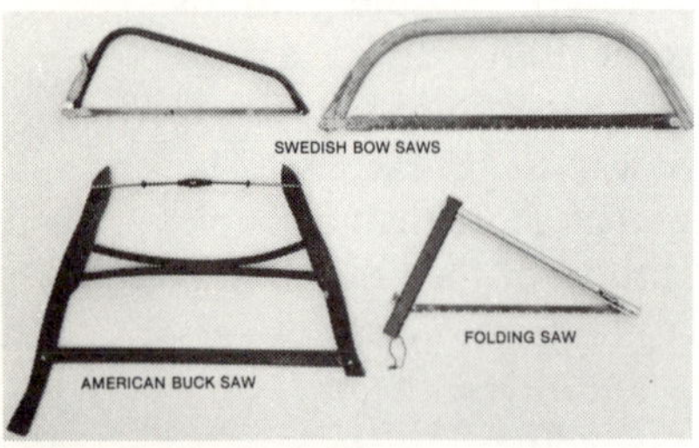


**SMALL-SIZE** crosscut saws (above), which are handy for the cutting of small-diameter logs, are equipped with replaceable blades. The folding types are especially handy for backpackers (below).

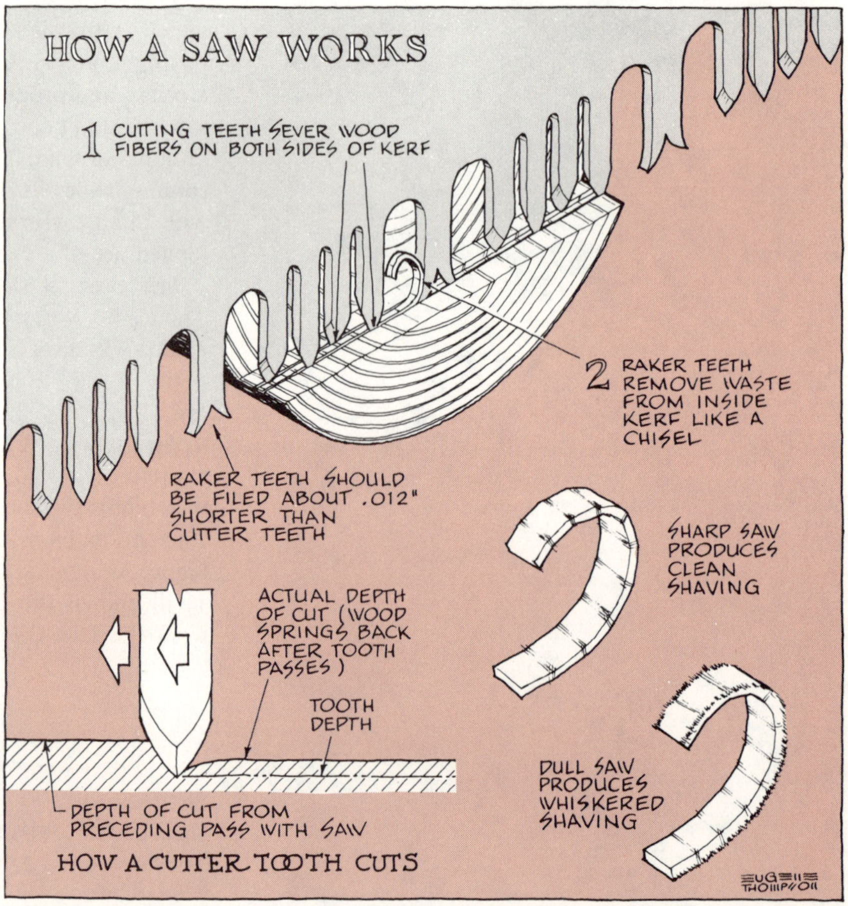

lengths from 3 to 6 ft., are available today in 3-, 3½- and 4½-ft. lengths.

■ Two-man saws are symmetrical and have a handle at each end. Two types exist—the felling saw for dropping timber and the bucksaw for cutting the dropped tree into shorter lengths. A felling saw has a narrower blade and a concave back. It is lighter than a bucksaw and more flexible. Bucksaws come with a straight back and are thicker, stiffer and heavier than felling saws. The weight is desirable, since it helps the teeth bite deeper and speeds cutting. Stiffness allows the saw to be run by one person.

While many felling saws and bucksaws are still around, some modern blades have characteristics of both types and could be called utility saws. They work well on many jobs.

Today, long crosscut saws are available, but not everywhere. They were once produced by several large companies, but now only one U.S. firm—Jemco Tool Corp., Seneca Falls, NY—makes them. A typical 6-ft. saw costs $57, with one pair of handles. A 42-in. one-man crosscut saw with auxiliary handle is $35. (All prices are approximate and were in effect at the time this was written).

### HOW TO FELL A TREE WITH A TWO-MAN SAW

■ THE FIRST TIME I ventured into a woodlot with a two-man saw, it took two hours, a lot of head scratching and a good push to fell my first tree. I've learned a lot since. Here are tips for anyone gung-ho enough to want fell a tree with a crosscut saw.

**1.** If you've bought a new saw, don't assume it's ready to use. A factory grinding wheel used to sharpen the teeth often leaves burrs that need smoothing with a crosscut file.

**2.** Know the type wood (hard, soft, green, punky and so on) you'll be cutting so you can prepare your saw properly at home. It's hard to change the set on site.

**3.** If you have no experience in judging which is the best direction to fell a tree, bring along someone who does.

**4.** Besides the saw, bring a hatchet for clearing underbrush from the working area, kerosene for lubricating the blade, an ax for completing felling notches, work gloves and a file and setting device in case teeth should need touching up. Finally, if possible, bring a sawbuck for cutting logs into manageable lengths.

**TO DROP** a tree, cut notch in direction of fall. Undercut ⅓ diameter of tree and chop out a 30° notch.

**BACK CUT** (opposite notch) is made 1 to 2 in. above undercut level. Leave 2-in. portion (hinge) uncut.

**PRIOR TO** making either cut, chip away bark with a hatchet. Dirt and bark may dull saw quickly.

**IF SAW BINDS,** drive wedges as needed to free blade and continue sawing.

**BE CERTAIN** escape path is clear of obstacles *before* you start. Best angles of departure are 45° from fall.

**ONCE TREE** is on the ground, use sawbuck and one- or two-man buck saw to cut log into desired lengths.

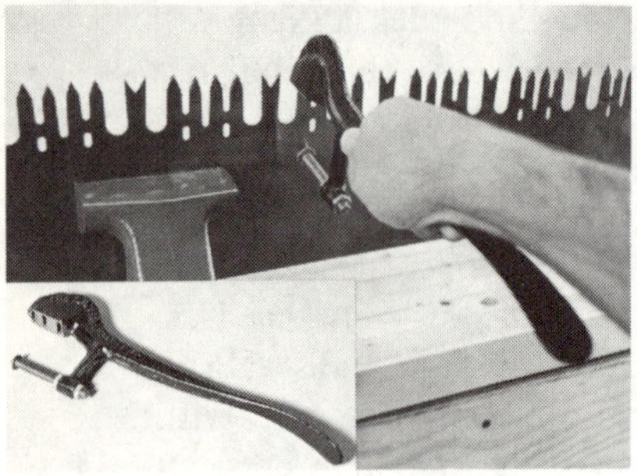

**SAW-SETTING TOOL** adjusts to set cutter teeth by repositioning a machine screw. Available with sharpening file from Crosscut Saw Co. (See text.)

**FILING CUTTER** and raker teeth is best accomplished with blade securely clamped in pivoting saw vise.

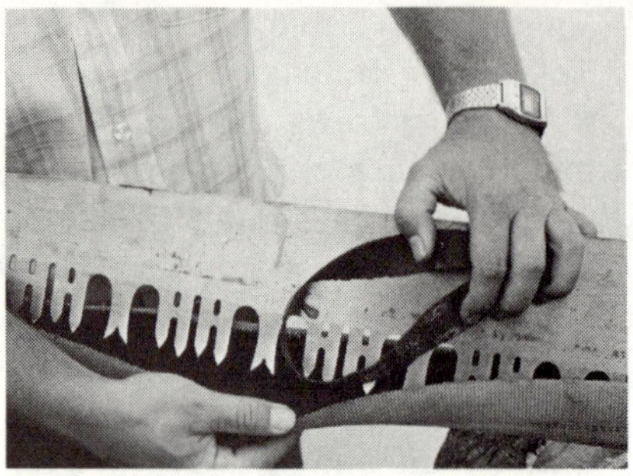

**A BLADE GUARD** for carrying your saw can be made from old fire hose or canvas. Hold with rubber bands from innertubes.

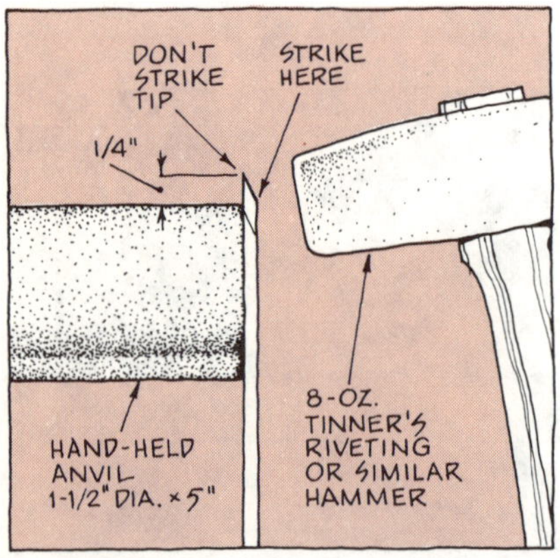


**EXPERTS** recommend using a hammer with a small strike face, anvil and spider gauge to set the teeth.

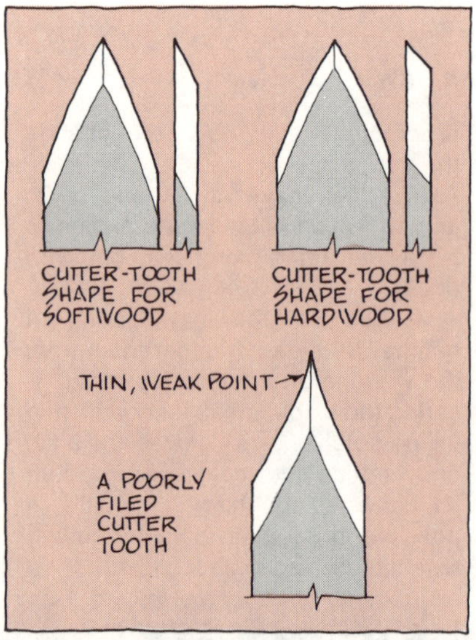


**CUTTING TEETH** filed slightly concave are easier to pull through wood. Use proper shape for wood type.

**CARRY SAW** on downhill shoulder with rear handle removed and teeth pointed away from neck. Walk last in line.

**IDEAL KIT** for sharpening and setting: 8-oz. tinner's hammer (A), anvil (B), spider gauge (C), jointer and raker combination depth gauge (D) and files (E).

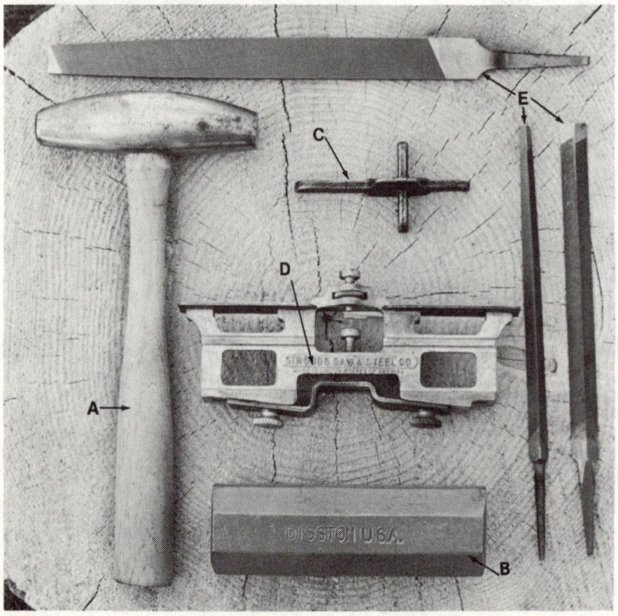


If your local hardware store doesn't stock saws and can't order what you want, write to the Crosscut Saw Co., 2 Leland Dr., Seneca Falls, NY 13148, for a catalog and price list.

If you can find them there, handsaws are least expensive at secondhand stores, garage sales, surplus stores and flea markets. Prices range from $10 to $60 for a used two-man saw, based on blade length, condition and whether it is sold with handles. The price goes up if the seller thinks it's an antique.

Avoid saws with pitted and rusty blades. Check a blade carefully—look for broken teeth, kinks or other signs that it has been roughly treated. If possible, look at several different saws before you buy, so you can recognize basic characteristics.

On many crosscut saws, a common tooth pattern features four cutter teeth to each raker tooth. The tooth lengths vary between brands; excessively short teeth may indicate the blade has been filed many times and is almost worn out.

**handling a crosscut saw**

While crosscut saws are safer than chain saws, several items should be remembered when using the blades. First, make a blade guard. A piece of fire hose or heavy canvas and large rubber bands cut from old inner tubes work nicely. Keep the blade covered until you reach the work site.

In a vehicle, remove the guard and sandwich the blade between two plywood strips. This keeps the teeth from punching through the hose and dulling against metal. Bolts and wingnuts secure the package.

Before you begin sawing, clear the area around the cutting site so the saw won't hang up on limbs or underbrush. Remove any bark at the point of cutting. Bark often contains dirt and grit that will dull teeth or jam the blade in the cut.

Evaluate potential safety problems before you start. Will a log shift or roll once you cut it through? Will a bent tree spring loose, once some weight is cut free? Are you on a hill? Cutting standing timber is particularly hazardous and should only be attempted in the company of an experienced woodsman.

Once the cut is started, remember the word "pull." If the saw is in good order, simply concentrate on pulling the blade toward you—your partner will pull it back. Pushing a saw may bend the blade and cause it to hang up in the cut, destroying the rhythm of your strokes. Once you achieve a consistent harmony with your partner, you may wish to experiment by adding some muscle on the push strokes.

The position of your hands on the handles affects the ease or difficulty you may have in sawing. A pull stroke is easier if the handle is in the "up" position and held near the end. Some saws have two mounting holes for each handle, allowing more adjustment to help you achieve the most efficient position.

If the wood you're cutting is green, sap may stick to the blade and cause it to jam. Lubricate the blade with kerosene when it begins to feel sticky.

**sharpening and setting**

If most of your cutting is in one place, a good sawbuck is worth building. It helps keep the blade out of the dirt, lets the cut open without wedging and permits a more comfortable stance for the sawyer.

One way to get your saw sharp is to have a professional do it, but if the classified pages don't turn up a sharpener (they're a disappearing breed), the alternative is to do it yourself. First, buy a copy of the Crosscut Saw Manual by Warren Miller for full information on crosscut-saw reconditioning, filing, maintenance and use. It also has a plan for building a sharpening vise. You can get this book from the Superintendent of Documents, U.S. Government Printing Office, Washington, DC 20402. Order stock No. 001-001-00434-1 and enclose $1.50.

Next, gather the sharpening aids which will make your task easier. Here's what you'll need:

■ A jointer-raker combination gauge for filing the cutting teeth to conform to the arc of the blade and for setting the depth of the raker teeth. A .008-in. depth is desirable for hard or dry wood and .030 in. is recommended for soft or springy wood. A good average starting figure is .012.

■ A setting tool or anvil and hammer for setting the end of the cutter teeth (see drawing, page 882). Set varies depending on the saw and the wood being cut. Generally, the harder the wood, the less the set—to a minimum of .010 in. Soft, punky or green wood requires a greater set, .030 in. or more for some saws. A little experimentation is required. The small gauges which are known as spiders made accurate setting easier.

■ A 7- or 8-in. crosscut file and saw vise for sharpening. Attempt to maintain the cutter-tooth bevel supplied on the saw.

Unfortunately, makers of jointing and raker depth-setting tools are no longer around. Jointing is often done with a long file and raker-depth setting is also improvised, using a gauge for gapping sparkplugs.

**small-size crosscut saws**

If you are not quite ready for a crosscut saw, but still need a saw for lighter-duty tasks, one of the following may serve your needs:

The traditional American bucksaw, always found near Grandfather's woodpile, features a 30-in. blade and a hardwood frame. See page 188 for how to build or buy one.

The Swedish bow saw has a tubular-steel frame and comes in various sizes and tooth patterns. Mostly, these have replaced the bucksaw in today's hardware stores. Prices run from $5 to $10. Replacement blades cost $2 to $4 in all sizes.

The Sven saw, a lightweight bow type, has a 20-in. blade which folds into the handle when not in use. Favored by backpackers, it costs $9 at outdoor sports stores and through mail-order catalogs.

Replacing an expensive oxyacetylene rig, this crucible furnace will melt virtually any metal, yet costs under $25 to make. It's a great way to get started in metal jewelry making

# Build a superhot furnace for metalworking

■ THE GREATEST OBSTACLE for someone who wants to get started in metal sculpture or jewelry-making is usually the high cost of equipment for melting metal. An oxyacetylene torch with the necessary tips, tanks, gauges and pressure regulators is a sizable investment. But you can make a crucible furnace like this one for a fraction of the cost.

SEE ALSO
**Cutoff machines . . . Metal casting . . . Metalworking . . . Power hacksaws . . . Sheet metal . . . Tin-can crafts . . . Torches**

It can provide temperatures ranging from about 900° F. to over 2700° F. That's hot enough to let you work with pewter, zinc, aluminum, bronze, brass, copper, precious metals and even iron and steel.

The combustion chamber is made of high-duty (about 3600° F.) insulating firebrick and, for mortar, an air-setting, high-alumina-content, refractory cement. It is assembled from eight bricks—two used as is, six cut to the shape shown. The cutting is done easily with a jigsaw, bandsaw or sabre saw. Begin assembly by soaking all the bricks in clean water until thoroughly sodden. Premix the mortar with clean water, in a clean container, until it has a smooth and creamy consistency like that of cake batter.

**WHEN THE CRUCIBLE** is glowing brightly, use tongs to put in an ingot of metal.

**STIR THE MOLTEN** metal with a green stick to bring the dross (oxides and dirt) to the surface.

**USE LARGE TONGS** to remove the crucible full of molten metal from the furnace. Use safety equipment.

**POUR METAL** from the heated crucible into your mold using shorter tongs.

Hand-dip the two uncut bricks in mortar and place them side by side to form a flat 2½ x 9 x 9-in. base. Use a small paintbrush dipped in mortar to smooth out any lumps and fill any holes. Add the other layers, two mortar-dipped bricks at a time, alternating the direction of the joints and using the paintbrush and mortar to smooth and fill.

Bake the combustion chamber at 400° to 500° F. in the kitchen oven until it is completely dry. The tuyere hole is cut through the second-layer wall on a tangent to the inner surface. A scrap of 1-in. pipe, turned by hand, will quickly and neatly make this opening. Finally, add a galvanized sheet-iron case to protect the brittle firebrick.

**making the burner**

The burner consists of an air-gas mixing chamber and nozzle (tuyere) and forced-air blower with speed control. Make the orifice pipe from a 3-in. long nipple of ⅛-in. black pipe. Drill a 3/32-in. hole through one wall at the midpoint.

The tuyere is made from an 8 or 9-in. length of 1-in. black pipe, with holes to accommodate the orifice pipe drilled through both walls 6 or 7 in.

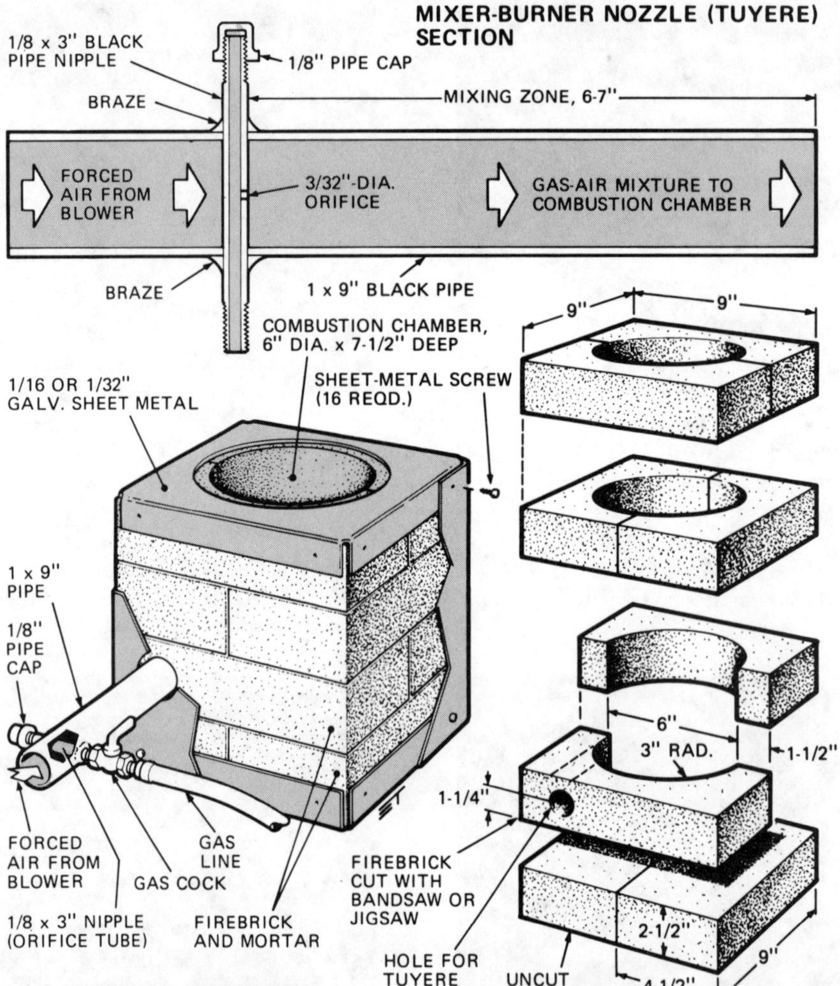

FURNACE ASSEMBLY

from one end. Braze the orifice pipe in place with the orifice facing inward. Cap one end and install a gas cock on the other. The blower is taken from any hair dryer, and a solid-state light dimmer is added for a speed control.

**installation and use**

Any site that is suitable for welding will serve, assuming that it has good ventilation and that natural gas and well-grounded electrical service are available.

Set up the combustion chamber on the floor and insert the tuyere into the combustion chamber—to, but not past, the inner wall. Connect the blower and speed control. Ground the tuyere and combustion-chamber case. Connect the natural-gas line.

Prepare for operation by assembling molds, crucibles, tongs, asbestos gloves, safety goggles and the metal to be cast. Place the crucible in the center of the combustion chamber; this aids heat circulation and makes the crucible easier to remove. Start the blower, then open the gas cock a little and ignite the burner immediately from the top of the combustion chamber. Over a 30-minute period, increase the gas flow to maximum, continually adjusting the blower speed for a pale blue flame.

When the furnace has reached its maximum temperature, the inner wall will glow a brilliant yellow. Once the crucible is glowing hot, you can put metal into it.

**COMPONENTS AND INFORMATION**

Insulating firebrick, refractory cement: A.P. Green Refractories Co., Green Blvd. Mexico, MO 65265.

Dimmer: Lutron Electronics, Box 154, Sutter and Jacoby Rds., Coopersburg, PA 18036.

Crucibles, tongs, asbestos gloves, safety goggles: Swest, Inc., 10803 Composite Dr., Dallas, TX 75220.

Publications No. 86A, *Ovens and Furnaces,* and No. 86B, *Industrial Furnaces,* National Fire Protection Assn., 470 Atlantic Ave., Boston, MA 02210.

Chemical Engineers Handbook, John H. Perry, Editor-in-Chief, McGraw-Hill Book Co., 1221 Avenue of the Americas, New York, NY 10020.

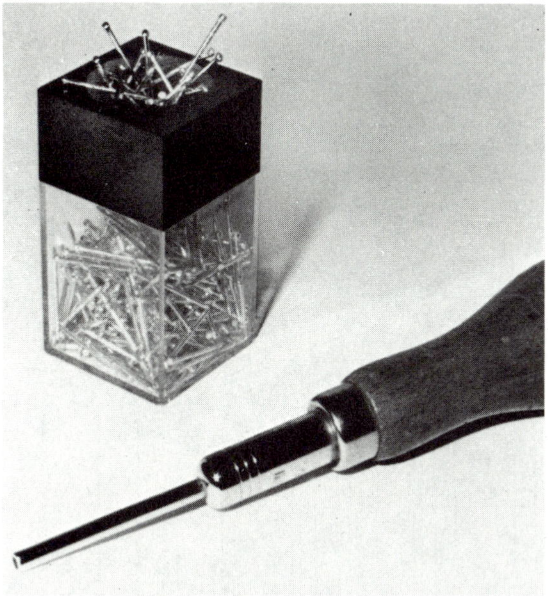

**MAGNETIZED PAPER-CLIP** containers of the type sold in most stationery stores are handy to have in the shop for storing a variety of small parts made of ferrous metals, such as the wire brads shown. When the container is tipped upside down, the brads are there, ready to use.—*C.H. Maxwell, Vancouver, WA.*

**TO TRANSFER LARGE DRAWINGS** onto plywood or other materials, you can use the classified pages of your newspaper, rubbed with a thin coat of paraffin, instead of carbon paper or pencil rubbing. Newsprint will not rub onto hands, and the close spacing of ads in small type will produce a followable line.—*Frank E. O'Connor, Gulfport, MS.*

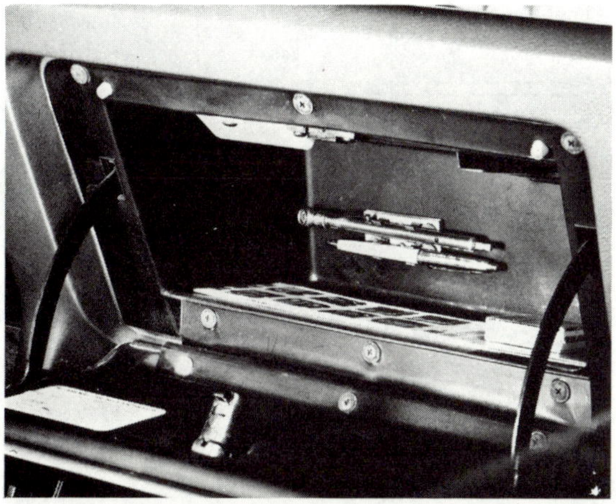

**A DOUBLE FUSE BLOCK** of the spring-clip type (sold in auto-supply stores) can be mounted in your car's glove compartment to allow neat, convenient storage of a tire-pressure gauge and a pen or pencil. Use pliers to bend the clips out wide enough for the articles they will hold.—*Kenneth M. Kaufman, Elbridge, NY.*

**YOU CAN DIVIDE A DRAWER** in half without nails, screws or brackets. A length of wood or heavy cardboard fitted diagonally between two opposite corners will halve the drawer exactly. It is self-securing (cut and try for best fit) and can be lifted out for easy cleaning.—*Allen Wilks, Matawan, NJ.*

# Make a Colonial cupboard for your china

**By WAYNE C. LECKEY**

■ CHARMING, COLORFUL and Early American in appearance, this fine version of a Colonial cupboard offers the perfect setting for displaying your best china. It's made of clear pine, a wood that's easy to get at any lumberyard. The piece consists of two basic units, a base and a top, built separately.

The sides of the glass-door cabinet—the upper unit—are recessed into the top of the base unit and the upper unit's back fits into a rabbet in the top of the base. This and a few screws along the back of the top unit weld your Colonial cupboard into a single, reliably rigid combination. Yet, if you decide to move, the whole cupboard breaks down easily into two separate units. You'll find them easily manageable on moving day.

The solid-pine ends and top for the base unit require wide pieces which must be built up of two or more boards. You can join them by simply butt-gluing the edges, but ⅜-in. dowels make the strongest joints. After sanding smooth, cut the ends to the sizes given, then run dadoes on the inside 2⅜ in. up from the bottom and rabbets in the top and rear edges; the rear ones are for a ¼-in. plywood back. You can use fir plywood for the bottom if you wish; it will save gluing-up boards. Use glue alone to hold the bottom in the dadoes and nails plus glue to attach the 2½-in. cross rails in the rabbets at the top. Check the assembly with a square and hold it with a diagonal brace across the front while you cut and add the plywood back.

Round edges of the top along three sides with a portable router or hand plane and run a rabbet in the rear edge as shown to later receive the back panel of the upper unit. Use No. 8 x 1¼-in. flathead screws up through the front and back cross rails to attach the top, but add the top last as this will make it easier to reach in and install the drawer guides.

SEE ALSO

**Chests . . . Desks . . . Drawers . . . Dry sinks . . . Fasteners . . . Finishes, wood . . . Gossip benches . . . Gun cabinets . . . Hinges . . . Hutch tables . . . Routers . . . Servers**

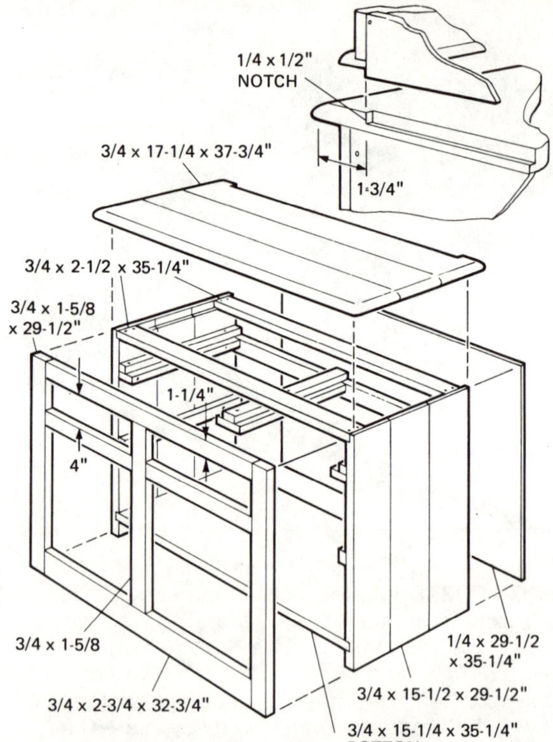


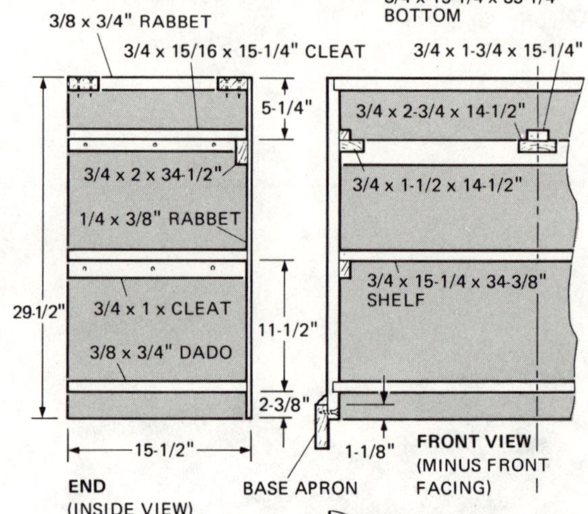


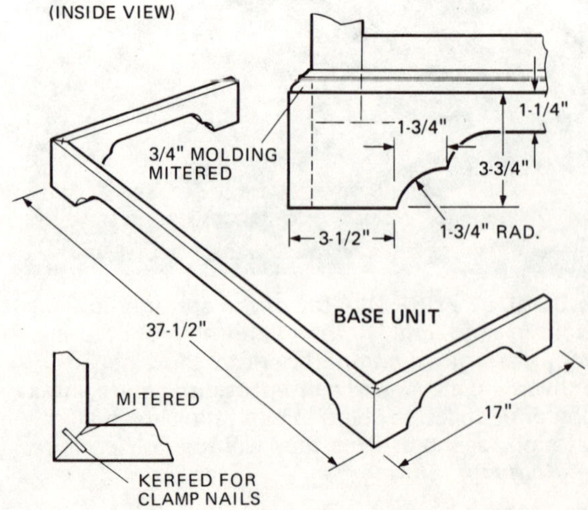

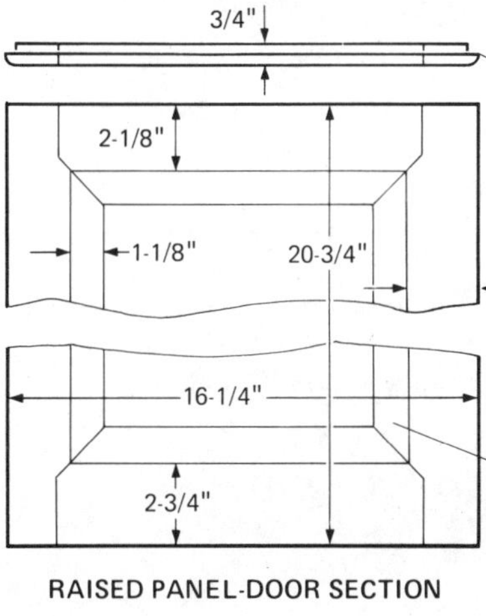


RAISED PANEL-DOOR SECTION

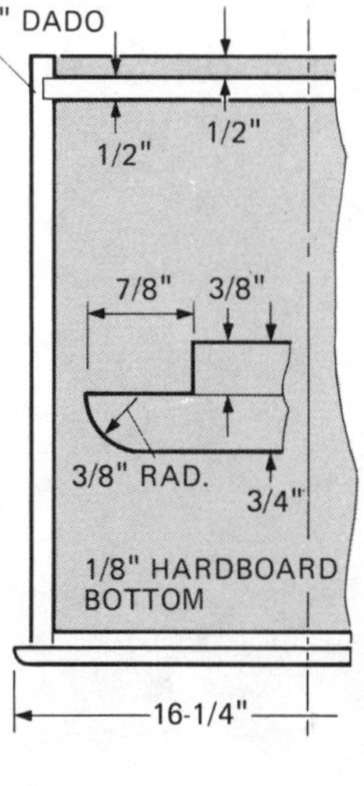


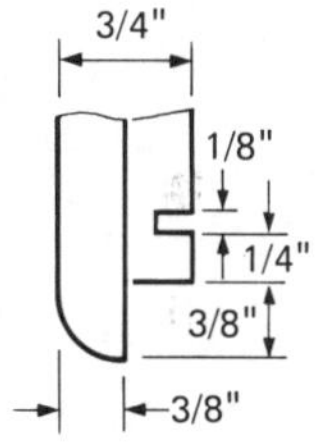


**NAIL DRAWER** sides to the fronts in deep end rabbets. Bottoms rest in grooves cut in front and side pieces. Backs fit into side dadoes.

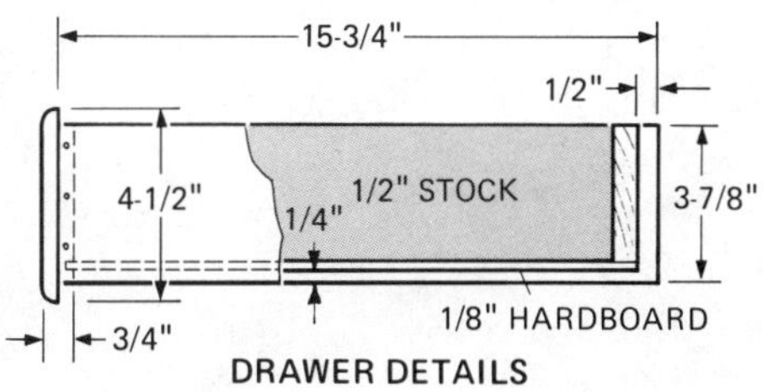


DRAWER DETAILS

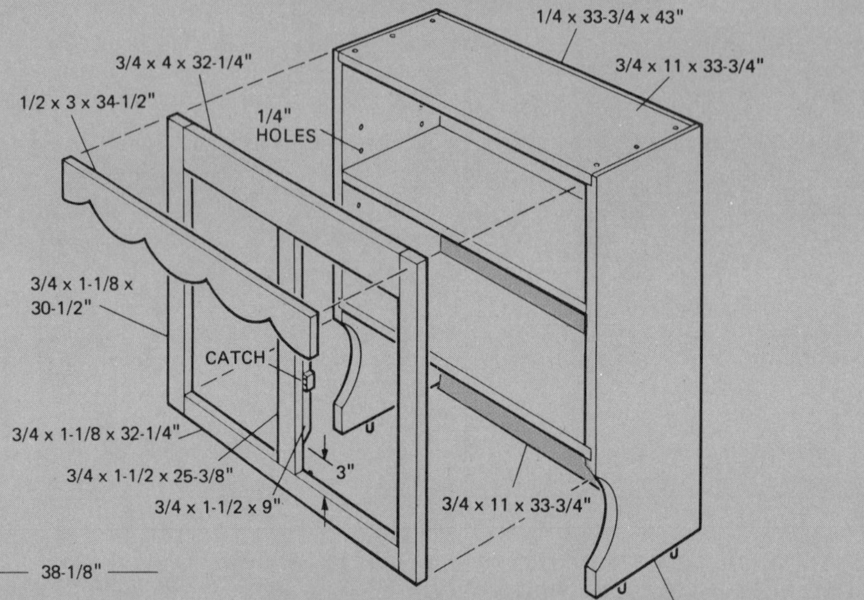


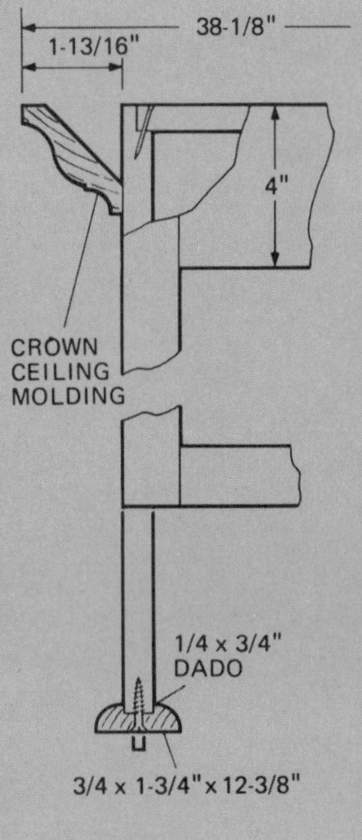


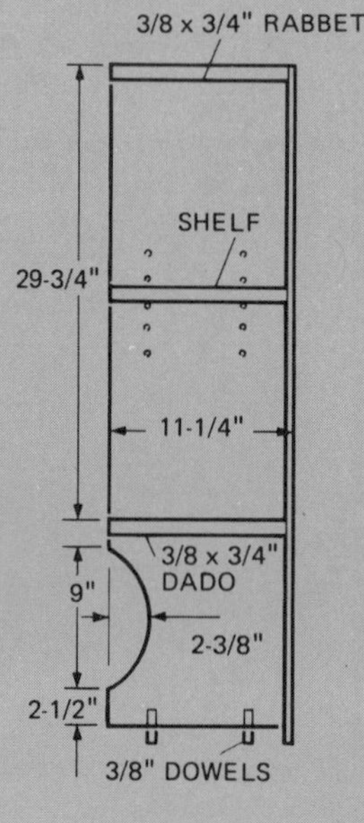


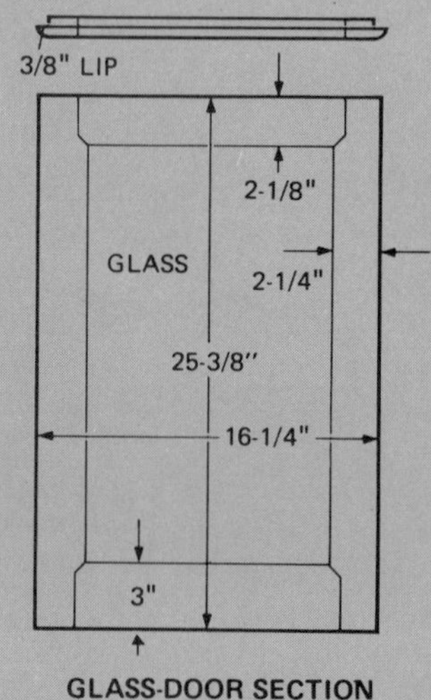


GLASS-DOOR SECTION

## PARTS LIST

**BASE UNIT**

| No. | Size | Use |
|---|---|---|
| 2 | ¾ x 15½ x 29½" | Ends |
| 1 | ¾ x 15¼ x 35¼" | Bottom |
| 1 | ¾ x 15¼ x 34⅜" | Shelf |
| 1 | ¾ x 17¼ x 37¾" | Top |
| 2 | ¾ x 2½ x 35¼" | Cross members |
| 1 | ¾ x 2¾ x 32¾" | Front facing (bottom) |
| 2 | ¾ x 1⅝ x 29½" | Front facing (sides) |
| 2 | ¾ x 1⅜ x 15 7/16" | Front facing (center) |
| 1 | ¾ x 1⅝ x 25½" | Front facing (vertical) |
| 1 | ¾ x 1¼ x 32¾" | Front facing (top) |
| 2 | ¾ x 1¼ x 14½" | Drawer guides |
| 2 | ¾ x 15/16 x 15¼" | Drawer guides |
| 1 | ¾ x 1¾ x 15¼" | Drawer guide |
| 1 | ¾ x 2¾ x 14½" | Drawer guide |
| 2 | ¾ x 1 x 15¼" | Shelf cleats |
| 1 | ¾ x 2 x 34½" | Back cleat |
| 2 | ¾ x 3¾ x 17" | Base apron (sides) |
| 1 | ¾ x 3¾ x 37½" | Base apron (front) |
| 1 | ¾ x ¾ x 72" | Base molding |
| 1 | ¼ x 29½ x 35¼" | Plywood back |

**UPPER UNIT**

| No. | Size | Use |
|---|---|---|
| 2 | ¾ x 11¼ x 42" | Ends |
| 2 | ¾ x 11 x 33¾" | Top and bottom |
| 1 | ¾ x 11 x 33" | Shelf |
| 1 | ¼ x 33¾ x 43" | Plywood back |
| 1 | ¾ x 1⅛ x 32¼" | Front facing (bottom) |
| 1 | ¾ x 1½ x 25⅜" | Front facing (vertical) |
| 2 | ¾ x 1⅛ x 30½" | Front facing (sides) |
| 1 | ¾ x 4 x 32¼" | Front facing (top) |
| 1 | ½ x 3 x 34½" | Scroll facing |
| 1 | ¾ x 3 x 68" | Crown molding |
| 2 | ¾ x 1¾ x 12⅜" | End feet |
| 1 | ¾ x 1½ x 9" | Door-catch cleat |

**DRAWERS**

| No. | Size | Use |
|---|---|---|
| 2 | ¾ x 4½ x 16¼" | Fronts |
| 4 | ½ x 3⅞ x 15¾" | Sides |
| 2 | ½ x 3½ x 15" | Backs |
| 2 | ⅛ x 15 x 15" | Bottoms |

**DOORS (BASE)**

| No. | Size | Use |
|---|---|---|
| 4 | ¾ x 2¼ x 20¾" | Side stiles |
| 2 | ¾ x 2⅛ x 12¾" | Top rails |
| 2 | ¾ x 2¾ x 12¾" | Bottom rails |
| 2 | ¾ x 12½ x 16¾" | Raised panels |

**DOORS (UPPER)**

| No. | Size | Use |
|---|---|---|
| 4 | ¾ x 2¼ x 25" | Side stiles |
| 2 | ¾ x 3 x 12½" | Bottom rails |
| 2 | ¾ x 2⅛ x 12½" | Top rails |
| 2 | ⅛ x 12½ x 20½" | Glass panes |
| 1 | ¼ x ¼ x 11½" | Quarter-round molding |

**HARDWARE (BRASS)**

| No. | Item |
|---|---|
| 4 | 1"-dia. door knobs |
| 2 | 3"-wide drawer drop pulls |
| 8 | 2½" lip-door hinges |
| 4 | Spring-loaded, cupboard-door catches |

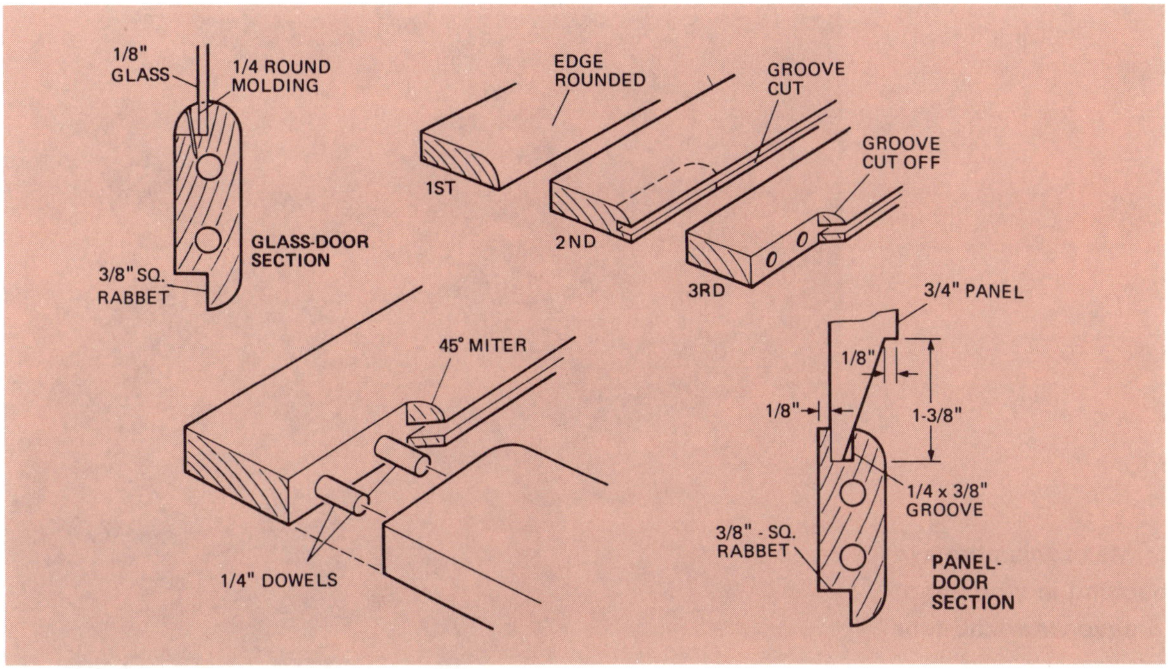


Front edges of the cabinet are covered with a ¾-in.-thick frame. Clamp it together as a separate unit, using dowels and glue to join its seven members. Apply the facing so it is even with the cabinet ends and top cross rail. Use glue, clamps and finishing nails to attach it, then set and putty the heads.

Next, install the drawer guides and shelf cleats following the end and front plan views. Notice that the drawer guides are supported at the back by a 2-in. cross member and placed so they will be in line and even with the drawer openings in the front frame.

The drawers have lip fronts that lap the openings. Use ¾-in. pine for fronts, ½-in. for sides and backs, ⅛-in. hardboard for bottoms. Fronts are rabbeted ⅜ in. top and bottom and ⅞ in. at ends.

The three-piece mitered base laps the front and ends 1⅛ in. Rip it 3¾ in. wide, scroll-cut it and glue and draw the mitered corners together with clamp nails. When dry, attach it from the back with No. 8 x 1¼-in. flathead screws. Finally, miter, glue and brad a molding to finish off the top edges.

The upper unit is simpler to make since the ends, top and bottom are cut from 1x12 boards. Run dadoes and rabbets in the end pieces as before. Sabre-saw the half-moon cutouts and bore a series of ¼-in. holes ¼ in. deep and 1 in. apart for shelf supports. Rip the top and the bottom 11 in. wide to allow for the ¼-in. back which sits in a rabbet. Before gluing and nailing the two members in place, run plate grooves in the bottom shelf, one 2 in. from the back edge, another 5 in. Make similar grooves in the adjustable middle shelf. Make grooves wide and deep enough to suit your china.

A separate frame, glued and doweled together as before, covers the front edges. Glue it on and use a finishing nail here and there to help hold it. Glue a decorative facing, scroll-cut from ½-in. pine, to the front across the top, then miter crown molding to go around three sides. Finally, glue and screw grooved pieces to lower ends of the uprights.

Put the four door frames together with dowels and rabbet the outer edges so that doors lap the openings. The lower doors are grooved for raised-panel inserts; upper doors are like picture frames, with a rabbet cut all around the inside for window glass. In each case, the grooves and rabbets must be cut before assembly.

The pine-faced plywood back of the upper unit extends ½ in. at the bottom to fit into the rear rabbet in the base unit, and screws are used to hold the two together.

We finished the prototype with Minwax's Liberty blue Americolor, a one-coat, brush-on-wipe-off wood finish that gives an ageless patina effect. You also have a choice of Independence red, Lexington green or Conestoga white. Hardware is from Christensen Hardware Co., Caldwell, NJ 07006.

**Make this abrasive cutoff machine in your shop and save wear-and-tear on your arm the next time you tackle a tough cutting job**

By BOB ECKERT

# Make your own abrasive cutoff machine

SEE ALSO
**Crucible furnaces . . . Drill press techniques . . . Drills, portable . . . Metalworking . . . Motors, shop . . . Power hacksaws . . . Sheet metal . . . Torches**

■ CUTTING THROUGH 1-in. steel rod by hand is one of the most time-consuming, arm-wearying chores you can tackle in the shop. Since I frequently work with metals, I decided to build the handy little machine shown here to ease the task. I get a remarkably fast and accurate cut and a surface-grinder finish on the metal.

Spare parts lying around in my shop were used to build my machine. The only tools needed are a screwdriver, wrench, hacksaw, drill press (or portable electric drill) and a ½-20 NF (national fine) die.

Basically, the machine consists of a base, riser channel, angle brackets, rocker-base pivot assembly, combination depth-of-cut adjustment and handle and the belt guard cover.

Start construction with the machine base and the rocker base. Lay out all holes as shown in the drawing on the opposite page and doublecheck the pillow-block dimensions (distance between mounting holes for these may vary from those in

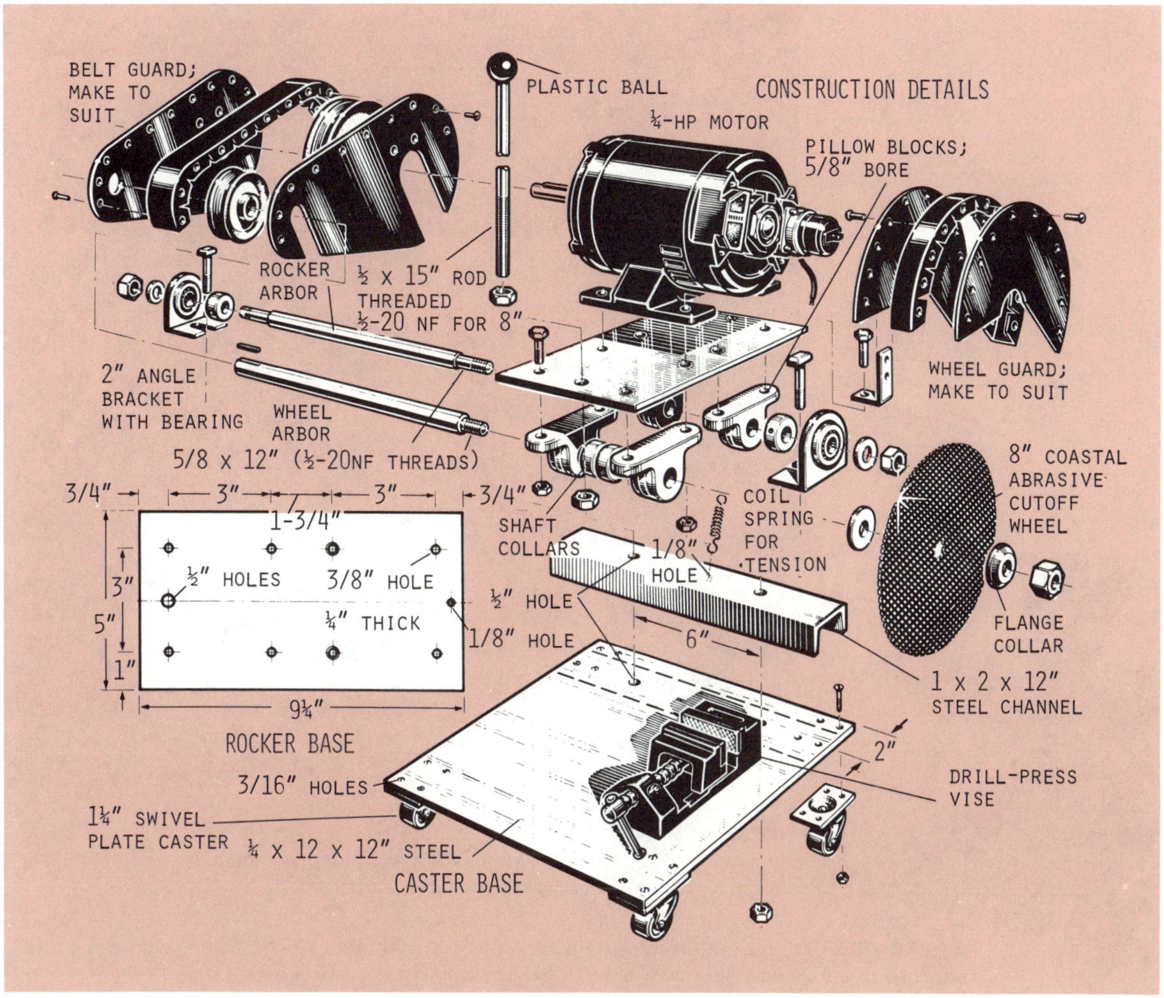


the drawing; just allow for any difference before you drill the holes). The ⅛-in. holes are for a tension spring needed to prevent the abrasive cutting wheel from being forced into the workpiece by gravity.

When drilling the rocker base, make certain the countersink is deep enough for the two ⅜-16 NC (national coarse) fh slotted machine bolts to lie flush within the plate surface. Make an error here and there's a good chance the motor's base might twist and break its weld from the motor when you're tightening it in place.

The combination depth-of-cut adjustment and handle regulates how far you can lower the cutting wheel, also keeps the wheel from cutting into the base. It also serves as the handle.

The belt guard cover, used for safety as well as looks, can be made of sheet metal; use Pop rivets to hold it together.

After making all parts except the belt guard cover, start assembly with the rocker base, regarding the end with the ½-in. drilled hole as the front. After the unit is assembled—mostly a matter of patience and trial-and-error fitting—install the power cord and mount the switch.

All shafts and pillow blocks can be obtained from local hardware stores. They come as a set for use as mandrels for buffing and the like. One shaft (for the rocker) from these sets should have a ⅝-in.-dia. bearing surface with both ends turned down to ½-in. diameter with ½-20 NF thread.

Attach any special wheel, such as the Coastal Abrasive Zippidi-Do shown, with large washers on both sides and secure it with a ½-20 NF hex head machine nut.

Adjust belt tension by sliding the motor back and forth. Don't make the belt too tight; pressed at the center, it should deflect about ½ in.

The machine throws a lot of sparks, so always put on safety goggles before you use it. A common drill-press vise is used to hold the work.

**THE SAW BEING USED** (above) to cut ½-in. steel rod. The side shield has been removed to show the cutting operation. In actual use, the side shield should always be fastened in place to protect the operator.

**A REAR VIEW** of the cutoff machine (left) shows how the portable saw is attached to the vertical supports. Since it isn't convenient to control the saw with its own in-handle switch, the switch is taped in the "on" position and the saw is controlled by a foot switch. It may be necessary to fasten the blade guard back out of the way.

# Portable saw pinch-hits as a cutoff machine

By WALTER E. BURTON

**This abrasive-wheel cutoff machine will tackle jobs that are too tough for a hacksaw to handle. It's made from a standard circular saw**

SEE ALSO

Abrasives . . . Blades, carbide . . .
Circular saws, portable . . .
Drill press techniques . . . Motors, shop . . .
Power hacksaws . . . Sheet metal

■ A PORTABLE CIRCULAR SAW is the heart of this cutoff machine. Its abrasive blade slices through metal rods, pipes, angle iron and bars of various shapes with ease, even through hardened steel that a hacksaw won't touch.

The machine consists essentially of a metal framework that supports the saw vertically and nose-down, with a swinging unit to which the material to be cut is clamped. Swinging this "workholder" through a short arc by a handle projecting upward from it feeds the work against the edge of the abrasive blade. Shields help provide safety and protect the user from sparks and particles generated by the grinding action.

A Rockwell No. 75, 7½-in. portable circular saw was used in the machine illustrated. The

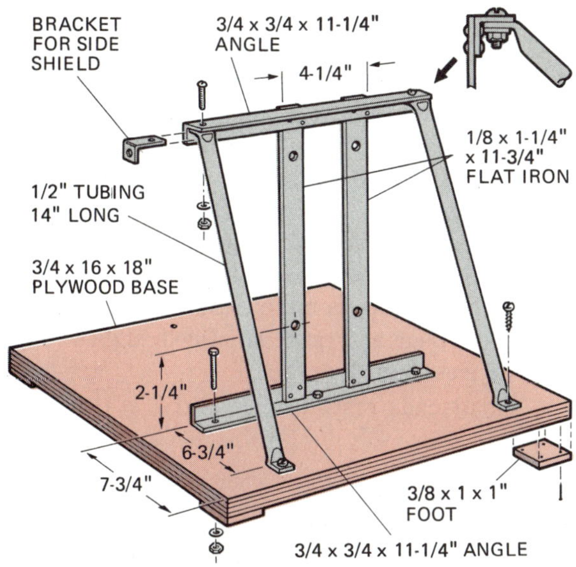


VIEW FROM REAR

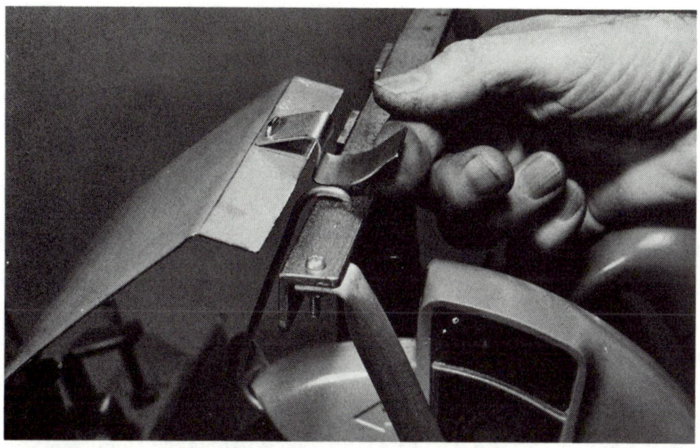

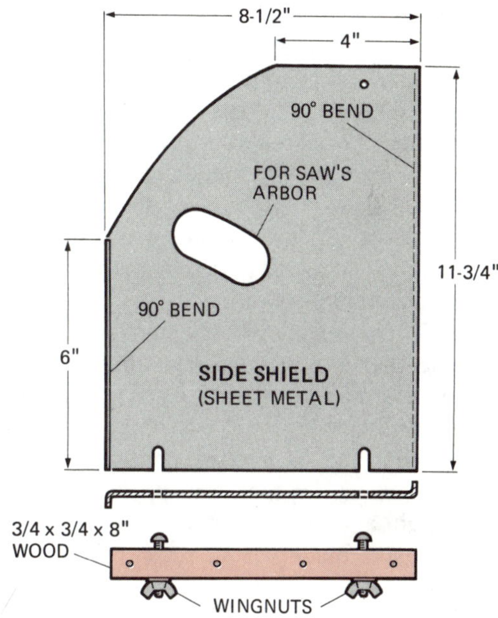


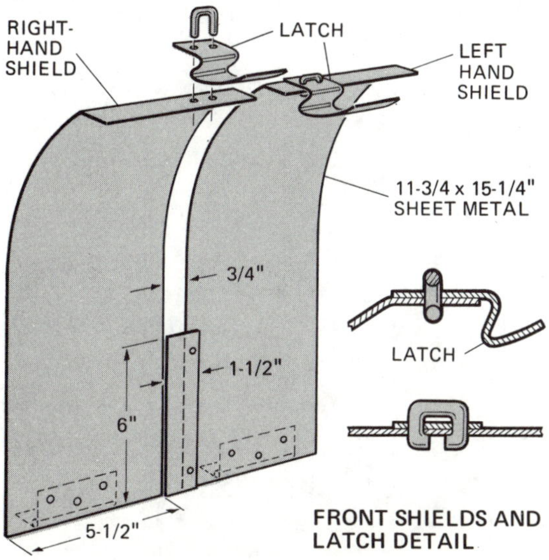


FRONT SHIELDS AND LATCH DETAIL

**AN ELONGATED OPENING** in the sheet-metal side shield (photo, top) accommodates long workpieces. The control handle has a plastic grip over the end.

**THE FRAME** which holds the saw vertically is bolted to the baseboard and held rigid by two diagonal braces as shown in the drawing at the upper left.

**A SIMPLE LATCH** holds each curved shield closed. The latch is easily flipped open, but will lock automatically when the shields are swung to their closed position.

abrasive disc normally used is an aluminum-oxide type designed for cutting steel and other metals. Dimensions given are for this particular saw but they can be altered easily to accommodate a saw of a different make.

The saw-supporting frame is made by riveting together two ⅛ x 1¼ x 11¾-in. steel bars and two ¾ x ¾ x 11¼-in. pieces of angle iron. The frame is mounted on a plywood base with three bolts, and braced by two lengths of ½-in.-o.d. tubing flattened at the ends. The bars are positioned on the angle pieces so that two holes drilled in each to receive 10-24 bolts will align with similar holes already in the base plate of the circular saw.

The bottom angle strip is fastened to the plywood baseboard with 10-24 bolts. So the lower ends of the bolts would clear the bench top, five blocks about ⅜-in. thick were glued to the baseboard (one at each corner and one near the center) to serve as "feet." In mounting the frame, the two tubular braces are positioned so the bars remain perpendicular to the baseboard.

The saw is attached to the frame with short 10-24 bolts, lock washers and nuts. It is positioned so its lower tip clears the metal angle by approximately ⅛ in.

The swinging workholder is made by bolting together two thicknesses of ¾-in. plywood. Dimensions are not particularly critical so long as the assembly can be swung without binding against the baseboard, and the V-groove for holding workpieces is at approximately the same height above the baseboard as the center of the abrasive blade.

The workholder pivots on a ½ x 10-in. steel shaft extending between two identical pillow blocks. A V-shaped channel, in which a piece of angle iron measuring 1¼ x 1¼ x 6½ in. is secured, is formed by the two 45° plywood edges. Centered ¾ in. up from the bottom edge is a ½-in. hole for the shaft. This hole can be formed by roughing a near-semicircular groove in each plywood half on a circular saw and finishing it with a gouge and rasp. The finished groove is a little less than ¼ in. deep.

Shaft ends rest in holes bored in the pillow

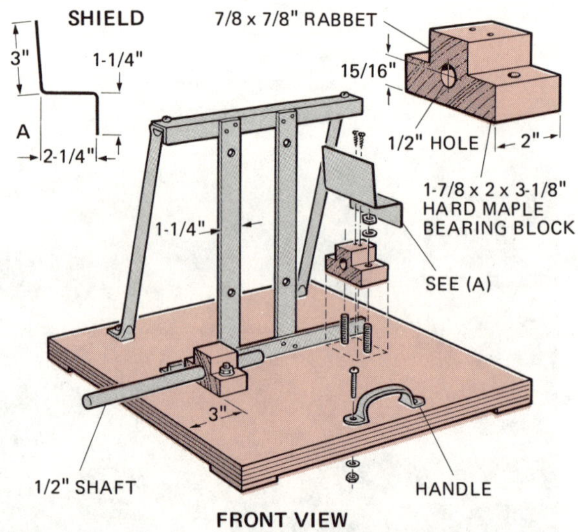


**HOLDDOWN CLAMPS** (below) are made from steel strips and attached with ¼-20 x 2-in. carriage bolts. Angle iron fits a channel formed by plywood pieces and is fastened with two flathead wood screws.

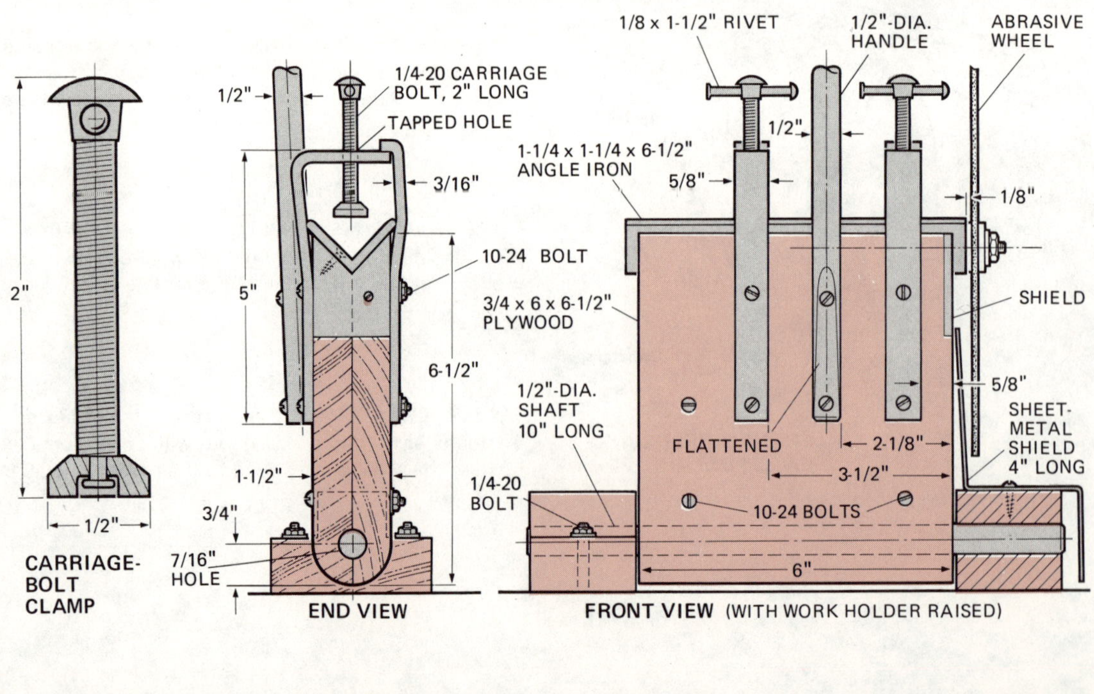

blocks and should be a rather tight fit. If you adjust the two lower bolts that pass through the plywood halves, friction can be maintained and all play eliminated. The shaft grooves are coated lightly with grease. In mounting the pillow blocks, holes were made oversize so the blocks could be shifted to eliminate end play of the workholder and to align the angle-iron channel with the saw blade.

Two screw clamps, made and installed as

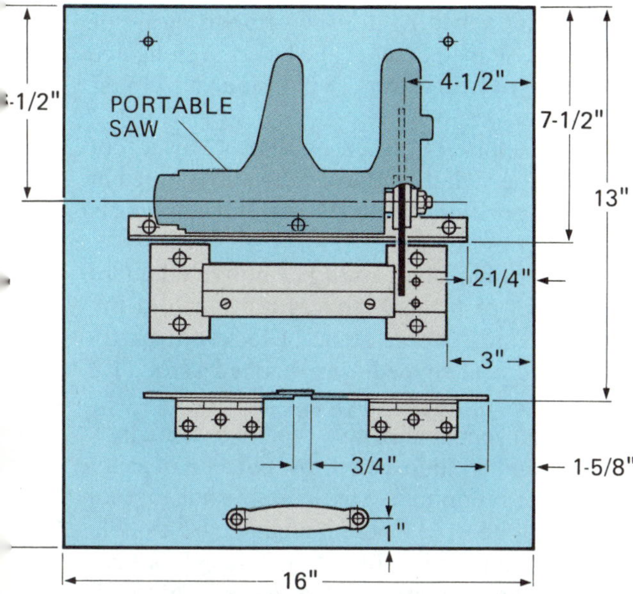


PARTIAL PLAN VIEW

**PILLOW BLOCKS** are mounted to position the shaft so that the work-holding assembly will clear the blade. The hinge is for one of the curved front shields.

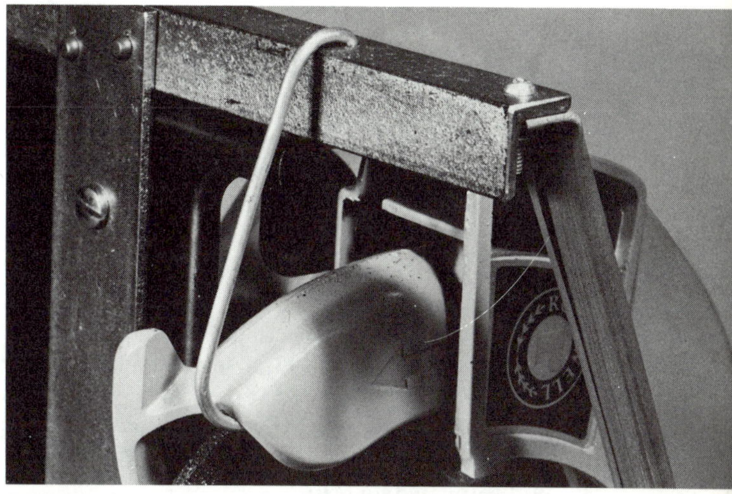

**A BENT WIRE** holds the spring-fitted guard of the circular saw partially open (above) to expose the saw blade to the work being cut.

**THE SWINGING WORKHOLDER** must position the workpiece perpendicular to the side of the abrasive blade if you are to be sure of obtaining a square cut.

shown, secure work in the channel of the swinging workholder. Both clamps are bent to an L-shape from 3/16 x 5/8-in. steel bar stock; and the clamp nearest the wheel is further stiffened by a "hook" made from similar material. This hook prevents the clamp screw from springing upward when tightened. Ideally, both clamps should completely encircle the V-channel as shown.

The clamp screws are made from 1/4-20 x 2-in. carriage bolts. The bolt tips are fitted with loose collars like those on conventional C-clamps. The collars are lathe-turned and the bolt ends turned down to fit loosely in the collar holes, after which the ends are peened over with the aid of a punch. The cross handles, extending through holes drilled just below the bolt heads, are 1/8 x 1 1/2-in. rivets.

The handle, which is attached near the middle of the workholder, is a 12-in. length of 1/2-in. steel rod, somewhat flattened at the lower end where two bolts are used to fasten it to the wood workholder. I added a length of plastic tubing to the end to provide a grip.

**installing the shields**

Shields made from heavy-gauge sheet steel help to protect against possible breakage, and against flying sparks and particles produced by the grinding operation. The curved front shield is 5 in. wide and positioned to be approximately centered with the blade. Its lower end is attached to the baseboard with a butt hinge so the shield can be swung out of the way when mounting or removing work.

While the swinging workholder fills the space fairly well on the motor side of the blade, I added a second curved shield in front of the machine and mounted it along-side the first with a space of almost 1 in. in between for the workholder lever. The lower 6-in. portion of this gap is blocked by a sheet-metal strip riveted to the right-hand shield.

At the upper end of each shield is a self-locking latch which engages metal angle to hold it in closed position. The latches are so shaped so they cannot be disengaged by outward pressure against the shield. They must be lifted by a finger.

Another sheet-metal shield is bent to fit over the pillow block beneath the abrasive blade to fend off sparks and grit. It extends upward between blade and workholder and overlaps a small metal shield nailed to the end of the workholder. Two wood screws fasten the pillow-block shield in place.

The side shield is at right angles to the curved shield and covers much of the side of the machine to intercept flying sparks and particles. Two notches in its lower edge engage 6-32 bolts that clamp it against a wooden strip fastened to the baseboard. The upper corner of the side shield is attached to the saw-supporting frame with an L-shaped bracket and bolt. An elongated opening permits long workpieces to pass through.

The machine is turned on and off by a foot switch. The switch in the saw handle is taped in the "on" position and all starting and stopping is controlled by the foot.

The portable saw I used has a pivoted guard that, if not restrained, covers too much of the blade in cutoff work. Hence I locked it partly open with a C-shaped wire hooked through a hole in the top metal angle.

A cutoff machine of this type is essentially a grinder, and grinders can throw out a lot of gritty dirt and voluminous sparks. So such a tool should not be used where it might cause trouble with other equipment or with personnel, or near easily ignitable material. No one should stand where, in the event of wheel breakage, flying pieces might cause injury. Children, especially, should be kept away. The machine should be checked frequently to determine whether all shields are in position and secured, and that other parts are functioning properly. The operator should wear approved safety goggles or a face mask, and a breathing mask (respirator) is recommended.

**choosing an abrasive wheel**

Manufacturers of portable circular saws often include abrasive blades among the accessories. Abrasive blades that are thicker than the regular saw blades may require a thinner inside washer to hold them properly in place. It is important that the saw speed in revolutions per minute should not exceed the recommended maximum rpm specified by the manufacturer of the abrasive wheel you are using. If the speed of the saw you are using is too high, consider purchasing a motor speed control that the saw can be plugged into. These are widely available at hardware stores and contain the proper circuitry to allow you to adjust the saw speed continuously from 0 rpm to the saw's maximum speed.

During cutting, especially of sizable stock, it is a good idea to stop and examine the clamps frequently to make certain the workpiece remains firmly held.

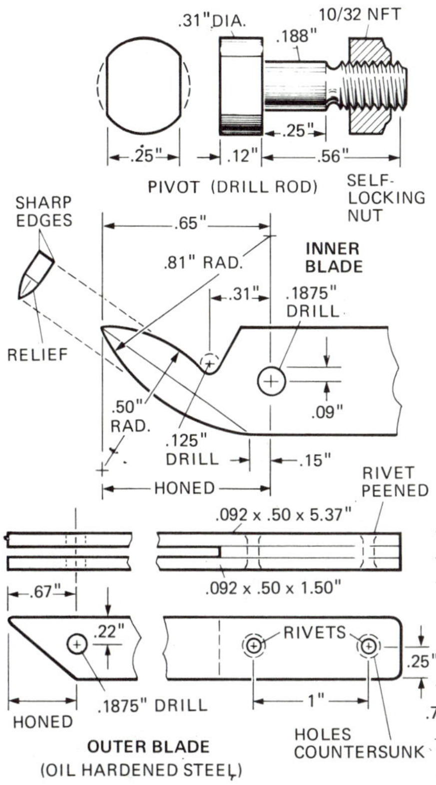


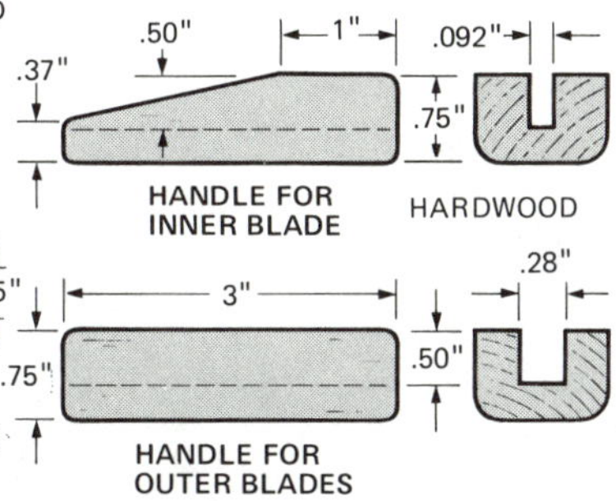


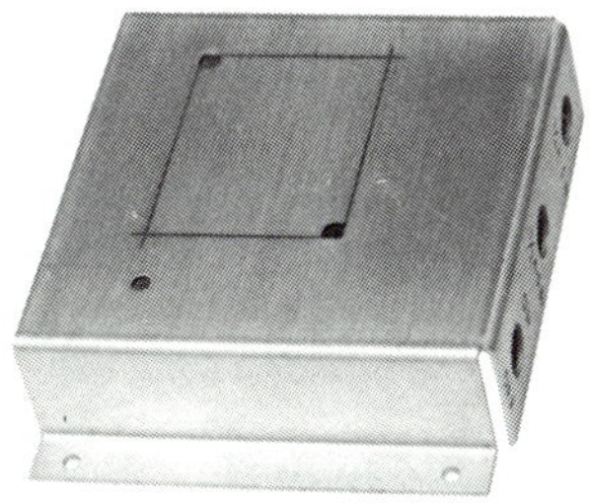

**FOR SQUARE** or rectangular opening, drill a .19-in. hole at opposite corners. Square the corners with a file as shown to permit the cutter to start on the line.

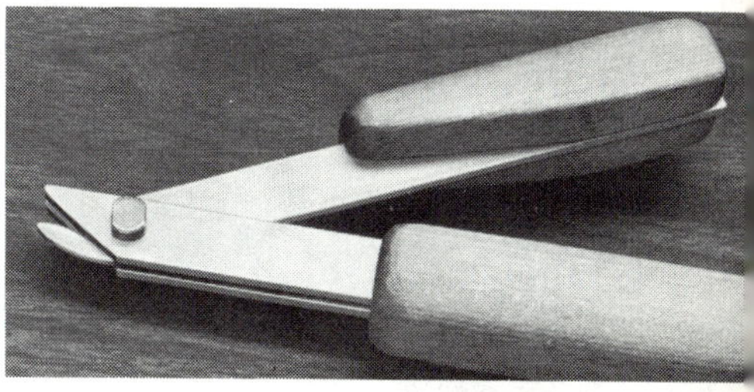

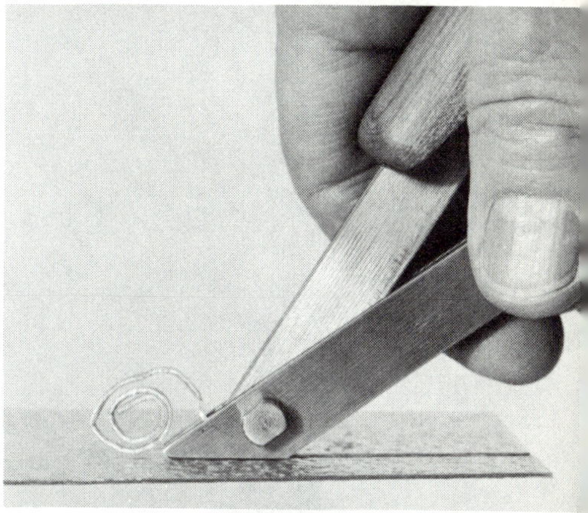

**CENTER BLADE** of cutter removes a narrow strip of metal in the form of a curl.

# Easy-to-make sheet-metal cutter

**You can start cutting right in the middle of a sheet of metal with this handy cutter. It makes a clean cut and will not distort the metal**

**By R. S. HEDIN**

■ THIS EASY-TO-MAKE sheet-metal cutter will do things you can't do with regular snips. It will cut in the center of a sheet with a .19-in.-dia. starting hole and cut on either the upper or lower side of the sheet, whichever is more convenient. It works best on straight cuts but it will cut a large radius.

As the blades cut, they curl a strip of metal ahead of the cutter. There is practically no distortion of the metal from the cutting action. The cutter will handle up to .06-in. aluminum or .02-in. soft-steel sheet.

The blades are made of oil-hardening tool steel. This steel is sold at machine-shop supply houses in strips two feet long. One strip is enough for one cutter. Finish the blades completely before heat treating as the steel will not distort during heating. To harden the blades, heat to a bright red (1475° F. to 1525° F.) and quench in motor oil. Draw the blades in a kitchen oven at 350° F. for an hour. Following the heat treatment, polish the blades and hone the cutting edges.

The hardwood handles are fastened to the blades with epoxy cement. Use a self-locking nut on the pivot bolt and adjust it so the blades work freely.

SEE ALSO

**Drill press techniques . . . Micrometers . . . Power hacksaws . . . Safety, workshop . . . Sheet metal . . . Shop techniques . . . Shop tools . . . Toolboxes . . . Torches . . . Tubing, metal**

Scoring picture and window glass squarely is easily done by aligning the edge with grid lines in the cutting board and drawing the glass cutter along the hinged nonslip straightedge

# Build a cutting board for your shop

**This multipurpose cutting board handles glass, cardboard, photo mats and roll paper. It features an adjustable stop and a replaceable cutting surface**

By C. E. BANISTER

A GOOD CUTTING BOARD is a valuable tool for both shop and darkroom work. Besides giving you accurate results every time, one will keep other surfaces from being marred by routine cutting jobs.

This board can be scaled to any size that meets your needs. Rather than incorporating a knife, it allows you to use the cutting tool most appropriate for whatever job you're doing by running it along a solid metal straightedge. The adjustable stop facilitates repeated cuts. If you are left-handed, you'll find the board easy to work with, too. The cost of materials is under $10.

Dimensions given in the drawing on page 902 are for a board about as large as you can work on comfortably. If you scale it down, the press bar should still be at least 13/16 in. high and 2 in. wide, and of a good grade of hardwood. For the baseboard, I used fir plywood, ¾ x 27½ x 30½ in., cut as shown. Note that the press bar and its extensions are 1 in. thick overall, while the anchor blocks are 1 3/16 in. thick. This allows material up to ¼ in. thick to be cut against the length of the fence. Thicker materials can be cut between the anchor blocks.

The 20-ga. sheet metal—I used galvanized—is 1 in. wide, rabbeted into the press bar so it is

**VERSATILITY** of the cutting board is demonstrated by its handling of a wide variety of materials. At top, picture mats with beveled edges are readily and accurately made. The bevel of the press bar makes the cutting angle precise. The middle photo shows the board with the stop removed to permit cutting of an extra-large sheet. A roll-paper holder, shown in use in the photo at the right, allows cutting of roll materials up to 24 in. wide, including photographic paper.

SEE ALSO
**Darkrooms . . . Frames, picture . . .**
**Glass cutting . . . Hardboard . . .**
**Mountings, photo . . . Prints, photo . . . Routers**

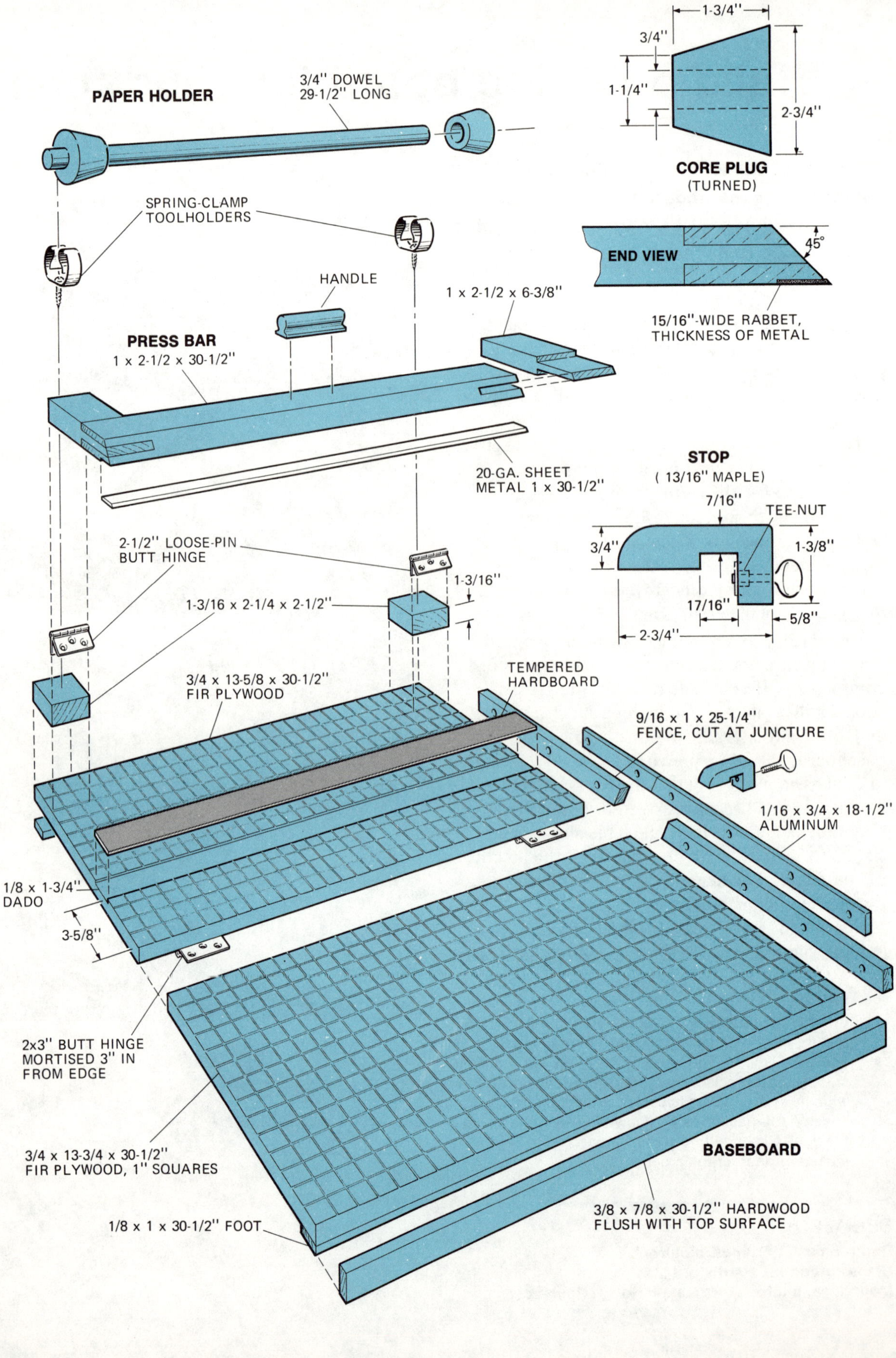
PAPER HOLDER
3/4" DOWEL
29-1/2" LONG
1-3/4"
3/4"
1-1/4"
2-3/4"
CORE PLUG
(TURNED)
SPRING-CLAMP
TOOLHOLDERS
END VIEW
45°
15/16"-WIDE RABBET,
THICKNESS OF METAL
HANDLE
1 x 2-1/2 x 6-3/8"
PRESS BAR
1 x 2-1/2 x 30-1/2"
20-GA. SHEET
METAL 1 x 30-1/2"
STOP
( 13/16" MAPLE)
7/16"
TEE-NUT
3/4"
1-3/8"
17/16"
5/8"
2-3/4"
2-1/2" LOOSE-PIN
BUTT HINGE
1-3/16"
1-3/16 x 2-1/4 x 2-1/2"
3/4 x 13-5/8 x 30-1/2"
FIR PLYWOOD
TEMPERED
HARDBOARD
9/16 x 1 x 25-1/4"
FENCE, CUT AT JUNCTURE
1/16 x 3/4 x 18-1/2"
ALUMINUM
1/8 x 1-3/4"
DADO
3-5/8"
2x3" BUTT HINGE
MORTISED 3" IN
FROM EDGE
3/4 x 13-3/4 x 30-1/2"
FIR PLYWOOD, 1" SQUARES
BASEBOARD
3/8 x 7/8 x 30-1/2" HARDWOOD
FLUSH WITH TOP SURFACE
1/8 x 1 x 30-1/2" FOOT

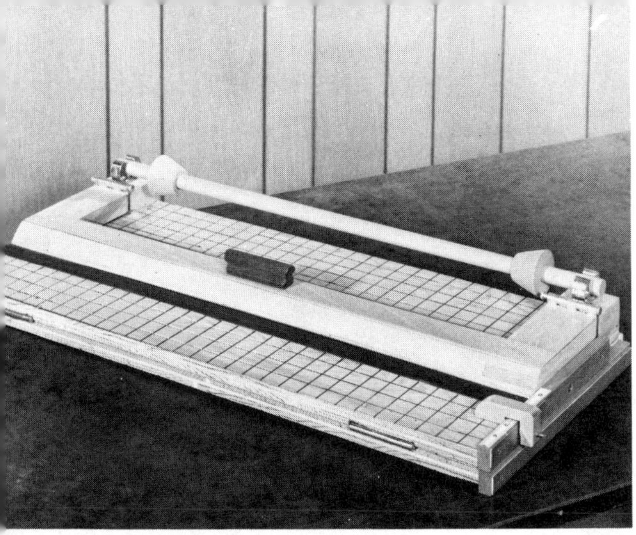

flush on the underside, and extends 1/16 in. beyond it. The metal is attached with contact cement; clamping is advisable for this step, and be sure there's always adequate ventilation when you're working with contact cement. The 45° cut on the press bar is made after the straightedge has been cemented in place.

The anchor blocks, attached to the baseboard with screws and glue, must be positioned accurately, since they will determine the ultimate squareness of the board. Small errors can be compensated for by shimming the hinges connecting the blocks to the press bar.

The routed or plowed 1/8 x 1¾-in. dado in the baseboard is for the replaceable tempered hardboard cutting surface, which should be cut for a snug fit. There are actually four different cutting surfaces, as the hardboard can be turned end for end, then turned over and finally turned end for end again before replacement.

The fence is secured with 1½-in. No. 10 screws, and the 1/16-in. aluminum, on which the stop rides, is attached to it with No. 4 screws. A commercially available metal tape with a pressure-sensitive adhesive back was used for the scale; a yardstick ripped to the proper width would be a suitable alternative.

Core plugs for the paper holder are turned on the lathe using the screw center and bored for ¾-in. dowel before being cut off from waste stock.

It is advisable to clamp the assembled anchor blocks and press bar to the baseboard before laying out the 1-in. squares. Measurement should start from the metal straightedge on the press bar for the lines that will be parallel to it, and from the upper edge of the baseboard or fence for the others.

Stain and finish the completed cutting board as desired. I used a clear resin sealer and urethane varnish.

**THE CUTTING BOARD FOLDS** for storage (top left), but can be built more simply when space is no problem. With the folding feature omitted, the 1/8-in feet, otherwise required by the hinge thickness, are no longer needed. In the middle photo, V-grooves are cut 1/32 in. deep with a thin saw blade set at 45°; a single pass will complete each V-cut. A molding head with V-knives could also be used. At left, grooves are darkened with a fine-point felt-tip marking pen before final finishing of the board. Paint or India ink would also work.

**NEED A SINK?** The Brooks Porta Sink (photo below) holds the three trays that you will need for your portable darkroom.

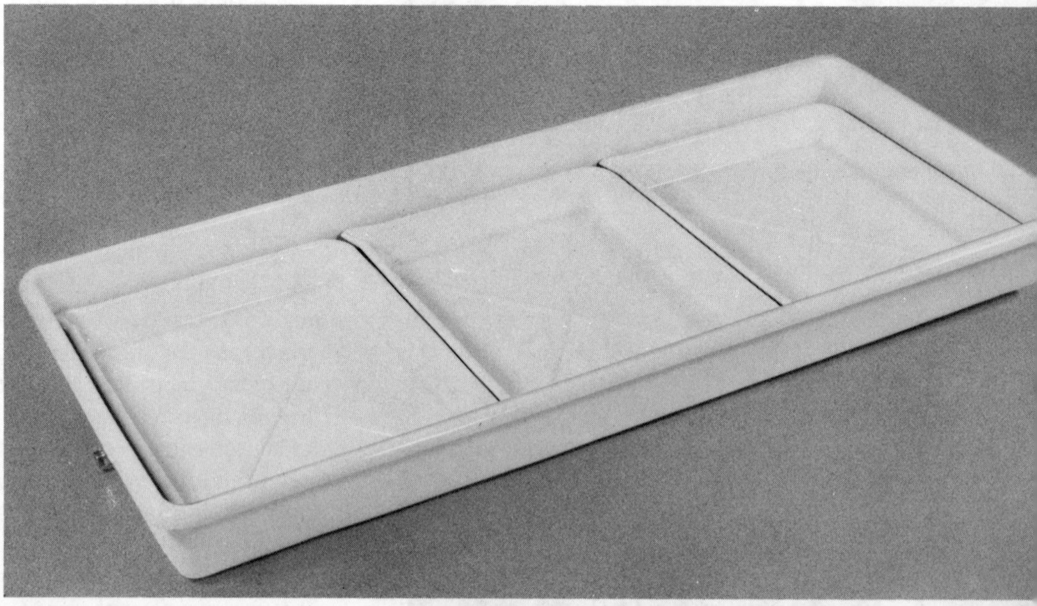

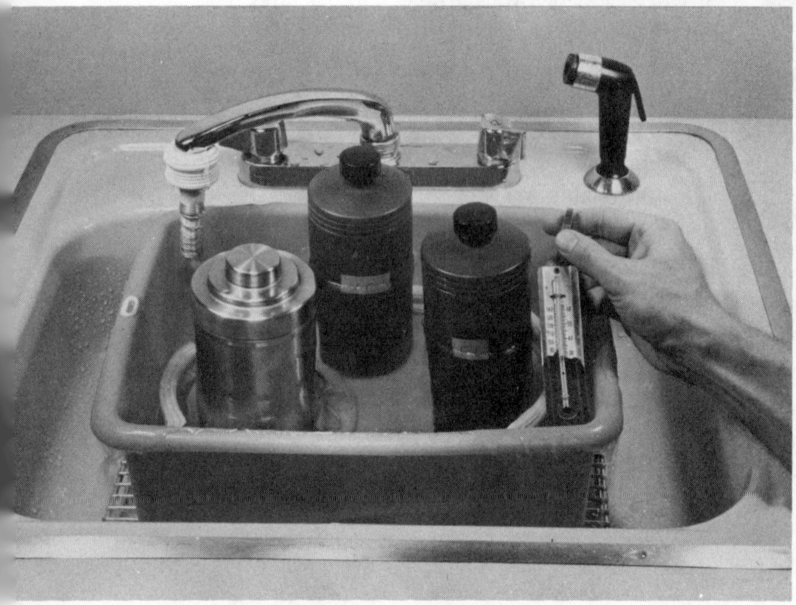

**TEMPORARY DARKROOM TACTICS** include the use of a plastic basin or dishpan as a carryall to carry each night's equipment to your workroom. It can also be used as a temperature-control bath (as shown above) and finally as a washer.

**THE WINDOWS** can be darkened with plastic lawn bags. It is suggested that the black plastic bags be used for daylight processing but the red-brown type will be satisfactory for nighttime developing work.

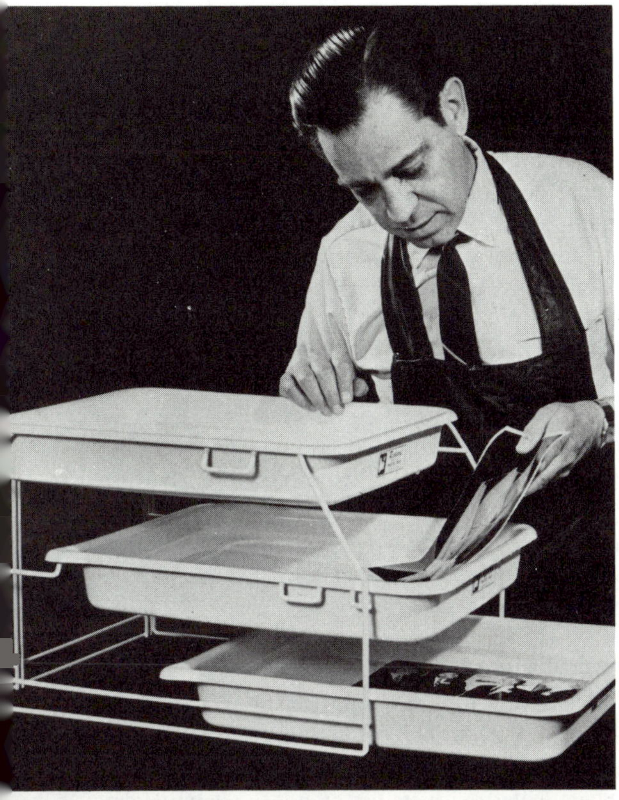

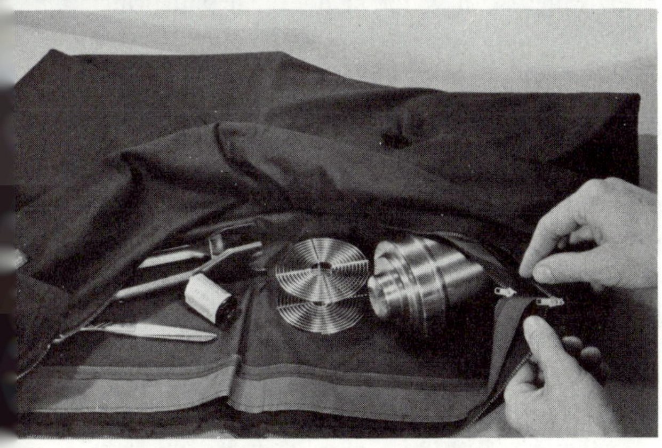

**THE TRAY-RAK** (top) holds three trays, step-fashion. The lower photo shows how a changing bag can be used for loading film-developing tanks of many different sizes.

# Borrow space for a darkroom

By ELBERT LAWTON

**Have you had trouble finding enough space in your home or apartment for a permanent darkroom? Here are some suggestions to help you purchase the proper equipment and set up a work plan for a portable darkroom which can be used almost anywhere**

IN MOST HOMES, finding space for a permanent darkroom is very difficult. When faced with this situation, many photographers find it easier to borrow space somewhere around the house for a few hours. One of the problems they encounter is that they are losing half their time setting up and taking down all the equipment which is necessary for developing and printing. If this is a problem you face, portable darkroom equipment and a work plan are what you need.

The first rule is to keep everything as simple as possible. Buy and use only the essentials—"time-saving" luxuries will seem a lot less luxurious if the time saved is then spent in moving them from place to place. Some photographers fear that using just the essentials will mean they

continued

SEE ALSO

continued from previous page

can't do as good a job as the guy with a permanent setup. This isn't true! However, it does mean that you can't count on quite as many prints per evening without cutting quality.

The second rule is to compartmentalize your work. This will involve careful planning as it simply isn't practical to drag out and set up *everything* each time you have a free hour or two to work.

It's better to break your darkroom work down into separate stages. Each of these stages can then be served by its own equipment and supplies. I divide my darkroom work into four such stages: chemical mixing; film processing; printing and print processing; and print drying, spotting and mounting. Limit yourself to one stage per work session (with the possible exception of the mixing stage). By using a method such as this you will find you accomplish a lot more than if you try to do everything at once.

**mixing the chemicals**

Chemical preparation takes little space and can be done in full room light. You can usually mix your chemicals the night you plan to use them, especially if you go to pre-mixed or liquid chemicals. Many powdered chemicals are supposed to be mixed at temperatures much higher than the standard 68°F. processing temperature. Mix them before dinner, and they'll be down to room temperature by the time you're ready for work.

You have the choice of the one-shot developers that are discarded after use or the kind you replenish. I prefer the one-shot developers as they're fresh each time—important when you do only occasional darkroom work.

Your equipment for this stage should include a quart graduate for measuring and mixing, a two-ounce graduate for adding replenisher (if you use it), a long-stem bar mixing spoon or mixing paddle, a funnel, a thermometer and plastic bottles. Some chemicals, which age more slowly (such as fixer and hypo eliminator), can be mixed more economically and conveniently in gallon quantities. This is especially true of fixer, which goes fast. If you do mix a gallon, divide it into quart bottles—the chemicals in the unopened bottles will last even longer, and you'll have less weight to lug around. If you can, always use separate graduates and paddles for mixing developer and fixer; otherwise, wash extra carefully between chemicals to keep one from contaminating the other.

Probably the best place in the house to do your mixing is the kitchen sink. And to carry your chemicals and equipment from storage to the sink and back, use a plastic dishpan—it will come in handy again in the next stage.

Now you are ready to do the actual developing. Developing film requires just a little additional equipment: a daylight-type developing tank, film reels, a changing bag, scissors, a length of hose (optional) from a bathroom hair-sprayer attachment, and (if you use 35-mm film) either a cassette opener or bottle-cap opener. The basic chemicals you'll need are film developer, stop bath (optional) and fixer. To speed up your processing, you can use rapid fixer instead of regular "hypo" type and a hypo neutralizer between fixing and washing to reduce washing time. Dip your film in wetting agent to speed up drying a bit and reduce the formation of water spots on the film.

Use a changing bag as a "dark-room." You will find that it is just big enough to hold the film, tank and reels. You can load the tank at your convenience.

**plastic dishpan is useful**

When developing, your plastic dishpan can serve double duty as a carry-all to bring your paraphernalia to the kitchen sink and as a water jacket. Filled with water at 68°F., it will bring all the chemicals and the tank to the correct temperature and hold them there for a period of time.

The best way to wash the film is to use a faucet's attached hose to direct a strong jet of water (still at 68°) through the center of the reels down to the bottom of the tank, where it will flush any impurities away. Some tanks come with hose assemblies, but with a little tinkering I have found that the hair-spray hose mentioned earlier seems to work well with many different kinds of tanks.

Printing takes a bit more equipment. You will need a developer and stop-bath tray at least as big as the largest prints you'll make as well as a larger tray for the fixing bath. You will also need tongs to agitate prints and carry them from one tray to another, and finally another deep plastic basin drilled with holes to serve as a washer.

Of course, you'll also need an enlarger and lenses for it. Unless you're sure you'll be shooting just 35-mm or 126 Instamatic photos for the rest of your life, it pays to buy the 35-mm-to-120 size—it won't be much more expensive. Look for one that can be disassembled easily for compact storage, but that is still of quality construction. The quality of your enlarger will directly affect the quality of your prints. If you want to get good sharp prints, buy a well-built enlarger. This is no place to save money.

You'll need enlarging lenses, too. You should get a 2-inch lens for 35-mm, or a 3-inch lens for 120 negatives. If you're trying to print both sizes but can only afford one lens at first, use a 3-inch lens, and attach a close-up lens to its front when you need bigger enlargements.

In enlarging easels, your best bet is the kind with calibrated, adjustable masking bands that let you use different paper sizes or crop your borders to precisely match the shape of your image. Most photographers agree that not all photos look best in precise 8x10 proportions. Look for an easel whose masking bands are supported on all four sides, not flopping in the air when you raise them to insert the paper. You should begin with an 8x10-size easel. Even after making bigger enlargements, you'll probably find that this size is easier to use when working with smaller prints.

**do without some "nonessentials"**

The only essential accessory left is a safelight. If you were setting up a permanent darkroom you would surely want to include such things as enlarging timers, paper safes and focusing magnifiers. But with your portable darkroom, you can do without them at first. Count seconds aloud (say "one-hippopotamus, two-hippopotamus . . ." to space the seconds properly) or watch the kitchen clock's sweep second hand. You can remove the paper sheets one at a time from the box, placing your body as a shield between the open box and the safelight. The focus can be checked with a conventional magnifier.

Once you have all your printing equipment ready, you are faced with the question of where and how you should set it up. For the "where" you have several choices: A basement location near the utility sink will minimize disruption of your family's life, provided the location is comfortable and free of dust. The kitchen is the next best bet because of its deep sink and its countertop space–but you'll have to wait till the dishes are washed, and teach everyone to knock before coming in. The bathroom is least preferable, since its sink is too small, its tub too low, and you'll frequently have to stop to admit other family members.

A sink isn't really needed till the final wash, though, so you can set up in a dry room–pick one with lots of space, few windows and low family traffic–just by adding another dishpan full of water to hold the prints till you can take a batch of them outside for washing.

Whatever room you pick, make sure it has a sturdy table or counter that won't shake under your enlarger. Keep your "dry" operations (enlarging and paper storage) separate from wet ones (developing, stop bath and fixing), either on opposite sides of the room or with a partition between them.

All that's left is darkness–and you need that only for enlarging. For daylight processing, cover the windows with large, black plastic trash bags from the supermarket, the red-brown type will do for use at night.

It is very important that the entire room be light-tight. If the room has a door, make it light-tight with weatherstripping. If not, cover the open doorway with more plastic, overlapping and taping the bags together. Carefully look to make sure there is no other light leaking into the room. At this point, ventilation can be a problem. My kitchen fan handles the problem for me.

Print drying can be left to the day after your printing session. It won't hurt the prints to soak, though the water should be changed a few times. Squeeze an electric print-dryer into your budget if at all possible–it's the only way to make sure that the prints you've spent hours making will look as good when dry as they did wet. For matte prints, you'll get a far more smoothly finished, wrinkle-free surface than you could with a blotter; and with ferrotype tins, you'll get good glossy prints much faster than you would with plain air drying. The best size for your dryer of ferrotype tins is 16x20 inches. It's big enough to handle big prints and will let you dry four 8x10s at once.

**the finishing touches**

For finishing touches, take the extra steps of spotting and mounting your prints. With just three bottles of spotting tone (in different densities) and a fine brush, you can render many dust spots and other imperfections invisible. For print-mounting, your best bet is to use one of the special adhesives sold in photo stores. Electric dry-mounting presses are bulky and expensive, and though a few hobbyists dry-mount successfully with a clothes iron, there's risk of damage to the print.

Useful mounting tools include a wallboard knife, a steel straightedge for trimming, and a board with a weight on top to press the paper down for a blemish-free surface.

# Roll-away bathroom darkroom

By RAYMOND D. JOHNSON

**THE MOBILE CABINET** stores your enlarger, dryer and other items in cleverly shaped compartments.

THIS QUICK-CHANGE SETUP turns a 5x8 bathroom into a handy darkroom in less than five minutes. If someone wants a fast shower, you can have the whole works knocked down and stored away in the same short time.

Heart of the system is a roll-around unit that

**WHEN NOT IN USE,** the cabinet parks in the kitchen where it doubles as extra counter space.

**SWUNG UP** over the tub, a hinged table holds the processing trays with a washer handy under it.

SEE ALSO

**Bathrooms . . . Camera bags . . . Camera care . . . Developing, photo . . . Dryers, photo . . . Photography . . . Prints, photo . . . Slides, photo**

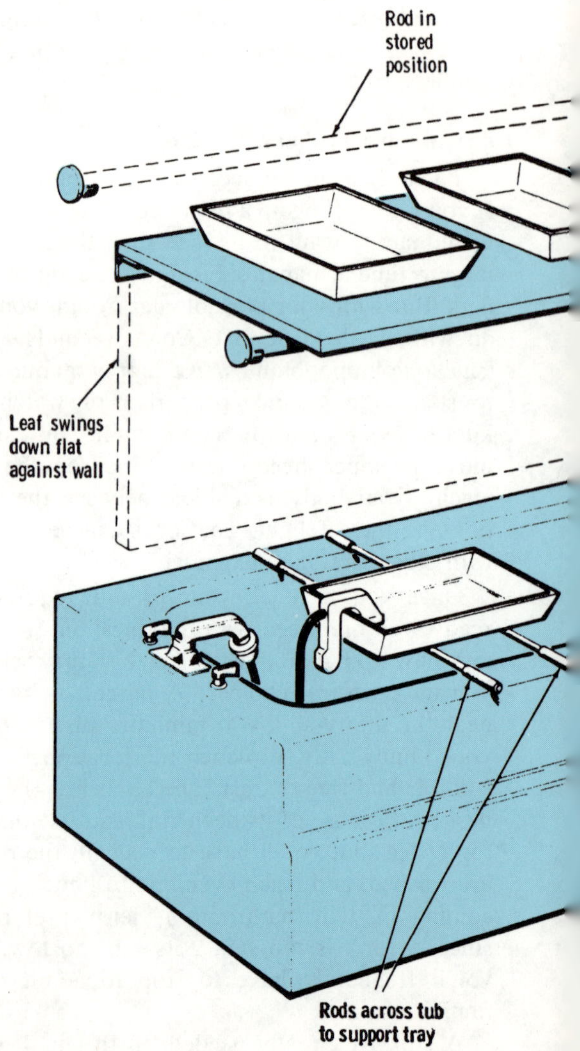

houses enlarger, print dryer, processing trays, paper, paper cutter and chemicals—all in a compact, counter-height cabinet only 20 in. wide by 24 in. deep. Ball glides on the bottom make it easy to move. Rolled into the bathroom, it becomes a stand for the enlarger, and a single-legged table hooks onto the side for added work space. The cabinet can be stored in a closet or parked in the kitchen.

Completing the setup is a drop-down counter hinged to the wall above the tub. This swings up and rests on a shower-curtain rod slipped into holders on the side walls. When not in use, the rod stores in a duplicate set of holders mounted near the back wall out of the way. The counter is purposely made slightly shallower than the tub so spills run off into the tub instead of on the floor.

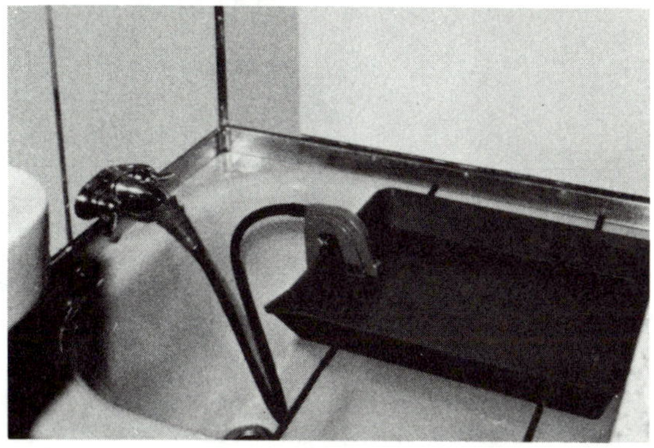

**IN THE BATHROOM,** the rolling cabinet becomes an enlarger stand. A hook-on table supports bulky equipment. Print washer rests on bars across tub where its overflow runs down drain.

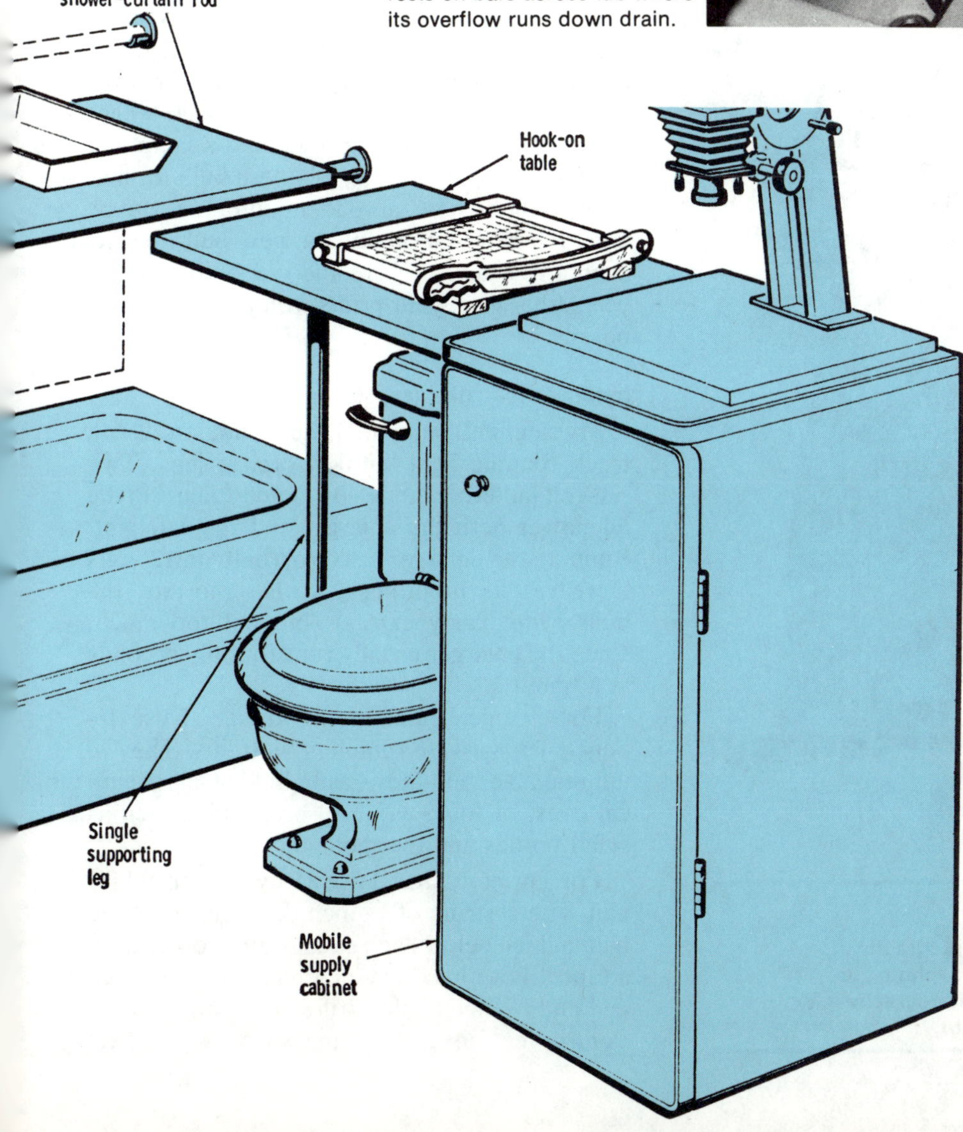

# Darkroom in a suitcase

By JAMES L. ABBOTT

SEE ALSO

Camera bags . . . Candid photography . . .
Developing, photo . . . Dryers, photo . . .
Filters, photo . . . Outdoor photography . . .
Photography . . . Prints, photo

■ EVER COME BACK from vacation only to find you or your camera hadn't been shooting properly—or that your local lab had finished *off* your pictures instead of finishing them?

That never happens to me. I take my darkroom with me—in one ordinary "two-suiter" suitcase measuring only 7 by 17 by 24 inches, and weighing less than 35 pounds. Within minutes I can set it up (even where no electricity is available) and start developing my day's color slides, or developing and printing black and white. If I've missed anything important, I know in plenty of time to reshoot the next day.

The case is adapted specifically to my equipment—you'll have to adjust its dimensions to your own. But the principles involved will be the same.

First principle is packing minimum equipment. I use the smallest enlarger I could find, the Durst J35 (no longer available). Like many small 35-mm enlargers on the market today, it disassembles quickly for packing. For U.S. travel, that and good quality are about the only strict requirements. For foreign travel, you might try to find an imported enlarger that can adapt for Europe's higher voltages (about 240 volts). I got around that by replacing my Durst's lamp and socket with a six-volt flash-lantern bulb for battery operation here, abroad, or outdoors. But be careful when you mount the new bulb that its center is exactly where the old bulb's center was; otherwise, your prints won't be evenly exposed.

**batteries for enlarger, safelight**

My safelight, built into the case lid, is a 12-volt truck running light with an orange lens. Two six-volt lantern batteries in compartments in the lid power both the enlarger and the safelight. Running the enlarger's six-volt bulb on 12 volts increases its brightness; it also shortens the bulb's life (carry extras)—but not too much, since the enlarger usually runs for only seconds at a time.

For chemical mixing and storage, I use 16-ounce Tupperware tumblers with lids. They're unbreakable, and they easily hold small chemical cans, or foam-wrapped breakables such as small bottles and thermometers.

For a print washer, I use a 9 by 12-inch baking pan with a string of ⅛-inch drain holes drilled half an inch below each edge; water comes from a faucet hose into a ⅜-inch pipe with a capped end and 1/16-inch holes drilled in a row along it. For a dryer, I invert the same pan over a low heat

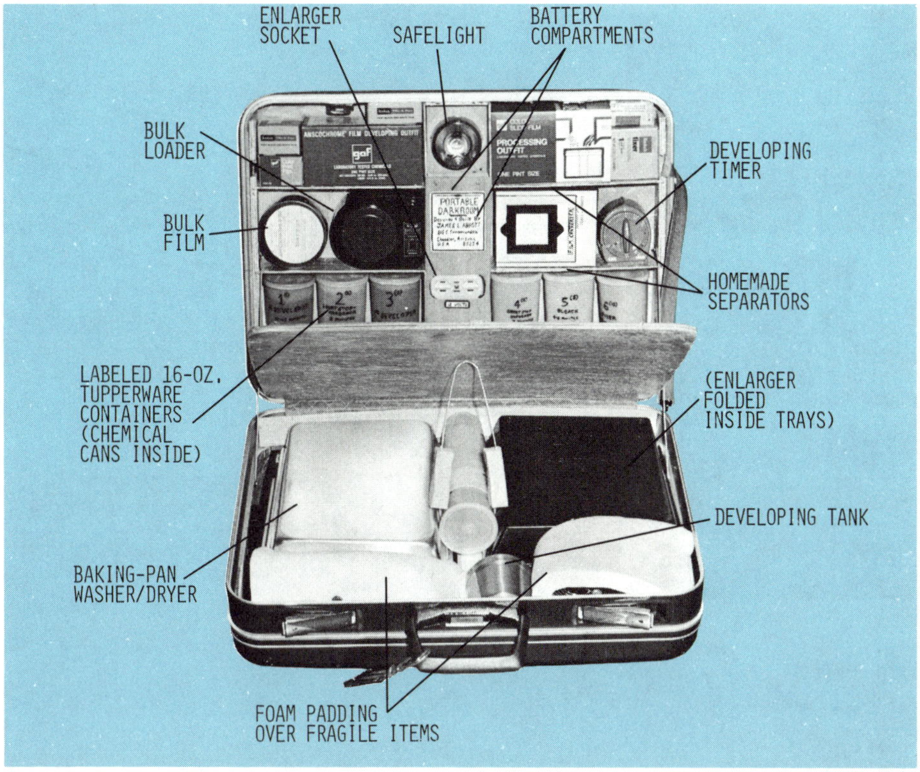


**IN THE SUITCASE** is a complete darkroom outfit, cleverly tucked away in homebuilt compartments, or one item inside another item.

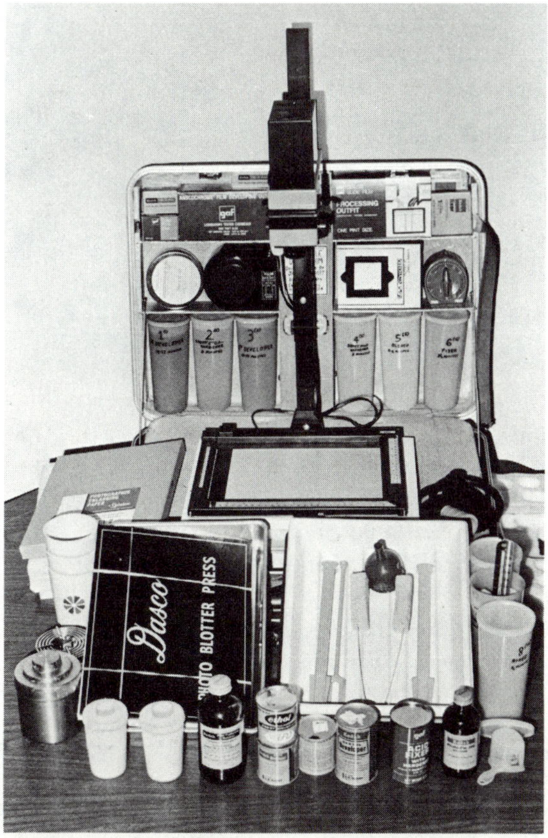

**UNBELIEVABLE AMOUNTS** of darkroom gear can fit in case; compact, take-apart enlarger is the key item.

**BATHROOM INTO DARKROOM** takes only blankets over the windows, the suitcase, and its contents.

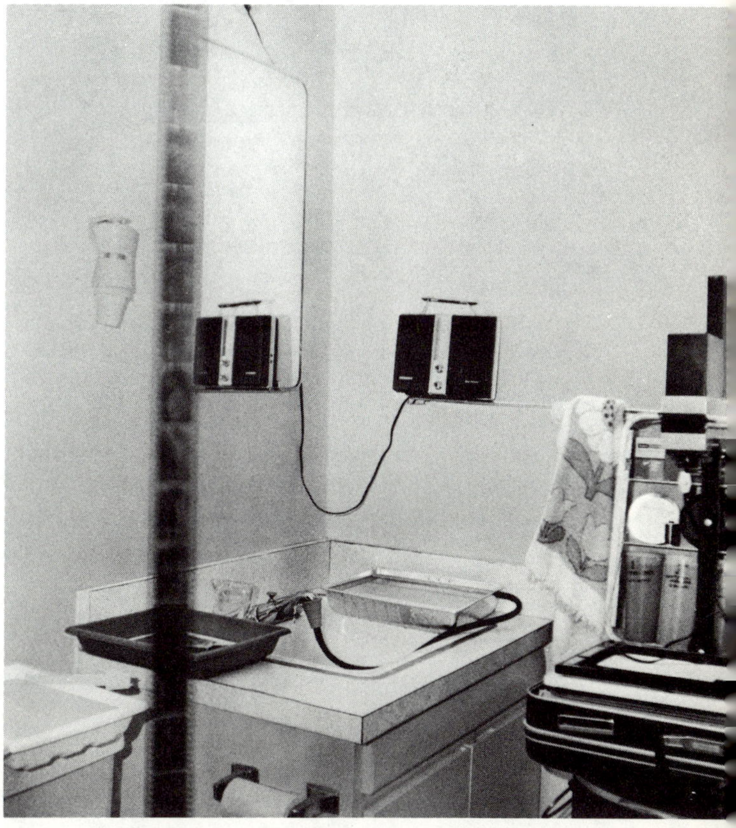

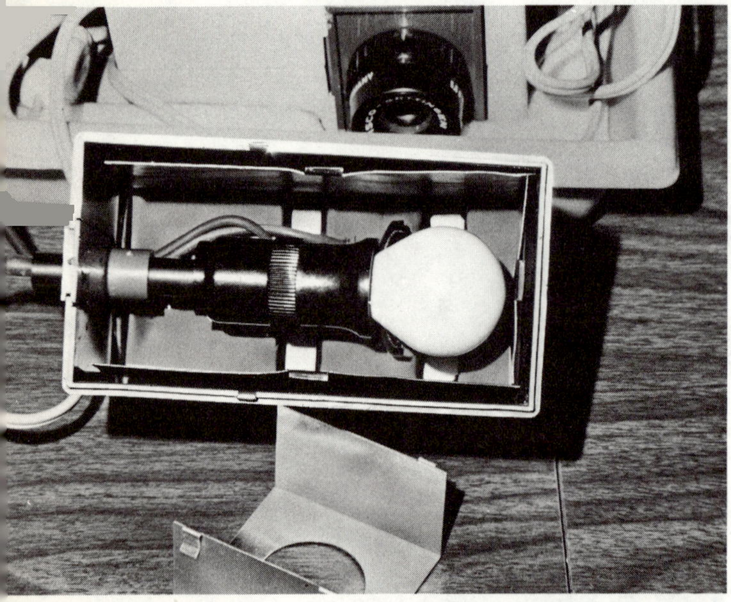

**FOR TRAVEL,** the enlarger's 110-volt bulb (top photo) is replaced with a six-volt flash-lantern bulb and socket, carefully centered in the old bulb's position so the print will still get even exposure. The six-volt bulb runs brightly on 12 volts from two lantern batteries in series——and battery power works in foreign countries with different voltages, or even in the outdoors if you are camping.

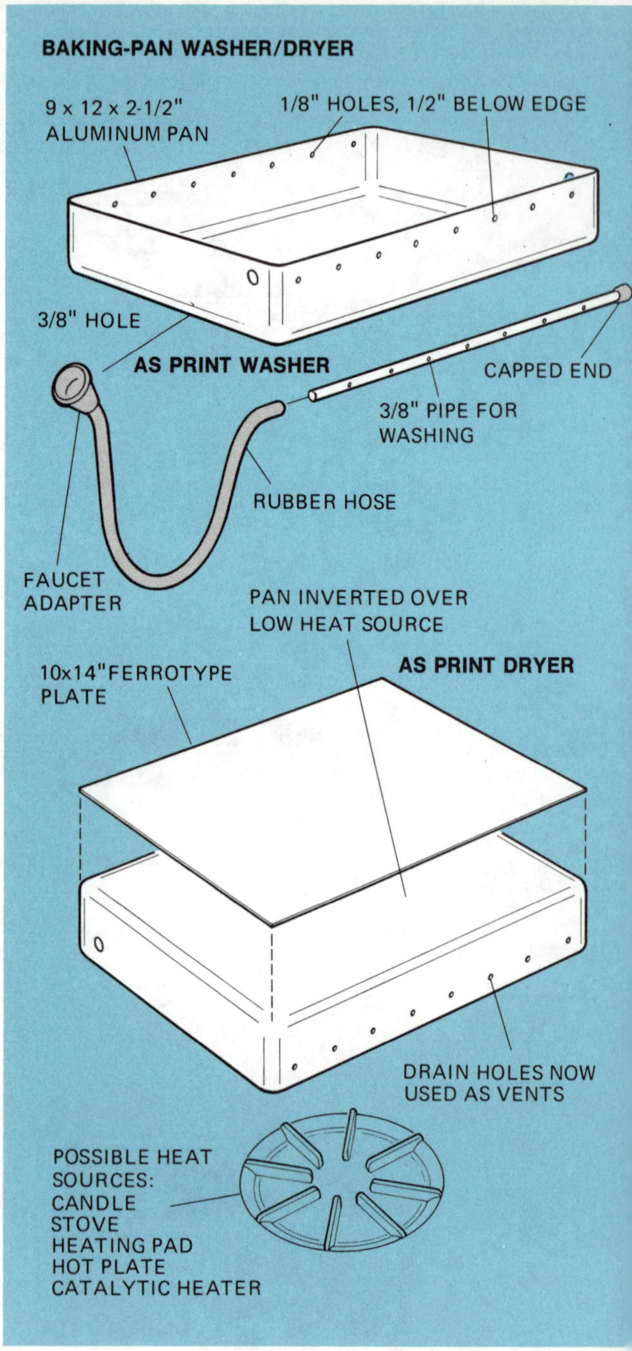


source (candle, catalytic heater or stove) and lay a ferrotype plate atop it; the drain holes now serve as vents. Using a 10x14-inch ferrotype plate, you should be able to peel off three 5x7 prints every five minutes or so at moderate heat (below 150° F.)

I keep my equipment to a minimum; any inconvenience resulting from that is outweighed by the convenience of being able to carry everything. Trays do double duty as containers for paper, the enlarger head is cushioned well with foam rubber. My chemicals are all 16-ounce sizes or smaller (Kodak's four-ounce black and white chemicals are great) in powder or concentrate form whenever possible.

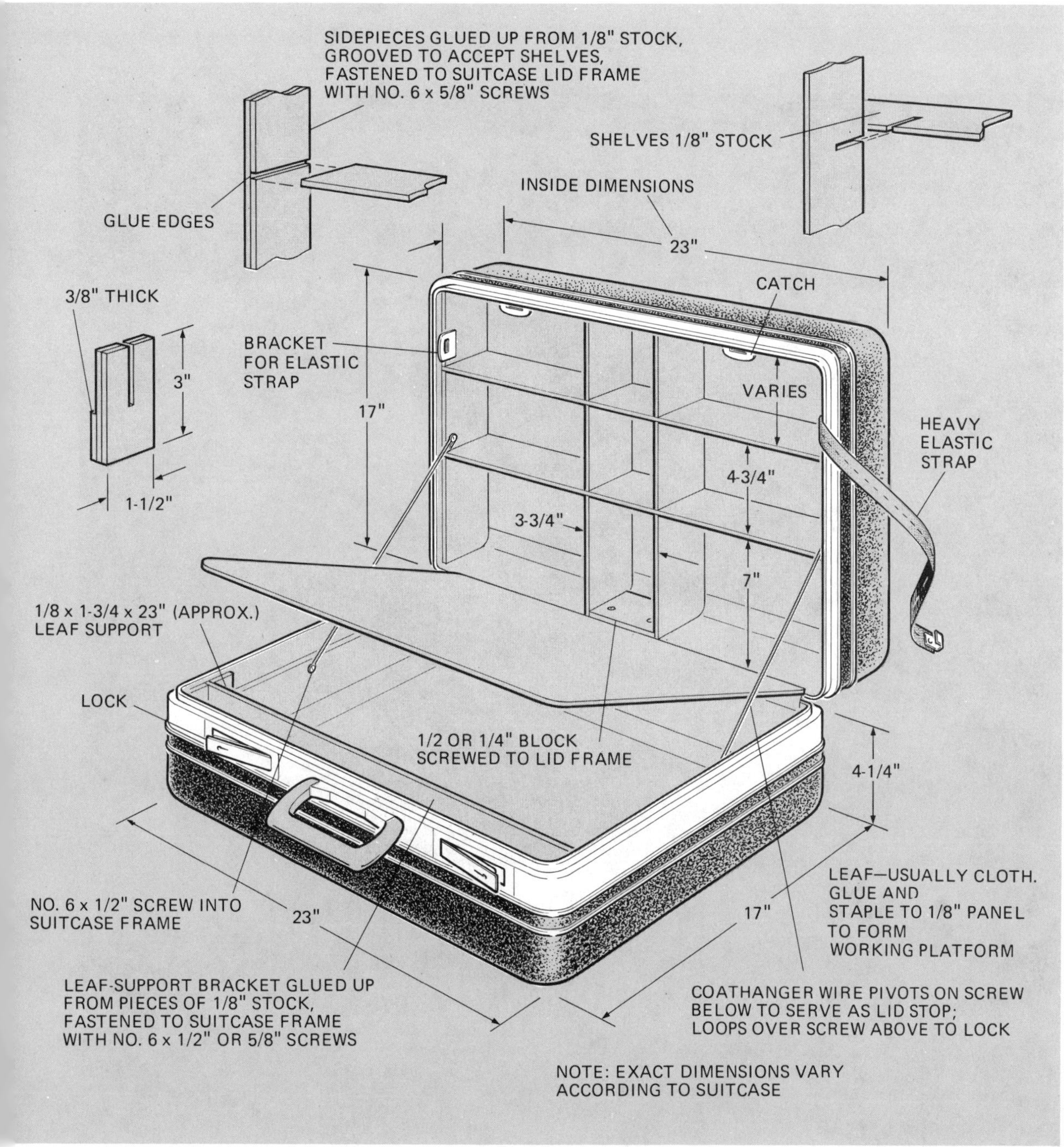


Since you can't always buy the film you want at the prices you're used to, and since some countries limit the number of rolls of film you can take in with you, I pack a bulkloader, spare cartridges and film in long rolls of 27½ to 100 feet (at about half the cost of the same film already loaded into cartridges). I also pack a changing bag—useful not only for loading the bulk-loader and developing tank, but for removing broken or jammed film from a camera without exposing it.

Of course, my suitcase only holds a darkroom setup, not the darkroom. But my changing bag takes care of anything that requires *absolute* darkness, and with blankets over the windows and paper stuffed under the door, any room can be an adequate darkroom for printing. You can even do it on an outdoor picnic table after dark.

To keep things from rattling around, the lid of the suitcase is divided into custom-fitted compartments by partitions of ⅛-inch plywood or hardboard, with a fold-down leaf keeping everything in place when you open the lid. The larger items are crammed tightly into the bottom of the suitcase; insulate anything that rattles with spare socks or other clothing items.

All this may seem a lot of trouble and expense. But my whole initial outlay, suitcase, enlarger and all, was just under $125 a few years back. My savings in film, processing and postage have run as high as $44 per trip since then.

# Enjoy the outdoors on an open deck

**With only the sky overhead, there's nothing like an open deck to give you that true outdoor-living feeling**

A WOOD DECK is simply a handsome platform on or above the ground. But it's a platform that adds much to the livability, beauty and value of a house.

A well designed deck can turn a hilly site into a useful, enjoyable outdoor living area at a fraction of the cost of adding an inside room. And there's no substitute for the style of living it can provide as an area for sunbathing, entertaining, dining, conversation, container gardening, children's play and parties.

As an aesthetic assist, good deck design eases the transition from house to garden and is a part of each. Where the land slopes upward from the house, the deck bridges the space with a usable level floor. Where the land slopes down and away, the deck extends the floor of the building out into otherwise wasted space.

Even on land that is generally flat, the deck can be a floor-level area gently leading to the garden a step or two below. Where paving of a flat area may be a practical expedient, a ground-level deck is often preferred for its resilient comfort and drainage advantages. For whatever reasons a deck is desired, it can also be counted on to add permanently to the value of a house as well as enhance its sale appeal.

Lumber selection for the various parts of the deck is based on its function. Thus, supporting elements are picked for strength, members visible to the eye for looks. Douglas fir or kiln-dried hemlock are good choices for beams, joists and the like. Or, if the advantages of redwood's natural resistance to weather are desired, a heartwood grade should be used. The decking, usually 2x4s on the flat, can be fir if it is to be painted, with redwood preferable if it is to remain natural.

Redwood can vary. In addition to the heartwood, there are clear all-heart, select-heart and construction-heart. A-grade, sap-common and merchantable grades permit the presence of some cream-colored sapwood. (*Note:* Sapwood is not decay-resistant and should only be used above ground.) If redwood is your choice for decking, you can use either clear all-heart or construction-heart, depending upon the appearance you desire.

The general approach to laying out a deck is to first decide on its size and then choose a pattern. Next, select the grade material you plan to

SEE ALSO
**Benches, deck . . . Cabanas . . . Fences . . . Garden shelters . . . Gazebos . . . Lumber . . . Measurements . . . Nails . . . Patios . . . Railings . . . Screened summer rooms**

**BENCH AND RAIL DETAILS**

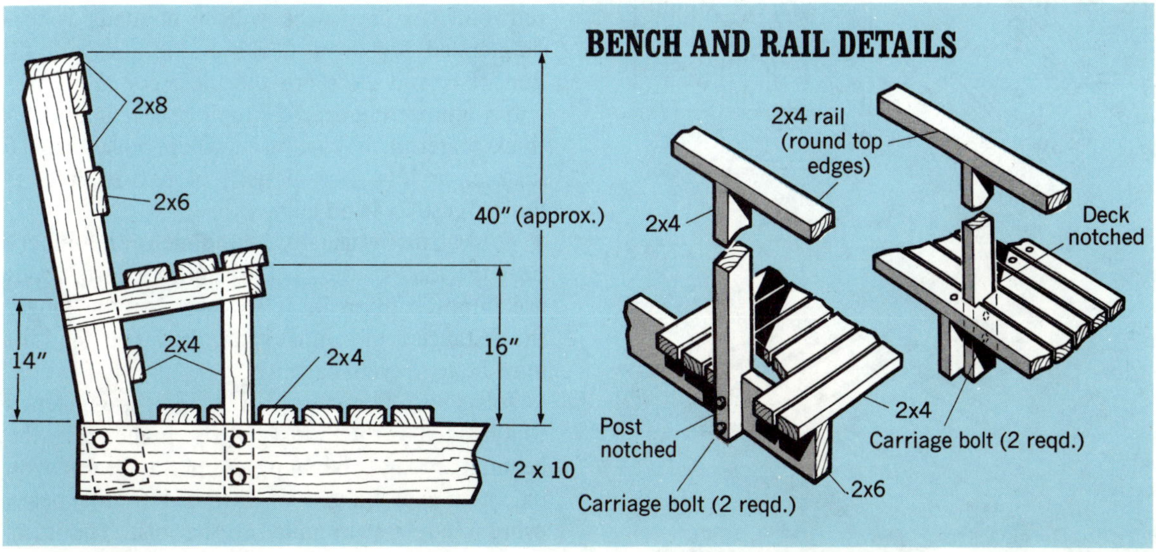

## FIVE DECK PATTERNS TO CHOOSE FROM

SQUARED HERRINGBONE

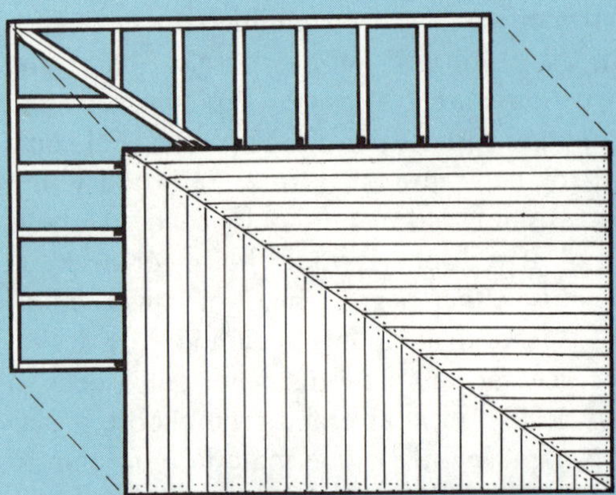

SYMMETRICAL

DIAMOND

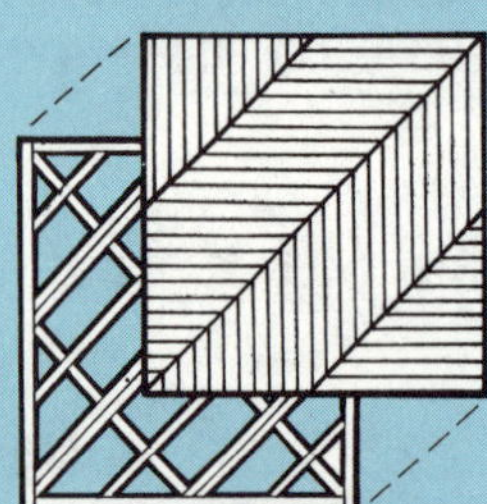

DIAGONAL HERRINGBONE

PERPENDICULAR SQUARES

**AS A SEPARATE PART** of the garden, an isolated ground-hugging deck (above) adds to usable yard space and offers low-maintenance landscaping.

use and determine the joist layout. With sketch in hand, visit your local building department. It will advise you about the size materials you will need for the structural members—posts, beams and joists.

• *Decking:* The deck surface—size, lumber grade and design—determines the arrangement and size of the framing. Two-inch (nominal) redwood (or fir if deck will be painted) is recommended for most decking situations. You'll find 2x4s and 2x6s are the most common sizes and minimize chance of cupping. Nominal 1-in.-thick material may be used where joists are 16 in. o.c. or less. If a pattern of narrow lines is desired, use 2x4s on edge.

• *Joists:* Joists (usually 2-in. dimension lumber) bear the load of the decking and whatever loads are imposed upon it. It follows that the longer the distance a joist must span, the larger the joist must be to prevent sagging.

Joists usually rest upon a beam or are fastened to a header. If they must not rise higher than the beam, they may be hung from the beam by a patented joist hanger or fastened to the beam using a ledger strip nailed to the joist. The joists

can overhang (cantilever) slightly beyond (outside) the beam for appearance or added size if desired. Overhang limit depends upon width of the joist and should in no case exceed ¼ of the joist's length. Bridging is usually installed at mid-span to strengthen joists.

• *Beams:* Beams rest upon the posts and support the joists. The size required depends upon the weight that will be imposed. However, a general rule is to utilize as large a beam as necessary in order to minimize the number of posts and footings. Beams of 4-in. thickness and greater are often used, and since these thicker members are not always readily available, it is sometimes necessary to construct a "built-up" beam by spiking thinner members together.

The beam can be fastened to post tops by a metal post-connector or a wooden cleat bolted or nailed to the post and beam. When the post must extend above the deck level to support a railing, seat or overhead shelter, the joists may be supported on paired members bolted to the posts. When the beam rests directly on footings, it should be anchored to the footings with nailing blocks or anchor bolts.

Where length of the deck requires splicing a beam, make butt joints over supporting posts and tie two beams together with cleats on each side.

• *Ledgers:* When deck height is of concern, joists can be supported by a ledger strip attached to the house or beam. Care should be taken to insure full bearing on the ledger strip. To prevent rain or snow from wetting interior floors the ledger should be located so that deck surface is at least 1 in. below the house floor.

• *Posts:* The posts bear the weight of the deck, transmitting it through the footings to the ground. For most low decks, the 4x4 is an adequate post. For steep sites, or for heavy loads such as large groups of people, snow, or plant containers, larger posts will be required to bear the weight.

Where a beam bears upon the top of a post, the length of the post must be carefully measured and trimmed to insure solid bearing for the beam. Accurate measurement may be achieved by carefully leveling the beam from a reference elevation on the house. Mark the level position, adjust for slope of deck, if any, and trim carefully. The post should be plumb when measured and installed.

Cross bracing may be necessary to prevent lateral movement of the deck, particularly if it is elevated high above the ground. Good connections between post and beam will help brace the deck structure, but diagonal bracing across

**DECK DESIGN** needn't be restricted to square and rectangular shapes. One of our editors built this fine five-sider (details below).

*open deck, continued*

corners or across the understructure may be the only way to achieve the stability required by local building regulations.

• *Footings:* The footing anchors the entire structure and transmits the weight of the deck to the ground. Building codes are specific on the subject of footings. Generally, they must extend to undisturbed soil or rock and, in cold climates, must be below the frost line (local codes determine depth). If concrete footings are site-poured, metal post-anchors or steel straps may be set in the wet concrete. Drift pins offer a concealed method of connecting the post to the footing when the underside of the deck is to be in open view. While anchors of metal are the most rigid and are recommended for high decks, wood nailing blocks imbedded in concrete usually are adequate for low decks.

Locations and placement of footings are determined by the design of the deck's structural members so that weight is properly transmitted to the ground. Placement points can be ascertained with a tape measure, a string, or a long, straight 2x4 and a wooden peg.

If the deck is to extend from a corner of the house, you can simply project a straight line from the nondeck side of the house out to where one corner of the deck will extend. Then measure and mark the points within the line where footings will be needed.

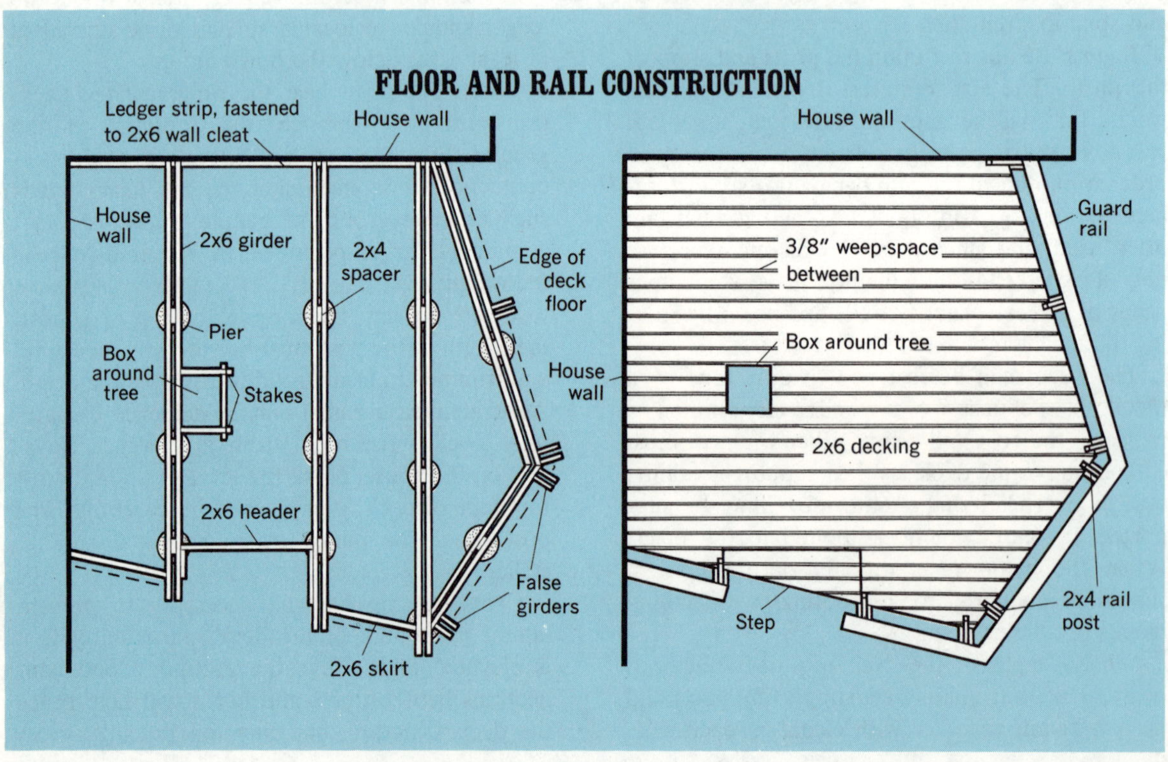

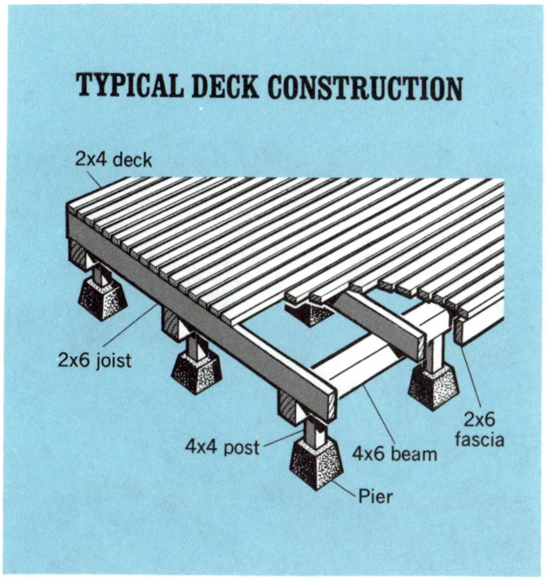


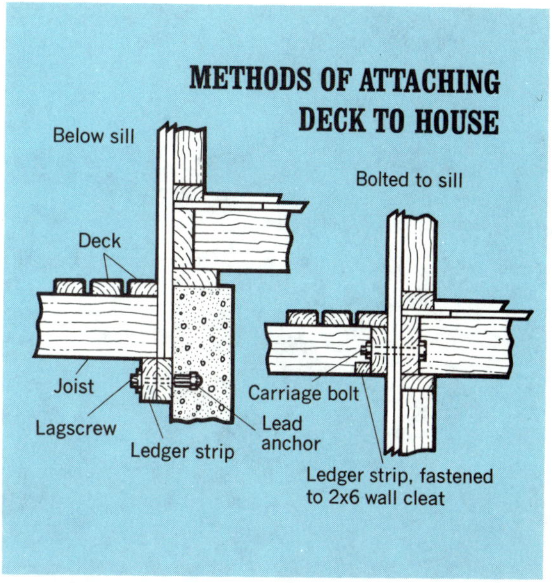


With this right angle (consisting of the line and the deck side of the house) established, two corners of the deck are determined. The length of the deck is then measured along the wall from the corner of the house. With a third corner thus established, location of the other corner footing can easily be fixed with tape measurement from these established points.

Accuracy of the four points can be proven by diagonal measurements between the farthest corners. If these diagonal distances are at variance, the deck is not square. This could be the fault of either an out-of-square house or inaccurate measurement. If the former, design the deck to match the house.

Here is another way to place footings:

If the deck is to project from a wall where a corner line projection is not convenient, a right-angle projection can be made by creating a mathematical right-angle triangle of 6x8x10 ft. or proportionally larger. This is done by marking a point (A) on the house wall which designates one corner of the deck. Measure 6 ft. from point A one way on the wall to establish point B. To establish the right angle desired between point A and C (8 ft.), the mathematical triangle which establishes this right angle can be created using a taut string approximately 2 ft. longer than the outside dimension of the deck. This string, nailed to a "batter board," should be pulled out from the wall. Then a long 2x4 marked at 10 ft. can be extended from point B to point C. The string and the marked 2x4 may have to be moved left or right until the marks on each match. When they do, a right angle has been created to use as a reference point for placement of footings where desired inside or outside the triangle. Other footings can be placed by measurements from this reference point and the wall reference points.

Lay out decking on the joists so that any butt joints that may occur are at random intervals and over joists. Joints should never occur on adjacent pieces of decking unless the pattern dictates. It is better to trim decking to size as it is used, rather than trimming first, in order to fit to any variations caused by installation of the framing or other decking. When decking is laid parallel to the house, make sure the first piece is properly aligned both with the house and at the proper angle to the joists.

Vertical-grain lumber is recommended for decking, but when flat-grained lumber is used it is important to make sure that the bark side of the piece is up. Either side of a vertical grain piece may be up when the piece is laid.

- *Nails:* Use only corrosion-resistant nails for secure holding power and to avoid rust stains on the wood. Stainless steel and aluminum never cause staining. If these are not locally available, hot-dipped, high-quality galvanized nails with a ring or spiral shank are adequate. For 2-in. decking, use 16d nails; for 1-in. decking, 8d.
- *Nailing:* Predrill holes for nails at the ends of decking pieces to avoid splitting. Seasoned decking material should be spaced a minimum of 1/8 in. apart for water drainage. Use only one nail per bearing, alternating from one side of the piece to the other. The nailing on alternate sides overcomes any tendency to pull or cup. Keep nails in alignment for best appearance.

# Simple details add beauty to your deck

**One of the least expensive ways to extend your living space is to attach a redwood deck to your house**

By HARRY WICKS

**AS IF TO PROVE THE POINT** that do-it-yourself construction isn't always as difficult as it may seem, the deck shown above—which is attached to a house parked on a hilly site in San Anselmo, Calif.—was built entirely by John Braun, age 18. John feels the project was worth the effort, as the family uses it much of the time.

■ FIRMLY ENTRENCHED as part of the American lifestyle, outdoor living can be as pleasant as you want to make it. Whether you attach a deck to your home to serve as a transition area from house to nature, to function as a sun trap, or to be an extension of indoor living, it is unquestionably the least expensive way to add living space to what you already have.

**A MULTILEVEL DECK** makes sense because it reduces the amount of furniture you will need when entertaining a crowd—you simply scatter pillows and use the steps. There are some basics you should be familiar with before taking on a deck project. For example, to get good appearance and high resistance to attack by insects and decay, you should consider using redwood throughout. And you can select from the lower-cost redwoods: "Construction Heart" is generally used for construction in or near the ground; "Construction Common" for decking and other off-the-ground members. Make certain you use either stainless steel, aluminum alloy or hot-dipped galvanized nails and fasteners. These won't rust and cause ugly stains on the wood. To finish the redwood, you have several choices: a clear water-repellent finish; bleach to hasten a driftwood-gray effect similar to natural weathering; or a pigmented stain which will let the grain show through.

*continued*

SEE ALSO

**Benches, deck . . . Cabanas . . . Fences . . . Garden shelters . . . Gazebos . . . Lumber . . . Measurements . . . Nails . . . Patios . . . Planters . . . Privacy screens . . . Railings**

**A FRONT VIEW** of the sturdy railing is what you see from the deck (above). Redwood planks which sandwich the rails are held together with bolts, washers and nuts. Notice that no attempt was made to conceal the boltheads. The fastening hardware has been left exposed to serve as an interesting architectural detail.

**THIS IS A BACK VIEW** of the architectural railing surrounding the deck. Alternate posts are fashioned using three lengths of 2x6-in. material per post. The posts in between are doubled-up. Since good deck construction calls for the use of noncorrosive nails and fasteners, hefty galvanized bolts were used.

**A BIG ADVANTAGE** gained with a multilevel deck is that the need for a great deal of patio furniture is eliminated—you simply use the steps for extra seating. This handsome deck has levels requiring three steps and some requiring two steps as shown above.

**SIMPLE, YET ELEGANT,** planters (above) are strategically located to divide the levels. These are well-stocked with plants to provide lots of color and create mood-setting decor. The potted plants rest on 2x2 rails to prevent rainwater from collecting.

In the past two decades patios and terraces have evolved from little more than drab slabs of concrete to the sophisticated-looking structure shown on these pages. Of multilevel design, it has many features you may want to adopt, whether your site is hilly or flat. Of particular interest are three outstanding features: steps, planters and the railing.

The deck shown here was constructed from redwood. Redwood was chosen because it weathers well. In addition, non-rusting fasteners were used throughout to avoid ugly rust stains on the wood.

A clear water-repellent finish is highly recommended. Easy to apply, it stabilizes wood color, retards weathering and reduces moisture effects. Varnishes aren't recommended; they deteriorate rapidly in outdoor use.

POST ATTACHMENTS

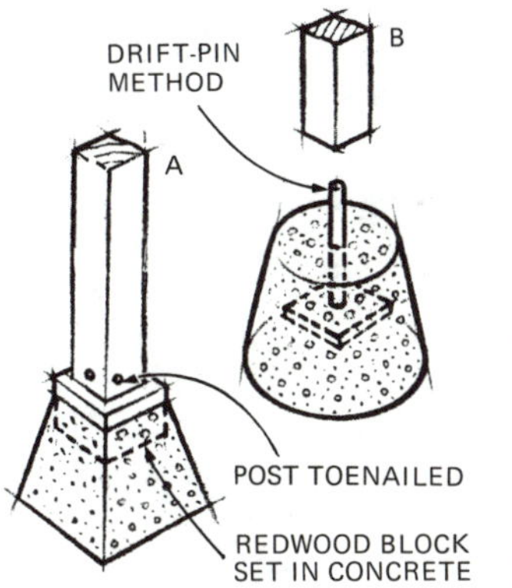


LEDGERS

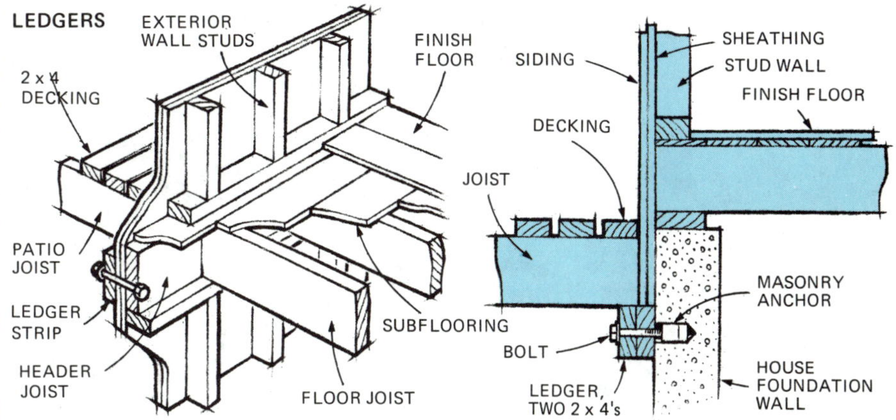


POST AND JOIST CONSTRUCTION

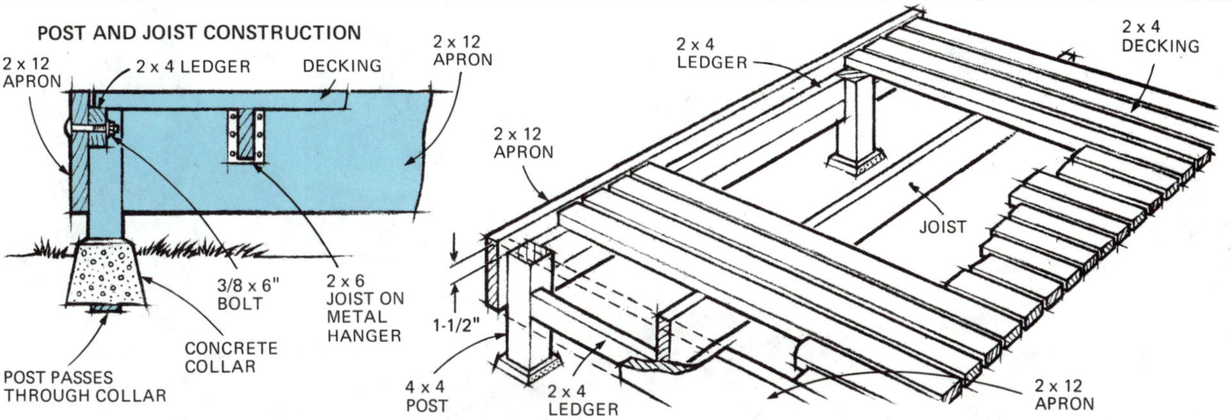


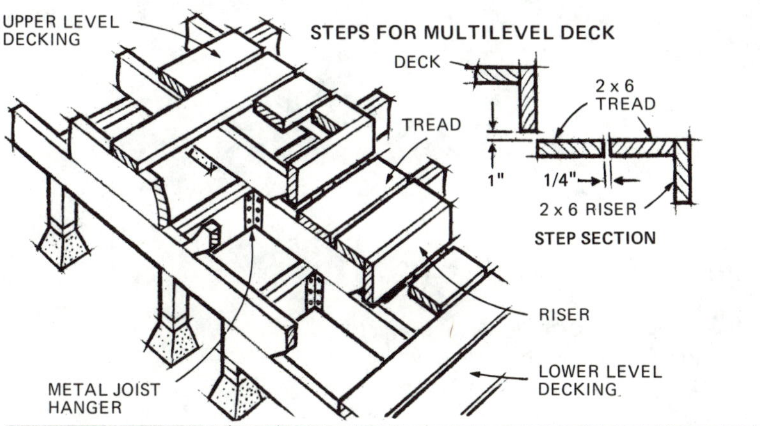


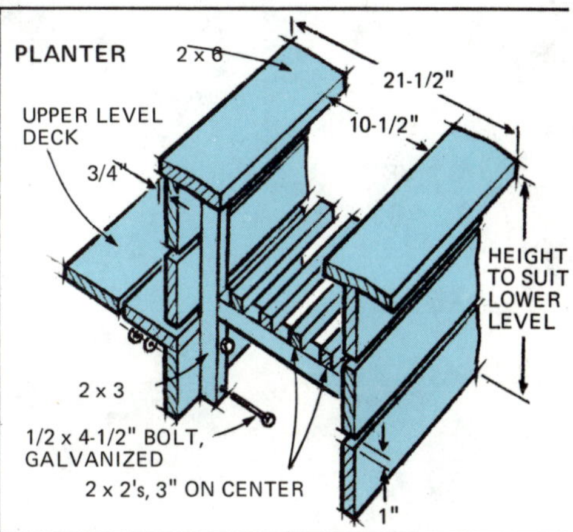


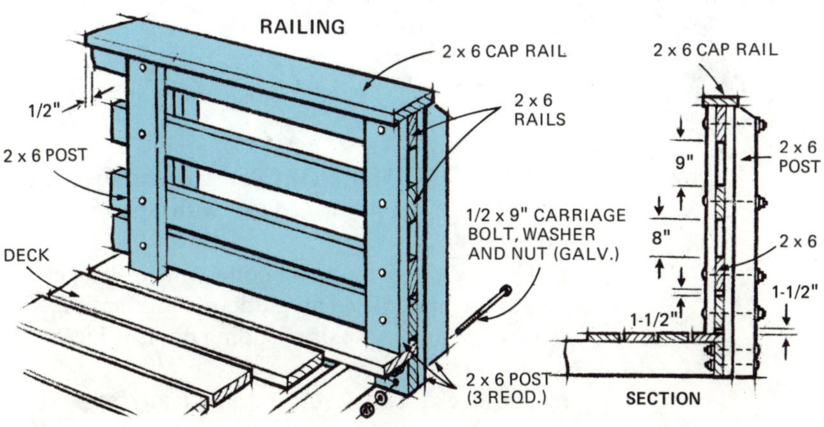

**FLOOR PLAN** (above, left) shows the well-thought-out layout. Access to the house and kitchen is through the sliding glass doors to the family room. The built-in gas-fired barbecue (left) is convenient to the dining table.

■ THIS UNIQUE DECK, created by Ira Grandberg, A.I.A., is loaded with special features:

■ The deck is a multilevel one which, in effect, makes the upper level an outdoor continuation of the family room. A pair of sliding doors is located between the two.

■ The deck's two levels automatically separate activities; there is a comfortable place for those

YOU CAN HAVE the best of all worlds on this deluxe two-level patio. Below: The sun-drenched lower deck provides a fine setting for a Sunday morning brunch. Near right: Awning-shaded bench provides solid comfort for a reading session. At far right is a view of the built-in table as seen from the second story.

# Sun or rain, you entertain—on a two-level deck

By JOSHUA MARK and HARRY WICKS

who want to pursue quiet activities on the upper level, while the lower level is fully exposed to the sun for sunbathing, entertaining, or just plain fun and games.

■ Deck longevity is assured through the use of Koppers Outdoor Wood. This pressure-treated lumber is highly resistant to decay caused by both insect infestation and moisture.

■ The handsome, functional awning installed

SEE ALSO
Benches, deck . . . Cabanas . . .
Carpeting, outdoor . . . Garden shelters . . .
Gazebos . . . Insect traps . . . Patios . . .
Planters . . . Privacy screens . . .
Screened summer rooms . . . Summer houses

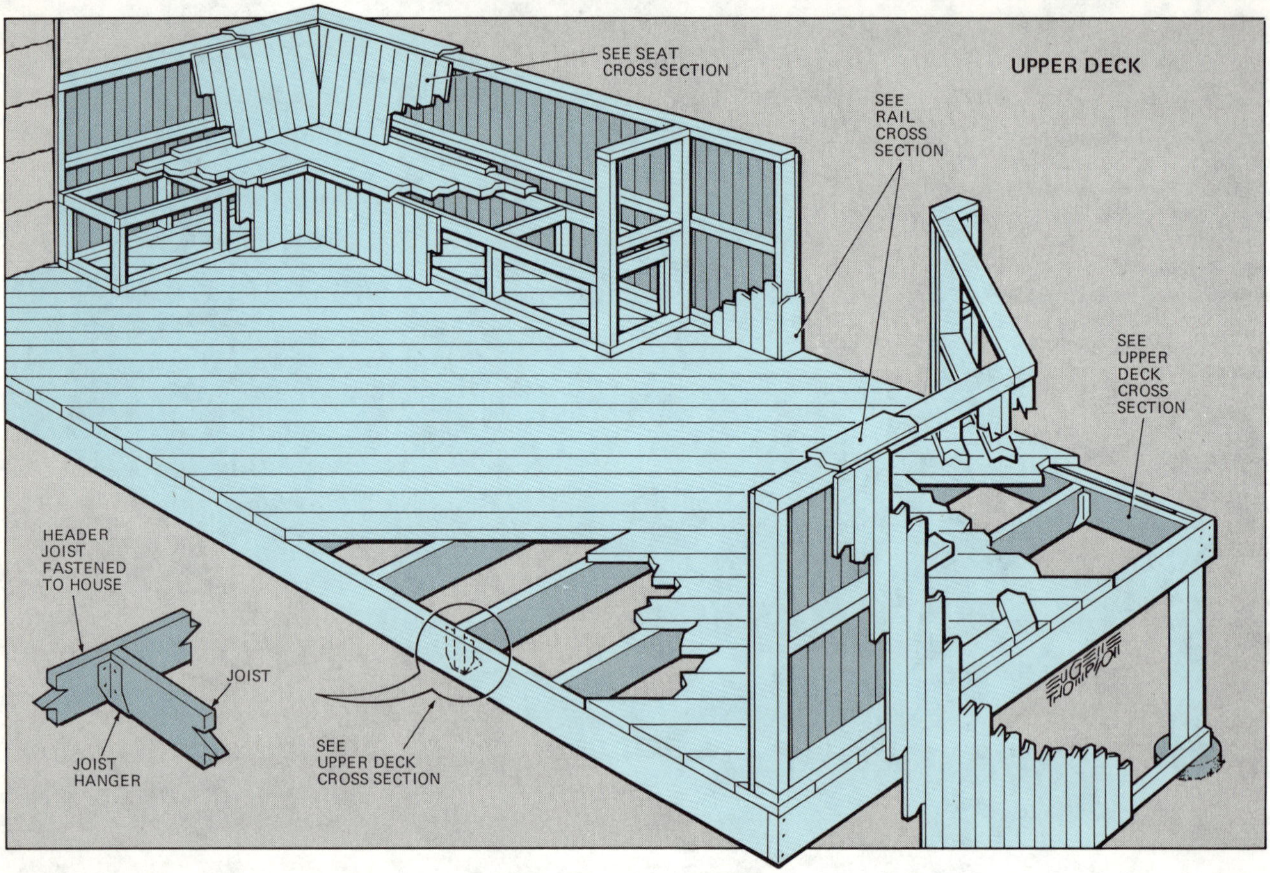


over the upper level means that you will never have to cancel a cookout because of the weather. If rain threatens, the party can be moved to a table set up beneath the awning.

**where to start**

Planning for the deck started with the family room at the rear of the house. The first floor elevation is roughly 36 in. above grade. This means that when the lower level is set on 2 x 6 joists, the upper level will be about 30 in. above. That height—which is the exact architectural standard for a dining table—inspired the built-in dining table here.

The upper deck was laid out to provide the all-weather aspect and a place was set aside for the built-in gas barbecue. The barbecue is located near the sliding doors, yet out of the flow of traffic across the upper level. Steps lead to the lower level, which boasts a deck with 2 x 6 boards laid diagonally over 2 x 6 joists.

Lay out your deck using mason's line and

**LOWER-LEVEL JOISTS** are fastened with two 16d galvanized common nails spiked through header joists. Use slate or pressure-treated wood as shims.

**SOIL** beneath the deck is covered with 6-mil polyethylene (or 30-lb. felt) to keep grass from growing through deck. Joists are spaced 16 in. on center.

**THE 2 x 6 DECKING** is installed with waste overhanging header. When all is down, a chalkline is snapped; decking is trimmed neatly with a portable saw.

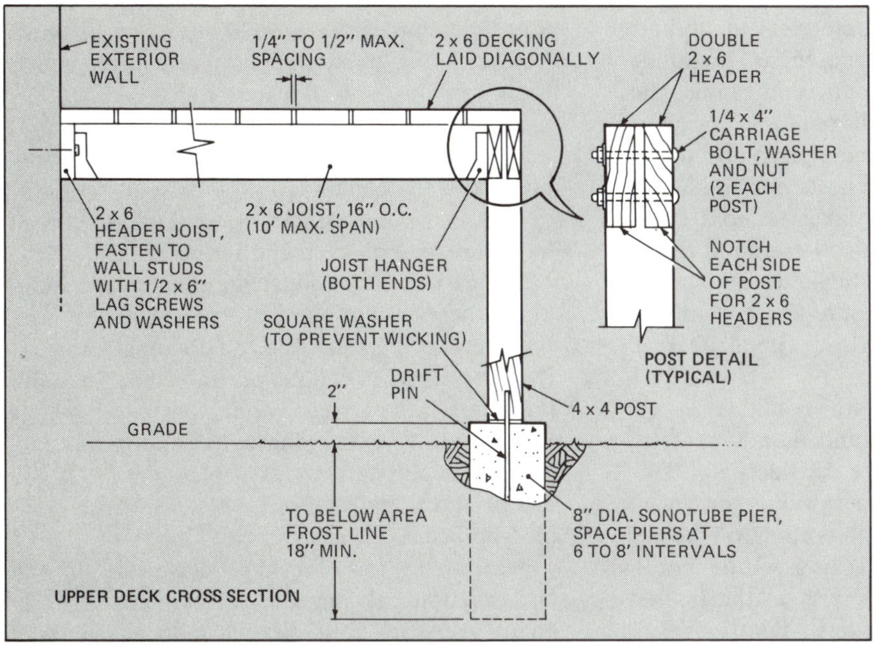

**THE 4 x 4 POSTS** for the upper level (upper right) are set over drift pins embedded in concrete piers (see drawing, above). Doubled-up 2 x 6s, serve as the header joist on the outboard end. The header joist along the wall of the house (lower right) is nailed to the wall studs. The joists are installed using metal joist hangers.

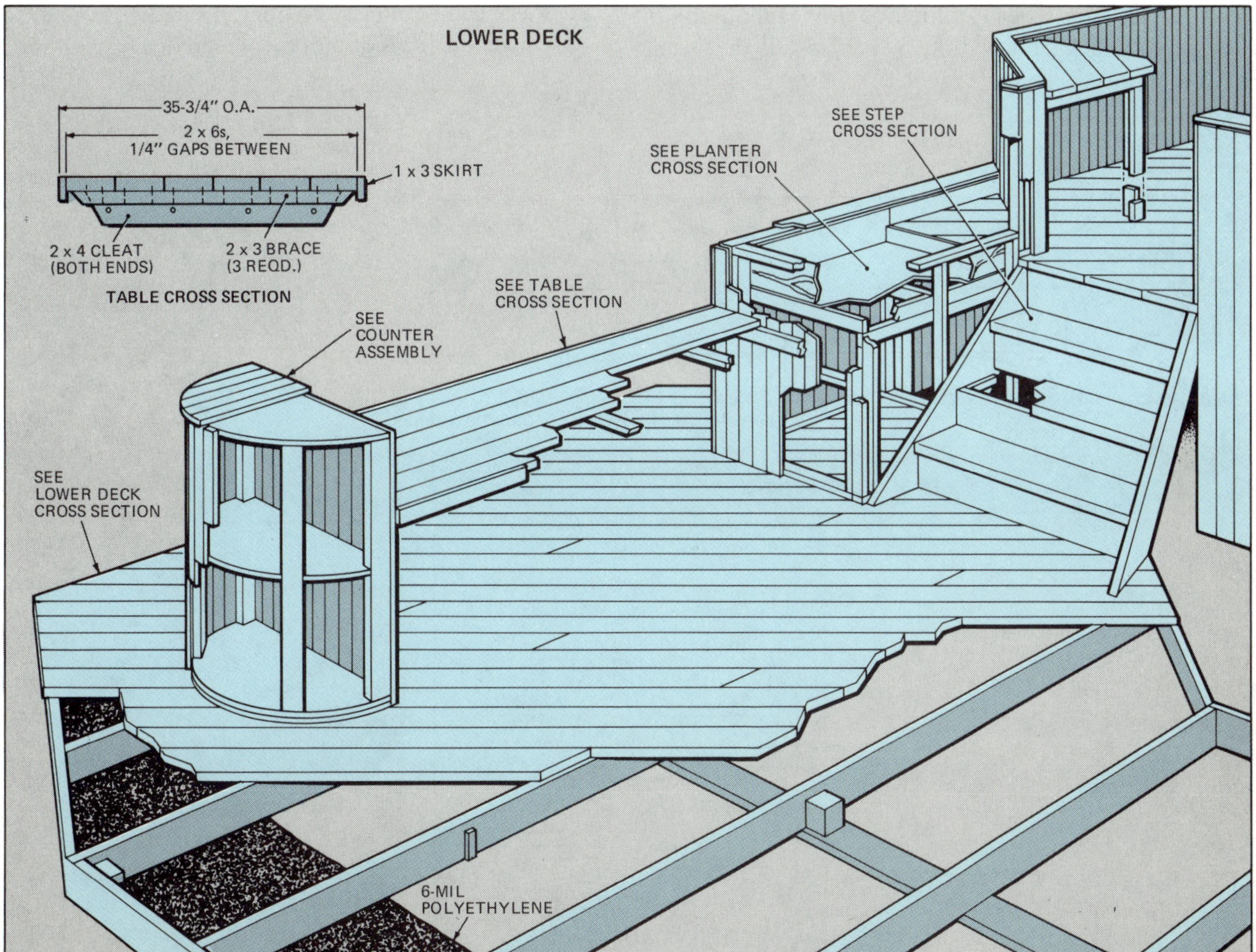

stakes. You will need concrete piers to support posts for the upper level and these should be spaced no more than 8 ft. apart. You can use the anchor-bolt method, which requires boring a centered hole in the lower end of each post to accept the bolt. Or, install the posts into the holes, use diagonal bracing and stakes to hold them plumb, and pour a concrete collar around them. Both methods are good, but the latter is just a bit faster. If you are using pressure-treated lumber, the posts can rest in the ground without fear of rot.

Metal fasteners, which are available at all well-stocked lumberyards and home centers, speed up the framing chore considerably. The easiest way to frame the upper deck is thus:

**1** Lay out for the header joist along the house wall. Do it so the finished decking will be 2 or 3 in. below the sill of the doorway to the house. Double-check your calculations. Snap a level chalkline along the house. Strip away siding or shingles so that the header can be installed flush against the sheathing. Re-snap the chalkline.

**2** Run a bead of high-quality caulk along the chalkline and, with a helper, install the header joist by nailing with 20d nails into the wall studs. Before nailing, make certain there is no chance of hitting any in-the-wall water or electric lines. Or, use lagscrews into the studs.

**3** Install the *inside header joist only* at the outboard end by toenailing into the posts.

**4** Next, lay out for and fasten the joist-hanger hardware, one on each end for each joist.

**5** Measure, cut and install joists one at a time. Since there is just one header joist at the outboard end at this time, you can obtain great rigidity by spiking a couple of 16d common nails through it into each joist end.

**6** When all joists are fastened, add the second 2 x 6 at the outboard end. Use plenty of 12d nails, driven at an angle, from both sides of the doubled-up beam.

**7** Finish by installing the decking as shown. Use two 10d galvanized common nails in each board over each joist. Set all nailheads slightly below the surface using a large punch or heavy nailset.

**8** When all decking is down, the overhanging waste can be cut off. To do it, partially drive nails above the outside edges of end joists and the

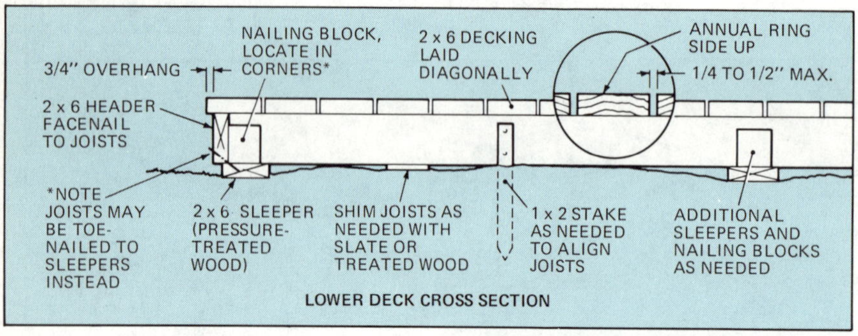

LOWER DECK CROSS SECTION

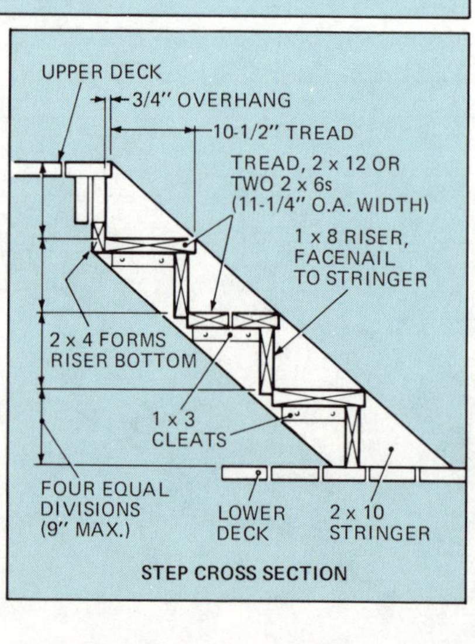

STEP CROSS SECTION

**PLANTER AND** utility table is framed with minimal number of 2 x 4s. One-inch siding, which follows, adds rigidity.

**HALF-ROUND COUNTER** is made with exterior plywood top and bottom and 2 x 4 studs. If desired, edges of 1 x 3 siding can be beveled for neat joints.

**CLEAT SUPPORTING** tabletop is fastened to counter to put dining table at 30-in. height. Use 1 x 3 boards for the tabletop, leaving a slight gap between boards.

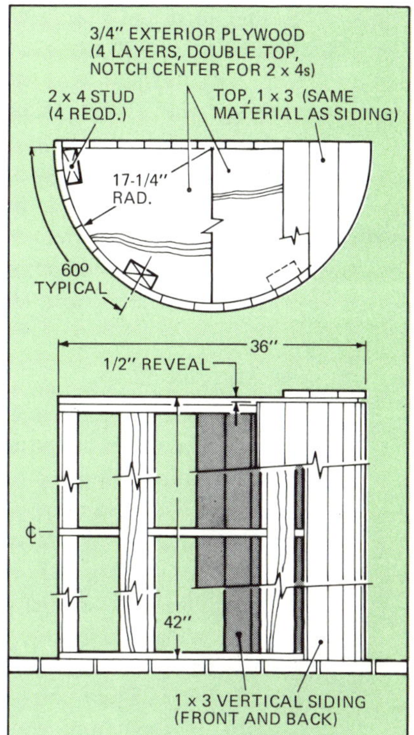


COUNTER ASSEMBLY

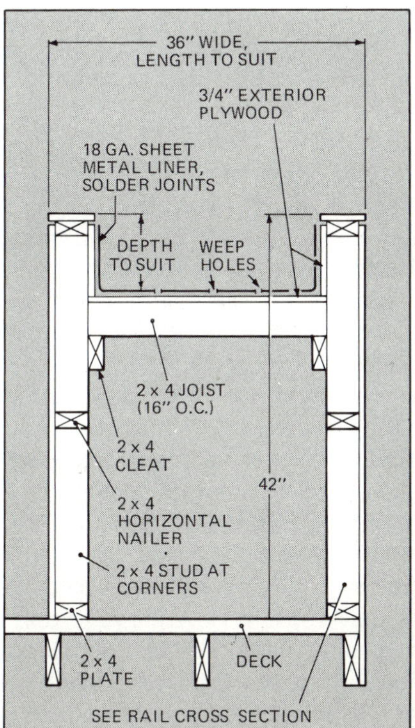


PLANTER CROSS SECTION

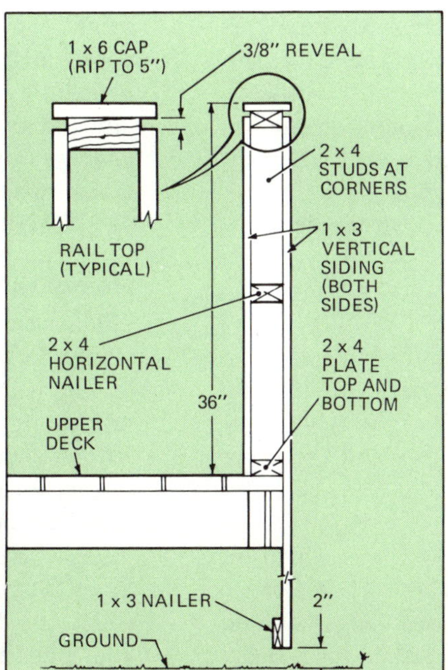


RAIL CROSS SECTION

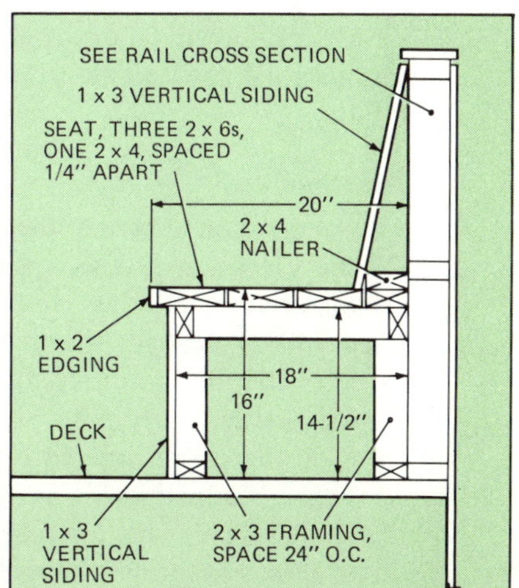


SEAT CROSS SECTION

header joist and snap a chalkline between nails. Make the cutoff using a combination blade in your circular saw with its blade set to just cut through the 1½-in.-thick decking. Cut on the outside of the waste line. If you make a wavy cut, you can true it up using a very coarse-grit paper (about 50-grit) in your belt sander. Don't start work on the upper-deck built-ins until after the lower deck has been completed. The stairs should be built only after both levels are finished.

#### the lower deck

There is nothing fancy or exotic about the way the lower deck is constructed. In fact, the simplest technique was used here because of the type of lumber.

With the deck's perimeter laid out, and corners checked for square, roll out either 6-mil polyethylene or 30-lb. felt. Either of these will keep grass from growing through the decking joints. Lay out the joists close to where they will be permanently installed. It will pay you to have a couple of long lengths of 1 x 3 furring on hand; these can be tacked across the top edges of the joists to keep them more or less in position, and on edge, while you get them all in place.

Once you have decided upon the elevation for the lower level, high ground spots will have to be excavated, if necessary, to bring a joist to the line. Conversely, a joist over a depression must be raised using either slate or pressure-treated wood scraps as shims.

You should also add stakes alongside joists at intervals to minimize deflection (bounce, as someone walks across the deck). The stakes are simply pointed 1 x 3s driven 18 to 24 in. into the ground and then nailed to joist sides. For rigidity, several 4 x 4 stakes were added at the corners on the deck shown. Once the diagonal 2 x 6 decking is installed, the lower level will have excellent stability.

#### the built-ins

As mentioned earlier, the dining table is at the same elevation as the upper deck, 30 in. The half-round counter at one end of the table is fitted with a cleat for the tabletop, and the other end of the top is secured to the upper deck, also with a cleat.

The top is constructed using 2 x 3s which, in turn, are skinned with 1 x 3 boards. The latter are installed with a slight gap between edges so food particles will drop through, rather than being caught between. The gap also makes it possible to clean the table using your garden hose.

The stairs between levels are easy to construct. They are built in conventional basement-stair fashion using 2 x 10 stringers and 2 x 12s for treads. Though the space between treads could be left open for an airy look, we installed risers on this prototype to hide the open space beneath the upper deck. The carriages (stringers) are not notched (cut out) to receive the risers and treads; instead, these are fastened to cleats securely nailed to the stringers. If you opt for notched stringers, you should use 2 x 12 stock for the stringers because there should be at least 3½ in. of solid timber beneath notches.

The stair assembly is fastened to the joist header at top by driving 16d nails through the stringers. The bottom of the stair carriage rests upon the lower level and is fastened to the latter with nails.

#### calculating riser height

There is a definite relation between the width of a tread and the height of a riser. If the combination of run and rise is too great, there will be too much strain on the leg muscles and heart of the user. Too small a combination and the user will probably kick the riser on every step. (In the trades, this is often called a tripper.)

A good rule of thumb for laying out stairs is: the tread width multiplied by the riser height in inches should equal somewhere between 72 and 75 in. If your ratio is anywhere near that, you will have a comfortable-to-use stairway. (Another rule is that the tread width plus twice the riser height should be about 25 inches.) To lay out your stairs, simply divide the elevation to be negotiated by 7½ (the optimum riser height) to obtain the number of risers. If the elevation from lower deck to upper is about 30 in., as ours was, this means that four risers are needed ($30 \div 7½ = 4$). With 7½ in. risers, a 10-in. tread is desirable.

#### professionals can help

The seating arrangement is obtained using straightforward, conventional framing. Once the seating is installed, the awning can go up. Since fabricating and installing an awning is a job best left to a professional, check the classified directory for the nearest awning dealer.

Rather than use a portable rollabout grill, we installed a fixed gas version by Arkla Industries. Since the pipe hookup should conform with local codes, it is best to have this connection made by your plumber. His bill will be lower if you have him do the roughing-in when the deck is just framed out, before the decking goes down.

# A stamp and pencil set

By C. WAYNE CLOSE

**POSTAGE-STAMP SLOTS** in the side of the block are cut through into the stamp wells with a thin-blade keyhole saw.

YOU'LL ALWAYS KNOW where to look for postage stamps when you have this novel dispenser on your desk. That goes for pens and pencils, too. It will hold two rolls of 100 stamps each, which are pulled out through slots in the side.

Wells for the stamps are bored in opposite sides of a hardwood cube (such as cherry or walnut) ½ in. up from the bottom and ½ in. in from the side. Entering kerfs are made through the side of the block with a thin-blade saw. Fancy metal buttons provide covers for the stamp wells and are held in place by small magnets that contact the heads of wood screws. The magnets are cemented to the backs of the buttons, and the screws around which the stamp rolls revolve are turned in far enough to bring the buttons flush.

Holes for pens and pencils are drilled down into the end grain of the block for a depth of 1½ in. and countersunk slightly. Complete by sanding the wood flawlessly, particularly the top of the block, and breaking the sharp corners. If the wood is open grain, you should apply a paste wood filler after staining, rubbing it off across grain. Finish by applying three coats of self-rubbing polyurethane varnish. When dry, glue a piece of green felt to the bottom of the block.

SEE ALSO

**Bookracks . . . Desks . . . Finishes, wood . . . Letter racks . . . Weekend projects**

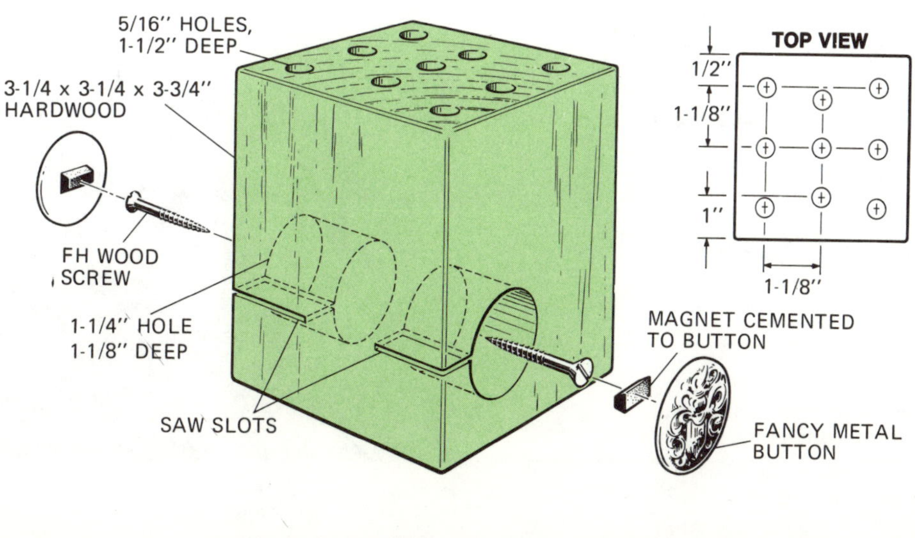

**Something different in holders —one for your shop, the other for your study. Both are eye-catching accessories you can make**

■ THIS NOVEL DRILL holder is fancy enough to use most anywhere to corral many things other than just drills. If you are familiar with the egg-shaped plastic containers in which L'eggs panty hose are packaged, you'll be quick to see that the ready-made dome shapes do the holding. As the two photos show at the right, you first drill a circle of holes in the top of each half shell, using each bit to drill its own hole, and drilling from the inside out. Then you cut a 2-in. Styrofoam ball in half, glue the pieces inside the half shells and finally cement the shells to a suitable wood base. Each drill bit is poked into the Styrofoam through a hole in the top of the shell.

Equally as eye-catching and handy as a desk accessory is the pen and pencil holder shown at the left. The twin cylinders are turned and grooved two at a time on a lathe from aluminum to represent revolver chambers, then bored from the top to accept pencils and ballpoint pens.

# Two gadgets to hold everything

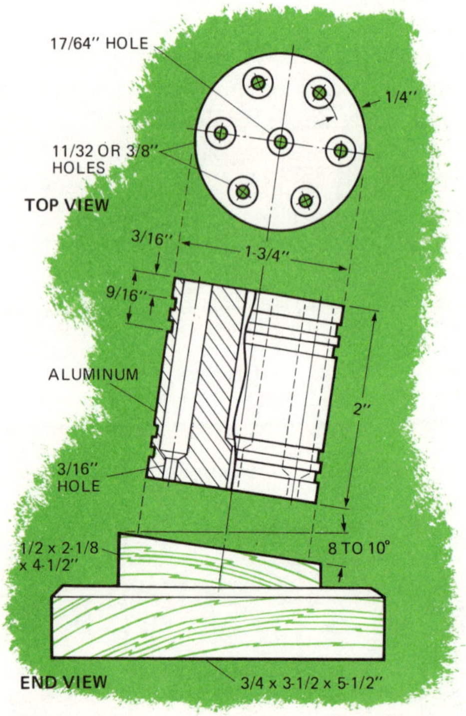


**PAD THE VISE JAWS** with leather when drilling the holes. Start with a small bit, then switch to a larger one.

SEE ALSO

**Bookracks . . . Desks . . . Drills, portable . . . Wastebaskets . . . Weekend projects**

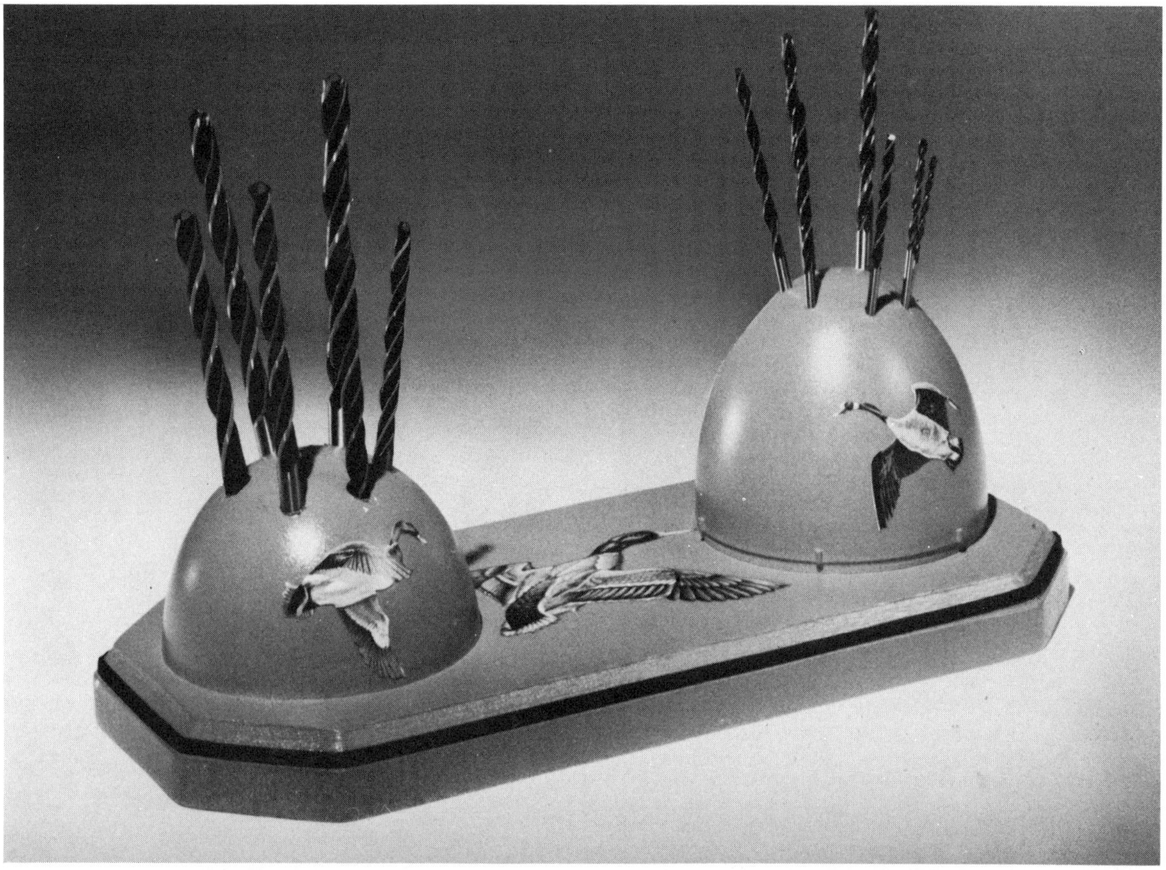

**LINE THE SHELL** with masking tape to keep the drill bit from wandering. Drill the holes from the inside.

**CUT THE STYROFOAM** balls in half and glue inside the shells. Drills are poked into the foam from the top.

Start with a $^3/_{16}$-in. drill bit to drill the seven holes from top to bottom, then redrill to final size with a larger bit for a depth of 1⅝ in. Drill a couple of holes at a time, take a coffee break to allow the metal to cool to avoid overheating, then continue. One cylinder should be drilled to hold slender pens, the other to take fatter ones.

After polishing with fine abrasive cloth and chamfering the holes a wee bit to remove burrs, attach each cylinder to a two-piece prefinished walnut base with a single wood screw down through the center hole.

By cutting the wood base longer, you can make the holder even more useful with a well between the cylinders to hold paper clips, stamps, or a rack to hold letters.

**WHEN YOU'RE DRAWING** rusty spikes and nails, iron pipe over the hammerhead increases leverage and avoids the chance of breaking your hammer handle.—*Henry Farr, Garnerville, NY.*

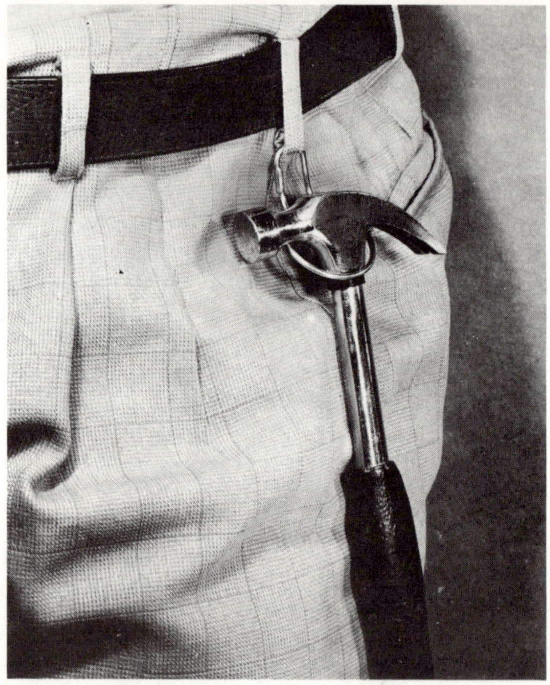

**FOR A CONVENIENT** hammer holster, clip a large metal shower-curtain ring, bent outward slightly as shown, to a belt loop.—*M.G. McMullen, Santa Margarita, CA.*

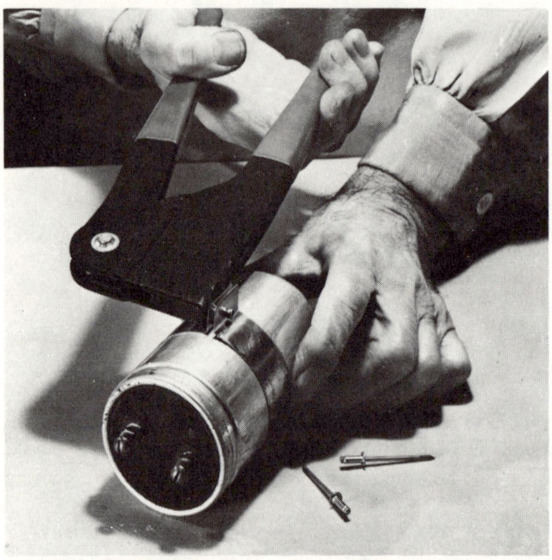

**A WAY TO CLAMP** a metal band tightly around a cylindrical object is to draw and fasten the ends together with Pop rivets. If less tension is desired, the rivet can be clinched part way and the shank snipped off. The tin-plate band shown on the condenser permits soldering to the supports.—*Walter E. Burton, Akron, OH.*

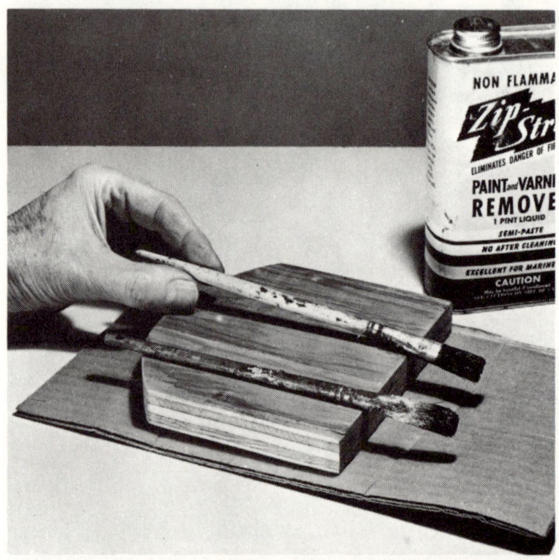


**PAINT-HARDENED BRUSHES** can be cleaned by dipping them in semi-paste paint remover, allowing them to hang over a board edge overnight, with a second application if bristles remain hard. A putty knife works out softened paint. Rinsing with mineral spirits completes the treatment.—*Burt Web, Skokie, IL.*

# Three unique designs for home offices

**These novel desks include one that folds against the wall, another that tucks into a corner, and a third that can turn your spare room into an executive's quarters**

**FOLDAWAY WORK CENTER** hangs on adjustable wall brackets, is easily placed at any desired height. In raised position (top), the hinged desk provides a roomy 36x39-in. surface—wide enough for two to work at when seated across from each other. When not in use, the leg folds up and top swings down against wall (bottom).

## 1. THE WALL-HUGGER

THERE ARE FEW families who don't need some little nook or corner for doing paperwork—a place for Dad to tackle the monthly bills and plan new projects, a kitchen organizer for Mom, a homework and hobby center for the kids. On these pages, we present three original ideas for home desks that are more than just desks. They range from simple to elegant, from small to spacious. Each offers a maximum of work and storage facilities in a minimum of space. Each is, in effect, a mini office in itself.

We call the three the "Wall-Hugger," the "Swing-Wing" and the "Split-Level." Each is designed to solve a particular problem or suit a special need. If you never thought you had space for such a unit, consider the possibilities shown here. Two of the three, the Wall-Hugger and Swing-Wing, take little floor space and fold away when not in use. The Wall-Hugger hangs on adjustable shelf brackets and features a drop-down desktop that stores neatly out of the way against the wall. The Swing-Wing sports two hinged extensions that open out to a 7-ft. width, revealing

SEE ALSO
**Cabinet furniture . . . Desk accessories . . .**
**Drawers . . . Hobby centers . . .**
**Modular furniture . . . Sewing centers . . .**
**Storage walls . . . Study centers**

**CLOCK, PHONE** and bulletin board add to unit.

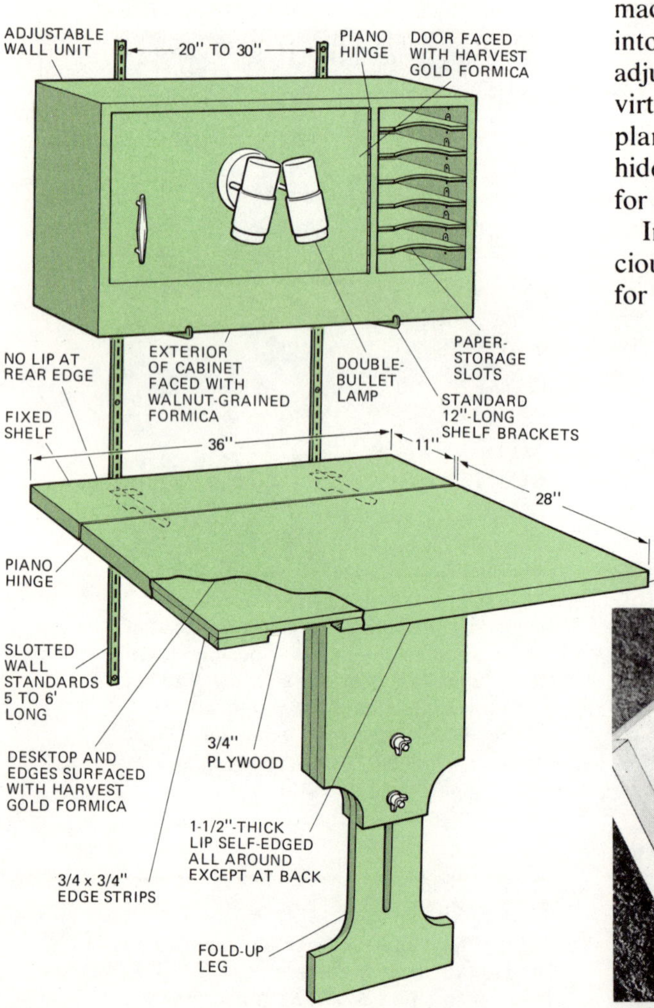


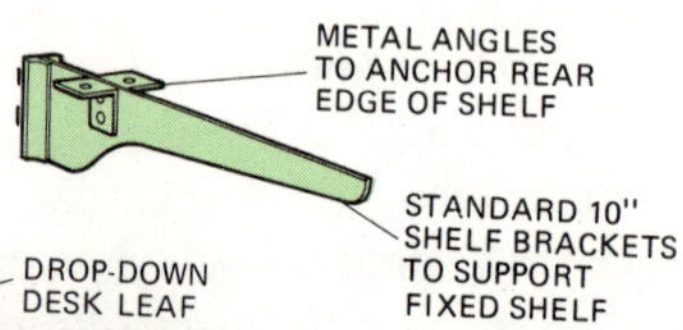


a desk, a two-drawer file cabinet, a retractable typewriter table and drawers for supplies. With the wings closed, it becomes a handsome, compact chest.

The Split-Level is a more elaborate classic design with rich, massive looks that would be the envy of many a company executive. It has a large main work surface at standard desk height, plus an L-shaped secretary return at a lower level for typing. While it requires more space than the other two units, it adds elegance as well as usefulness to a den or family room. All three designs are distinctive; they offer features not found in commercial units and can be built yourself for far less cost. Construction of the Wall-Hugger is shown on these pages. Details for building the Swing-Wing and Split-Level are in the next two sections.

The basic Wall-Hugger unit consists of two separate parts—a drop-down desk hinged to a wall shelf and a cabinet mounted above the desk. Both desk and cabinet are supported on ready-made metal shelf brackets of the type that hook into slotted wall standards. This makes it easy to adjust their height and enables them to be placed virtually anywhere—in a kitchen as a menu-planning center, in a master bedroom as a hideaway home office or in a youngster's room for study and hobby activities.

In its raised position, the desk forms a spacious 36x39-in. work area—that's large enough for two persons to share from opposite sides.

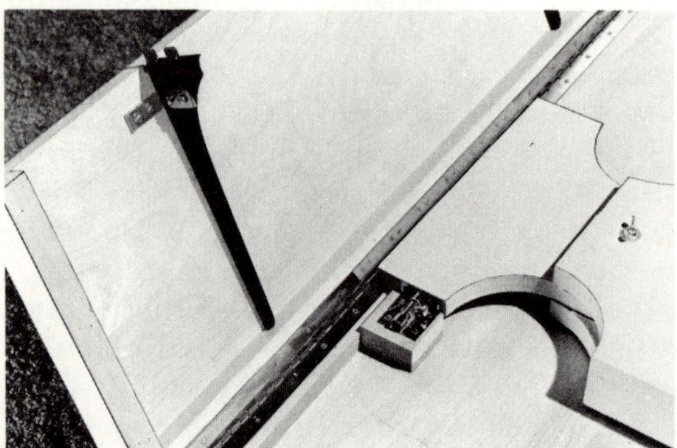

**UNDERSIDE VIEW** of desk shows how fold-up leg is held by latch bolt.

The cabinet above has open paper-storage slots at one end and space behind a door for a typewriter and other supplies. A double-bullet pinup lamp on the face of the door illuminates the desk, and a fluorescent fixture hidden in a recess under the cabinet provides additional down lighting to bathe the wall dramatically below it.

The flexible wall-track system makes possible a number of variations on the basic arrangement. A bulletin board, as shown on the facing page, offers an attractive and useful accessory and can be attached to the wall standards with clips made from regular shelf supports. If you'd like more shelves in place of the bulletin board, these, too, can be added easily between the desk and cabinet, again using stock brackets. Other possibilities include magazine racks, pencil drawers, even a drawing board—all mounted by means of the same hook-in shelf brackets. Typical mounting arrangements for such accessories are shown below.

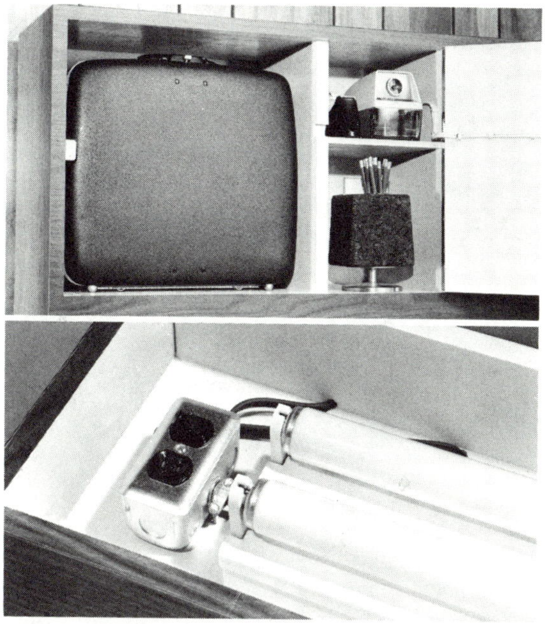

**WALL CABINET** stores typewriter, other supplies (top). Lower photo shows recess in underside of cabinet for a fluorescent light controlled by main switch in outlet box.

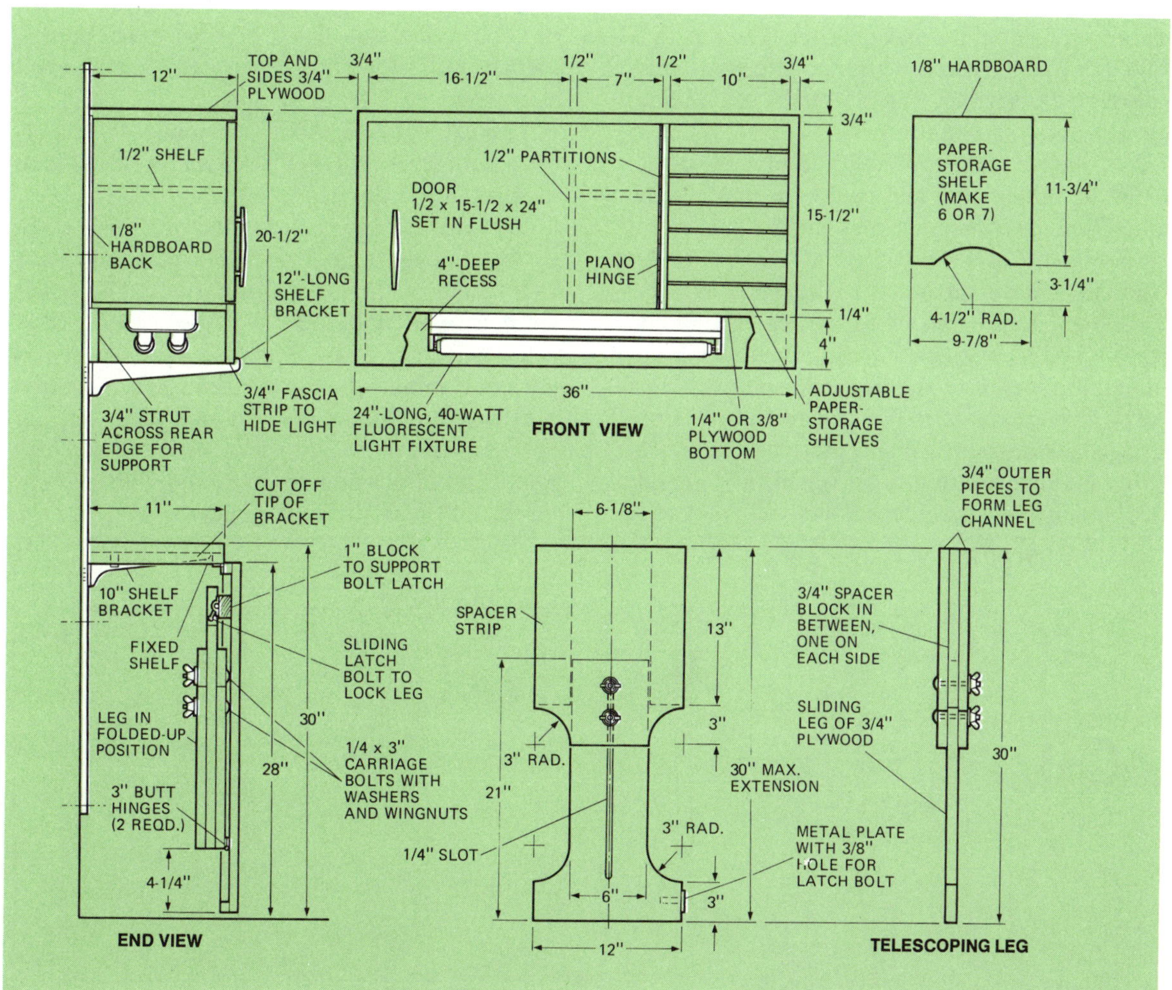

**FOR PERMANENT SETUP,** desk can rest on two-drawer filing cabinet, instead of folding leg.

The main parts for both cabinet and desk can be cut from a single sheet of ¾-in. plywood. The rear portion of the desk is anchored to two 10-in. shelf brackets with metal angles. This holds it in place so it can't slip off as the folding portion is raised and lowered. Edge strips are fastened under the desk to give it the smart, modern appearance of a double-thick counter. The top and sides are then covered with a countertop laminate such as Formica. We chose Harvest Gold, but any color can be used.

To collapse the drop leaf, the hinged leg is folded up underneath and held by a small latch bolt. The telescoping leg should slide smoothly but not be loose. If it binds, it may be necessary to add thin cardboard shims to the spacer blocks at the top. Adjust the fit so the leg just slides freely when the wingnuts are loosened. Tighten the nuts to lock it at the desired height.

The upper cabinet is 12 in. deep and rests on 12-in. shelf brackets. While most brackets are sturdy enough to support its weight, it's a good idea to screw the cabinet to the wall tracks to help carry the load and prevent any tendency for the cabinet to tip forward. With the cabinet positioned at the desired height, locate a pair of screws in the wall tracks behind it near the top, remove the screws and drill matching holes in the back of the cabinet. Then run the screws through the back and into the same holes in the wall tracks. If necessary, use longer screws than those supplied to assure a firm grip in the wall anchors.

The bullet lamp is fastened to the door with a short ⅛-in. pipe nipple. The wire runs through the door and is stapled along the back side to the hinge point, using insulated staples. Form a loop in the wire where it passes around the hinge to allow some slack. This permits the door to be opened and closed without the lamp cord interfering with its operation. (Note: While this method does not conform to accepted code practice for permanent house wiring, it is adequate in this case because the wall cabinet is not considered a permanent part of the house.) The fluorescent fixture is wired through a surface-mount duplex receptacle that provides a switch for controlling the light, plus an extra convenience outlet for plugging in an electric pencil sharpener, desk lamp or other appliance.

The cabinet is finished in walnut-toned Formica with Harvest Gold laminate on the door to match that on the desk.

You can build the basic units for a fairly modest figure, even including the Formica (half a 4x8 sheet each of the walnut and gold). The bullet lamp, a Sears Model 34 A 8702, is low-priced, as is the two-tube, 24-in. fluorescent fixture. If you wish to eliminate the Formica and go to a painted finish, you can save about 40 percent, but the laminate is well worth the expense as it hides joints, simplifies construction and adds a slick, marproof finish to the project.

**BULLETIN BOARD DETAILS**

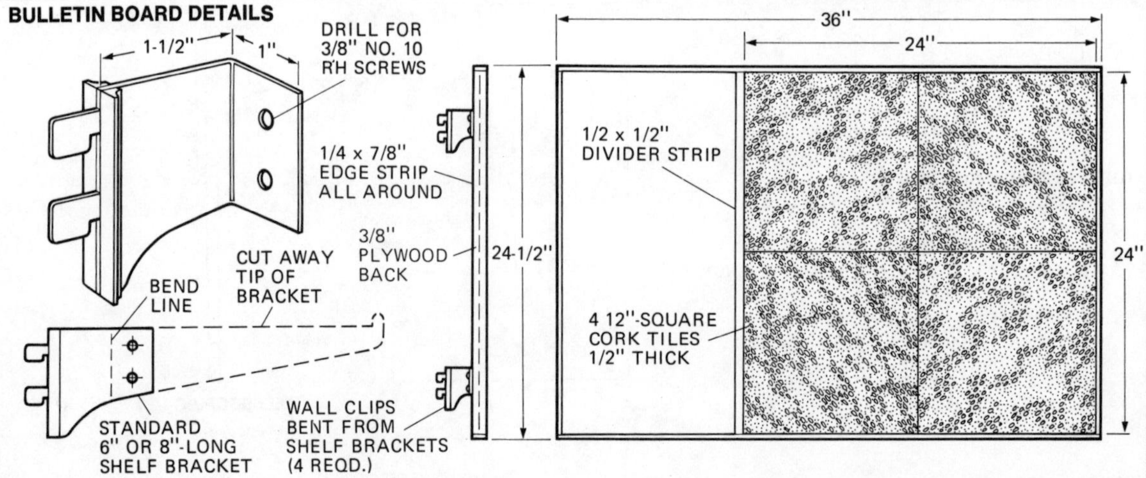

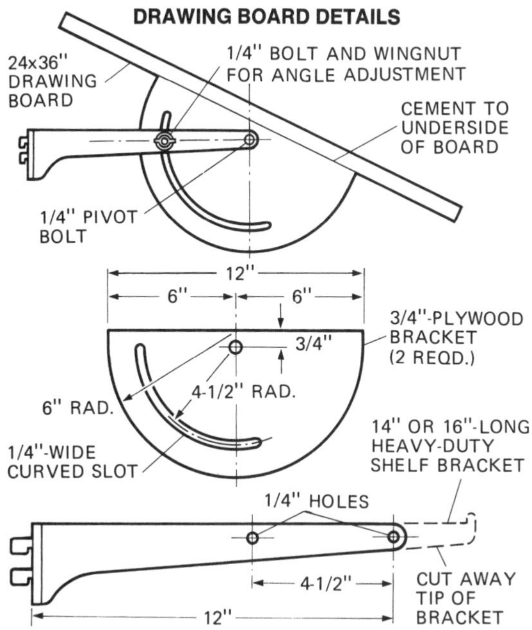


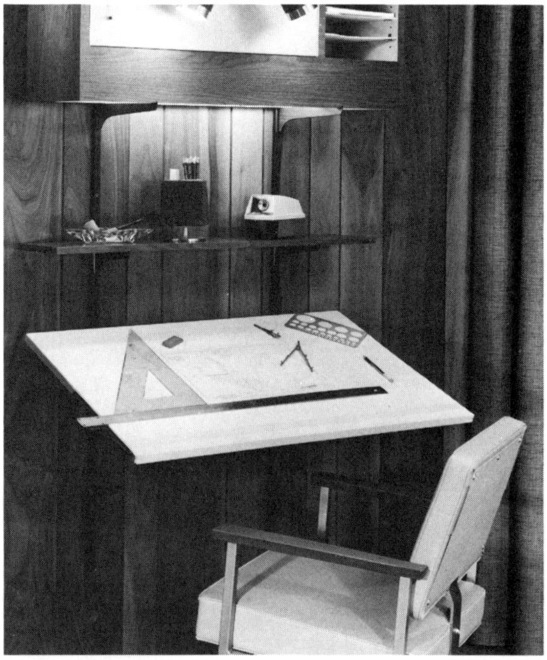

**DRAWING BOARD** can be mounted on shelf brackets, as at left, in a non-foldaway position.

## 2. THE SWING-WING

REMEMBER the old rolltop desk—how you could pull down the front and walk away without disturbing your work? You can do practically the same with this modern version which has wraparound wings that close like the twin doors on a refrigerator.

Posing as a king-size chest when closed, the desk features a swing-out shelf that provides a regulation-height typing stand. Two paper-storage compartments in the wings are within easy reach of your chair. A shallow under-the-desk drawer keeps pens, pencils, clips and the like extra handy. Important papers can be stored safely and locked in a fireproof steel filing cabinet. There's a shelf for a wastebasket and drawers galore for storing countless supplies. A built-in fluorescent light is supplemented by a mini typing spotlight.

The unit is designed around a two-drawer metal file cabinet and built largely from ¾ in. plywood covered with handsome woodgrain plastic laminate.

File cabinets come in various sizes, but to obtain a regulation desk height of 30 in. and a standard typing shelf of 26 in., you must select a cabinet that measures 29¼ in. high. Width and depth are not so important; the cabinet shown measures 15 in. wide and 27¾ in. deep.

The chest consists of three separate sections—a center section and two wings. The cutting schedule on page 944 shows how the 16 basic parts can be economically laid out on two 4x8-ft. sheets of ¾-in. plywood. Although it costs a bit more than common fir plywood, cabinet-grade, lumber-core plywood was used in the original. It is less susceptible to warping and has a smoother surface for painting.

Begin making the center section which includes parts E and F. Parts E are 14⅝ x 47⅝ in., part F is 14⅝ x 43 in. A ⅜ x ⅜-in. rabbet is cut along the rear edges of all three parts, and a ⅜ x ¾-in. rabbet is cut across each end of part F. Glue and nail part F to parts E. then enclose the back with a ⅜-in. plywood panel, 42¼ x 47⅝ in. Glue two 2 x 29¼-in. strips of ⅛-in. tempered hardboard vertically to the inside of part E (see top view, page 942) at points X, front and back. These will bring the file cabinet flush with the right-hand side of the desktop and provide clearance for the right-hand wing.

Make the desktop and drawer next, as detailed on page 944. Remember that dimensions given accommodate a 15 x 28-in. file cabinet. Note that the top is ⅜ in. wider at the back than the front

**WHEN WINGS ARE SWUNG SHUT,** office fits in a 29x43x48-in. chest. Swung open wide, wings provide spacious work center measuring 7½ ft.

**WINGS WRAP AROUND FILE CABINET** on one side (see above), desk on other. Swinging typing shelf parks under desk drawer when not in use.

and that it's made double-thick except where it rests on top of the file cabinet. A ¾ x 1 x 14-in. cleat is screwed to the inside of part E (29¼ in. high) to support the desktop along the left-hand edge. Holes are made in the bottom of the cleat for attaching the desktop with 1¼-in. No. 8 fh screws. Screw holes are also made across the plywood back and in the top of the metal file cabinet, although the desktop is not permanently installed at this time.

Except for being right and left-handed, with the left wing having a shelf at the bottom, both wings are made alike. Parts A measure 14⅝ x 46⅝ in. and have a ½ x ¾-in. rabbet along the front edges to accept parts B, which measure 21³/₁₆ x 46⅝ in. The latter are glued and nailed in the rabbets with finish nails and checked for squareness. Parts C measure 14⅝ x 21⁷/₁₆ in. and are rabbeted (⅜ x ¾ in.) along two edges to fit over and flush with the top edges of parts A and

B, then glued and nailed. Part D (the wing shelf) is secured with ¾-in.-square cleats glued and screwed to parts A and B. Screw holes for attaching shelf brace L are drilled through parts B and D for screws driven from the front and up from the bottom.

The actual length of part I is determined by the width of the file cabinet. In the original it measures 14 x 26⅜ in. and is anchored in place by a cleat at one end and the file cabinet at the other. Two holes are drilled through the side of the cabinet for screws from the inside.

The 14 x 21-in. swing-away typewriter shelf consists of parts H, J and K, assembled as detailed on page 943. Parts J and K are glued and screwed along adjacent edges of part H. A 10-in. length of piano hinge is used to hinge the assembled shelf to a ¾ x 2 x 10-in. wood block, which is later screwed and glued to the inside of part E, 26 in. up from the floor.

Now you are ready to cover the various parts and assemblies with plastic laminate. The original was covered with Formica's English oak, No. 343, finish No. 64. It takes about two and a half 4x8-ft. sheets.

If working with plastic laminate is a new experience for you, see the article on page 1760. The most professional (and fastest) trimming job is done with a portable router, using special cutters, but it can be done with a special hand tool made by Arlyn Industries, 6921 Stride Ave., Burnbay 3, B.C., Canada.

Only part L is covered with laminate on both sides, others just on the edge and one side. In each case, the edges are banded first. A good place to start is on parts D and L since these, particularly part L, must be screwed in place before part B can be covered on the outside. In the case of the wings, the extra width that the 1/16-in. laminate adds has been accounted for in

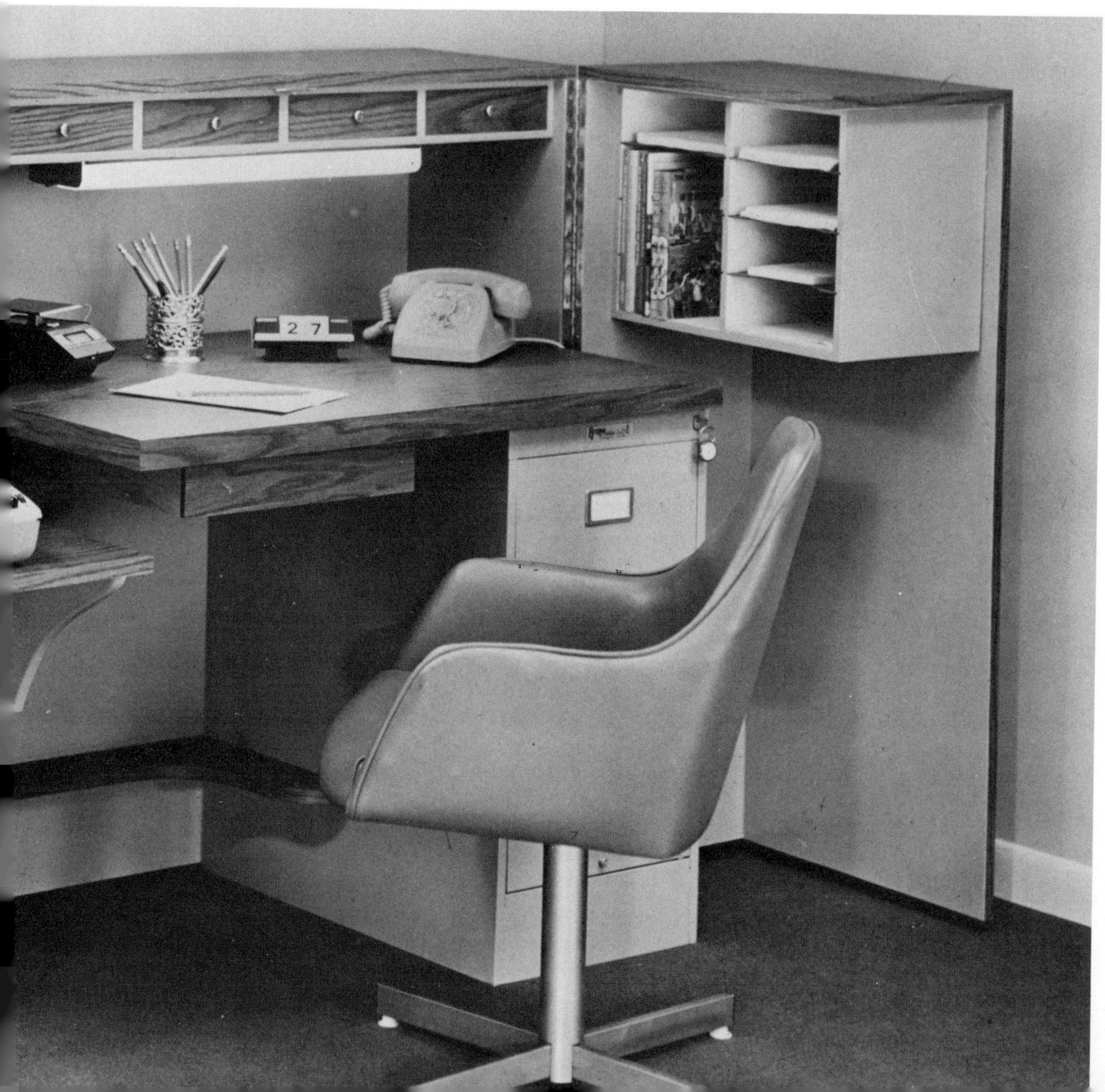

the overall sizes given for parts B and C. Inside surfaces not covered with laminate were painted olive green, as was the file cabinet. Here it's wise to paint the back panel of the center section before assembling the desk.

When all parts are covered with laminate, you can start putting the desk together. First lay the center section on its back and position the file cabinet against the ⅛-in. hardboard strips. Use two C-clamps to hold the cabinet in place and drill two screw holes through the sheet metal opposite each hardboard strip. Drill two more through the back of the file cabinet and the plywood back. Use ¾-in. No. 8 rh wood screws into the hardboard strips, and ¾-in. stovebolts through the plywood back.

Next install the desktop by turning screws up through the left-hand cleat, through holes in the top of the file cabinet and holes in the plywood back. Add the typewriter shelf by screwing the block to which it is hinged to part E at a point 26 in. up from the floor. The shelf should clear the desk drawer by ¼ in. Part I is added next and is held with screws inserted through its cleat, the side of the file cabinet and the plywood back.

Wings are hinged last with 46¼-in.-long piano hinges. It's best to hold the wings in their open position by clamping them temporarily to the sides of the center section. Hinges are surface-mounted.

The striker plate from a lockset is used to align the two wings with the top of the center section when they are swung shut. Two magnetic catches, screwed to the underside of the desktop at the front, are used to hold the doors shut. A third magnetic catch is used to hold the typewrit-

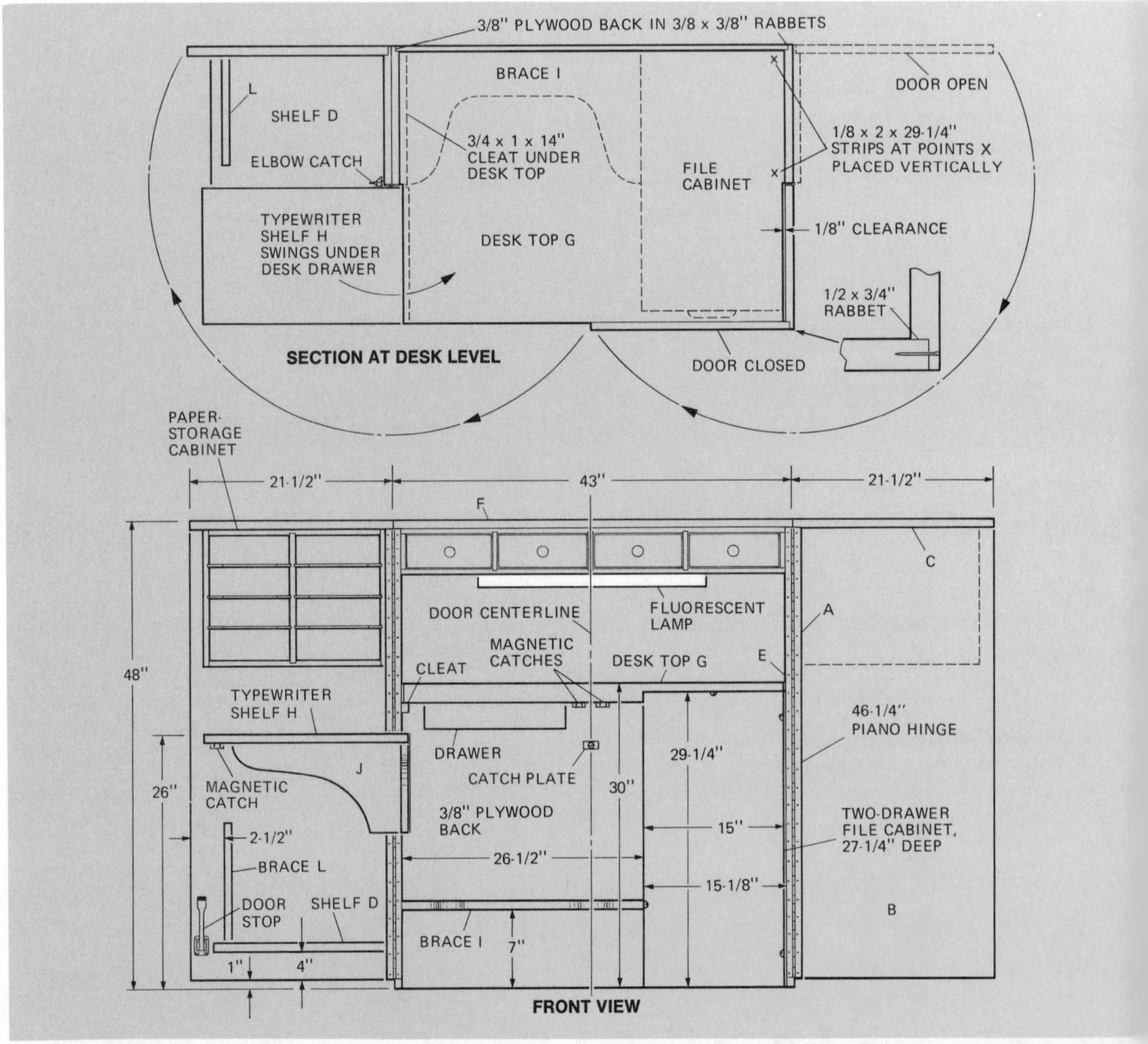

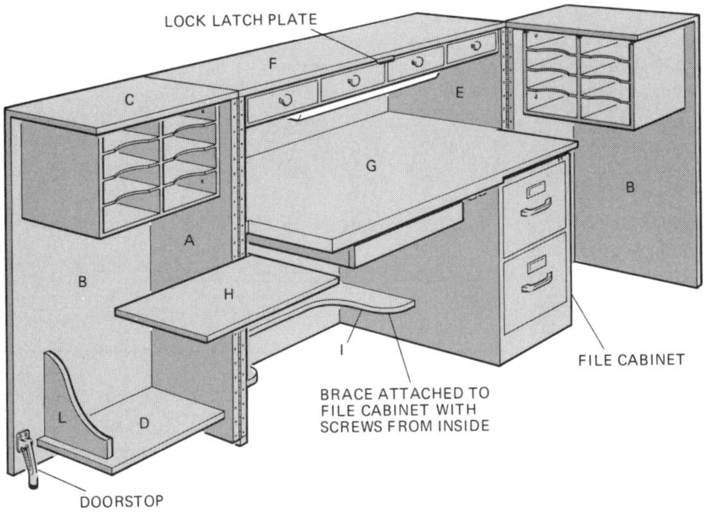


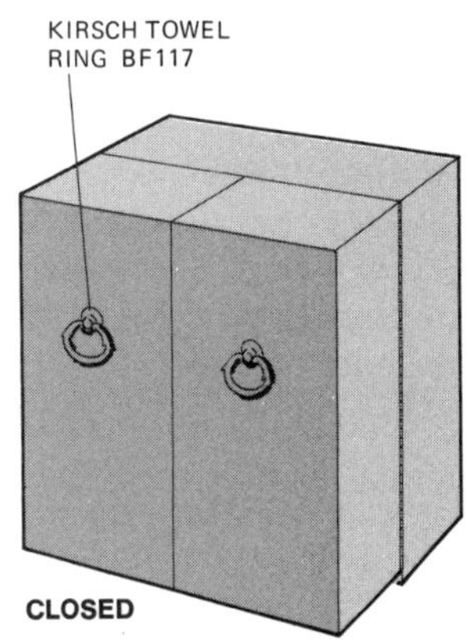


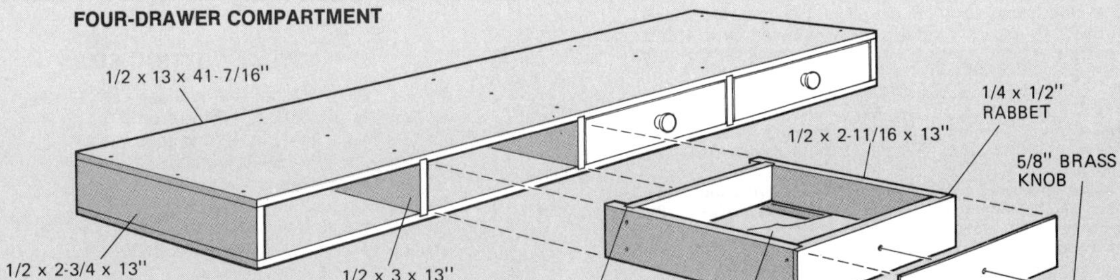


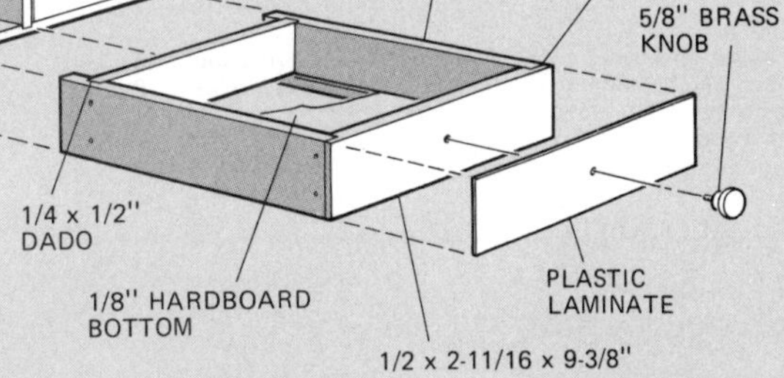


**FOUR-DRAWER COMPARTMENT** sits back 1 in. from front of chest to provide room for a lockset striker plate screwed to underside of part F and used to align wings with top of chest when closed.

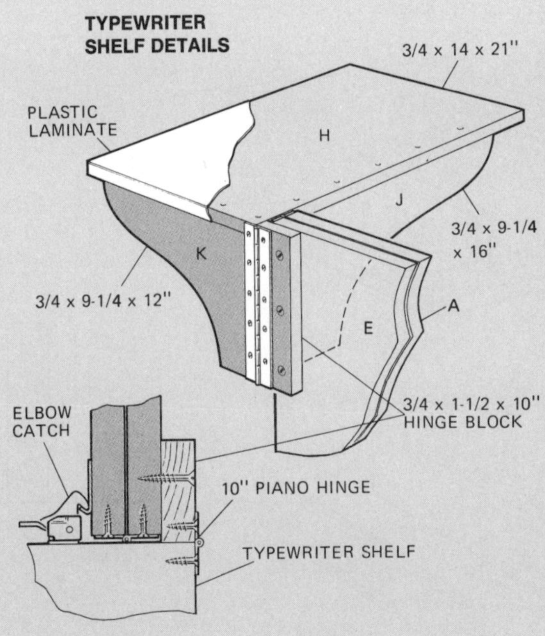


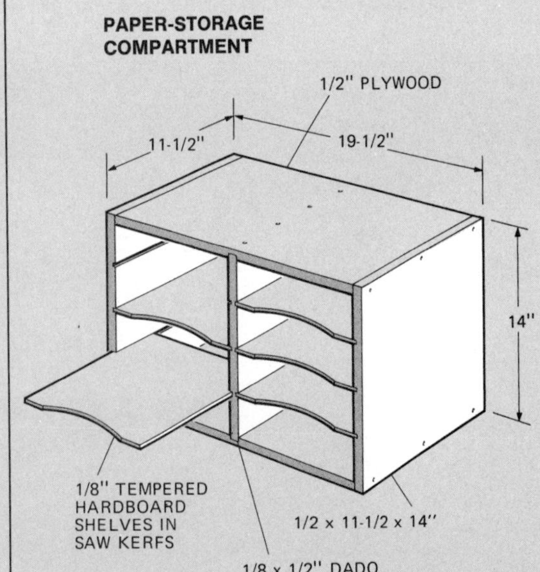

er shelf closed, while an elbow catch is used to lock the shelf in open position. The plate for the magnetic catch on the typewriter shelf is fastened to the plywood back with a short stovebolt. A pivoted doorstop is used to keep the left-hand door "locked" to the floor when the typing shelf is being used.

Twin paper-storage bins, and the four-drawer compartment, held in place by screws, are detailed on page 943. Large decorative towel rings are used for elegant wing pulls, and a regular 24-in. undercabinet fluorescent fixture attaches to the underside of the drawer compartment.

**MANUFACTURER'S PRODUCTS**

**Companion side chair**—Cat. No. C3KX7796N, olive green, Sears, Roebuck & Co.
**Portable electric typewriter**—Celebrity power 12, Cat. No. 3H5360N, Sears, Roebuck & Co.
**Plastic laminate**—English oak No. 343, No. 64 finish, Formica Corp., 120 East 4th St., Cincinnati, Ohio 45202.
**Pinup light**—Handymate PN-2, walnut, Swivelier Co., Inc. Nanuet, N.Y. 10954.
**Wing pulls**—Antique brass Chateau No. BF117 towel rings, Kirsch Co., Sturgis, Mich. 49091.
**Paint**—Velour semigloss alkyd enamel, olive green, Devoe Paint Co., Inc., 2 Oxford Drive, Moonachie, N.J. 07074.
**File cabinet**—two-drawer, full-suspension with lock, 15 x 28 x 29¼ in. Modern Steelcraft Co., 1101 Linwood St., Brooklyn, N.Y. 11208.
**Door holder**—5 in. dull bronze, No. J1235 DEZ, The Spartan Works Ltd., 27 Ludlow St., New York, N.Y.

**CUTTING SCHEDULE**

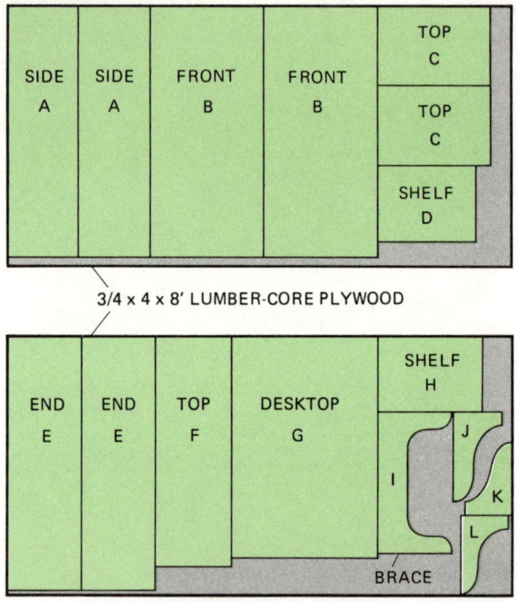


**ACTUAL CUTTING SIZES**

(A) ¾ x 14⅝ x 46⅝ in.—Wing sides
(B) ¾ x 21 3/16 x 46⅝ in.—Wing fronts
(C) ¾ x 14⅝ x 21 7/16 in.—Wing tops
(D) ¾ x 12 x 18¼ in.—Wing shelf
(E) ¾ x 14⅝ x 47⅝ in. —Chest ends
(F) ¾ x 14⅝ x 43 in.—Chest top
(G) ¾ x 28 x 40⅛ in.—Desk top
(H) ¾ x 14 x 21 in.—Typewriter shelf
(I) ¾ x 14 x 26⅜ in.—Brace
(J) ¾ x 9¼ x 16 in.—Typewriter-shelf brace
(K) ¾ x 9¼ x 12 in.—Typewriter-shelf brace
(L) ¾ x 9¼ x 11 in.—Wing-shelf brace

**UNDERSIDE OF DESKTOP**

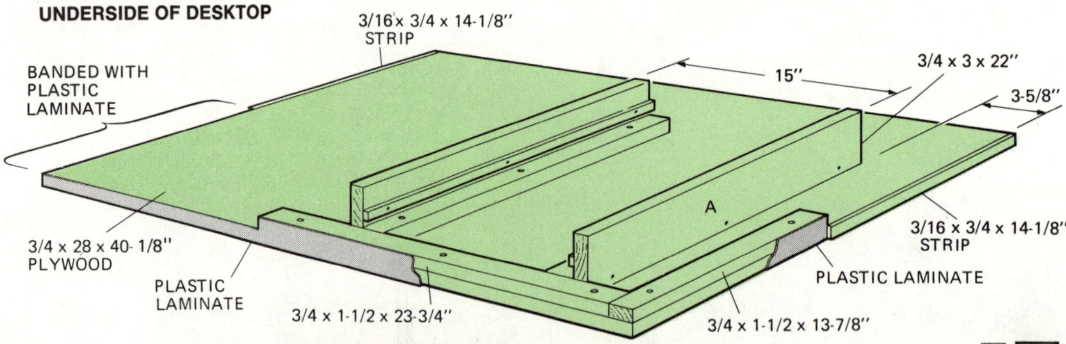


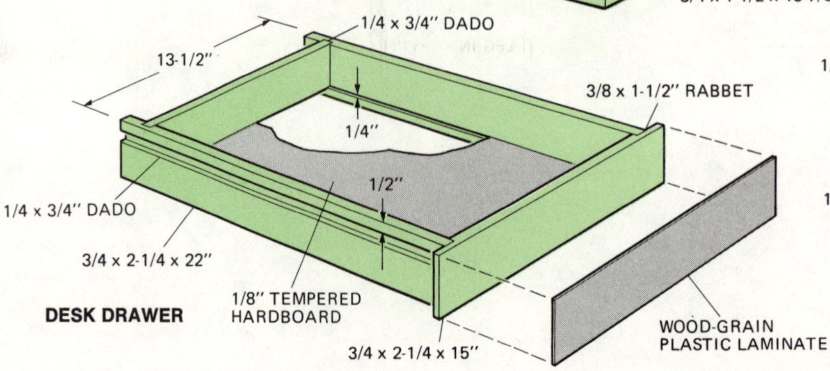


**DESK DRAWER**

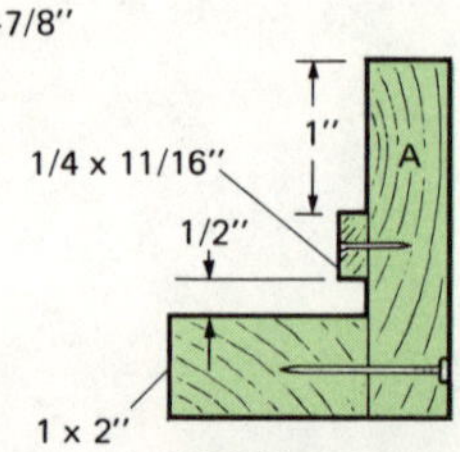


**DRAW-RUNNER DETAIL**

## 3. THE SPLIT-LEVEL

HERE'S A FUN PROJECT intended to brighten the environment of a home office, whether you use it full time or just for extra work that you bring home from time to time. The clean and simple design is devoid of frills and gingerbread.

Because it is extra sturdy, with plywood doubled up to obtain a 1½-in. thickness throughout, and entirely covered with plastic laminate, the desk is not "cheap." But similar units offered commercially are likely to cost at least twice as much as the desk you build at home.

You'll need six 4x8-ft. sheets of ¾-in. plywood plus four large sheets of Formica: two 4x8 ft., one 4x6 ft. and one 4x9 ft. Your local supplier may not stock them but can usually fill such an order in a week.

Be sure to lay out and mark all pieces of plywood for cutting; remember to allow ample waste for the saw-blade kerf. When laying out the Formica allow at least ⅛-in. extra overall to provide an overhang when the laminate is applied to the plywood. If the laminate is to be cut on a table saw using a carbide blade, lay out

**AS HANDSOME FROM REAR** as from front, the desk has clean, contemporary styling to go with almost any decor, while Formica surfaces minimize maintenance. Drawings on these pages illustrate construction details.

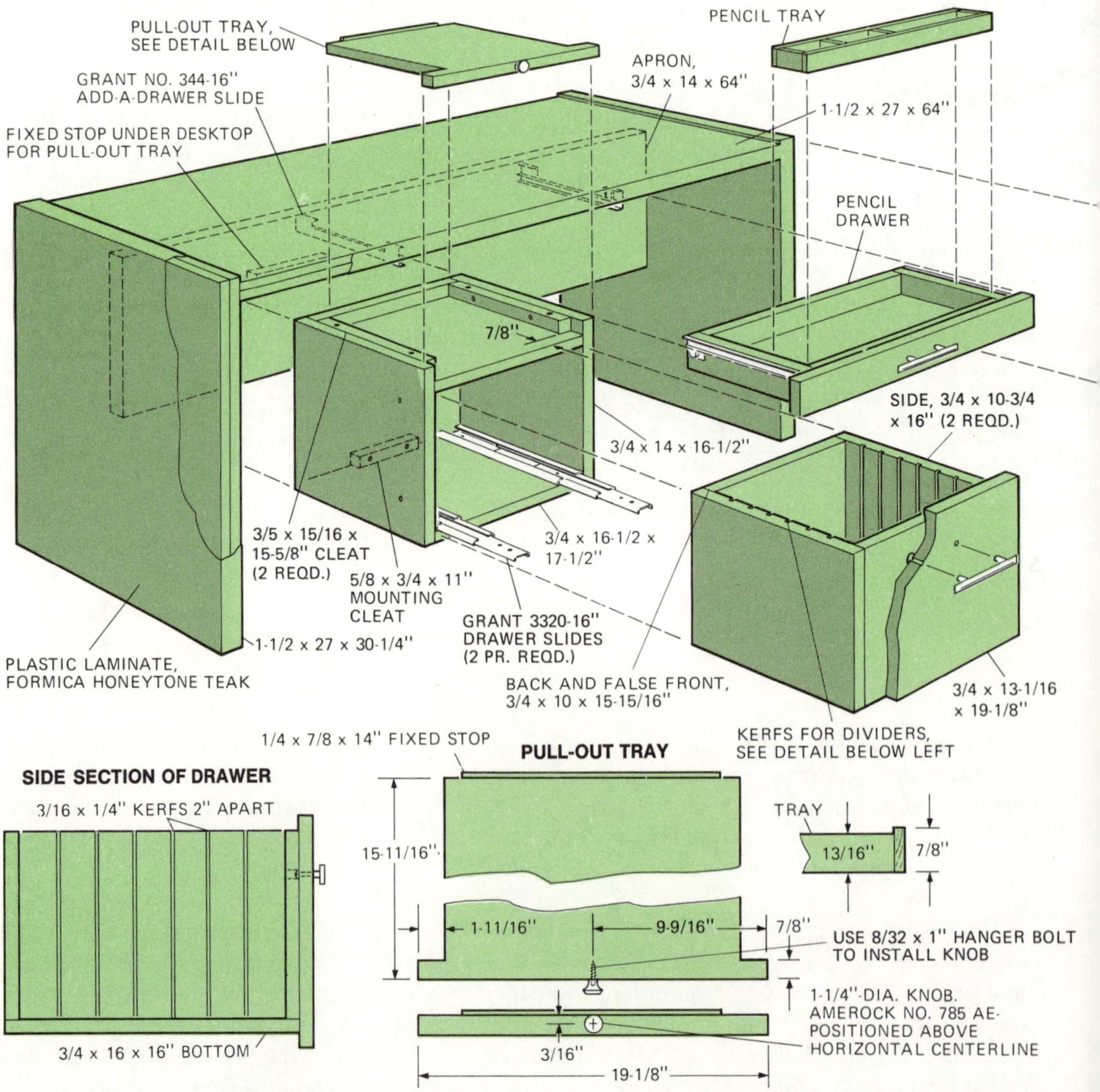

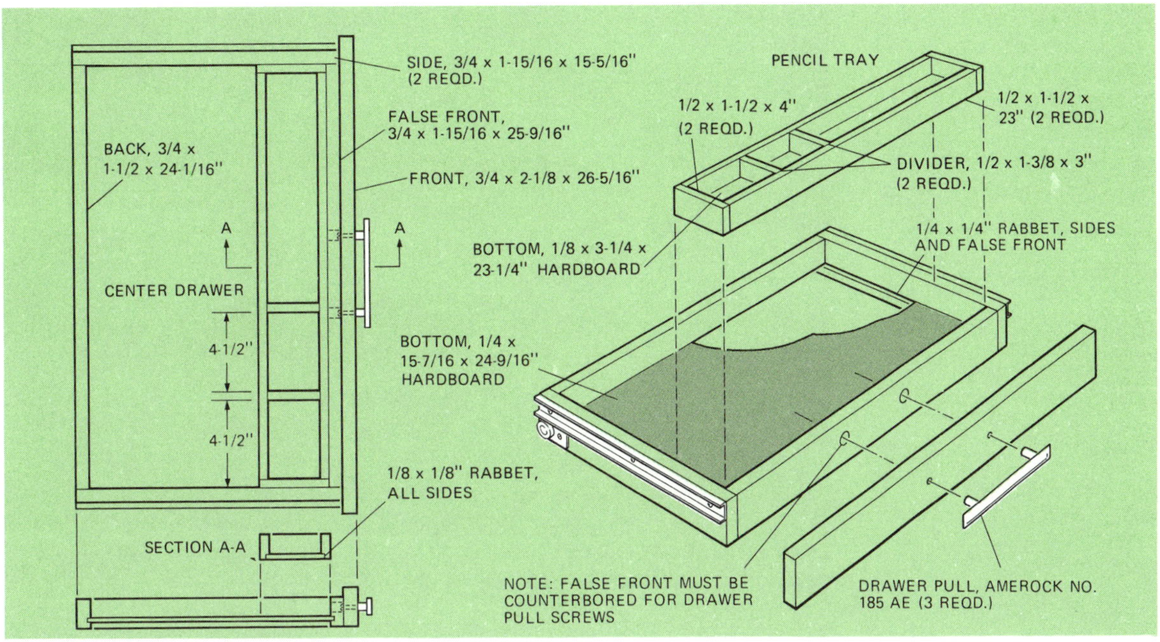


**Exploded view showing split-level desk assembly**

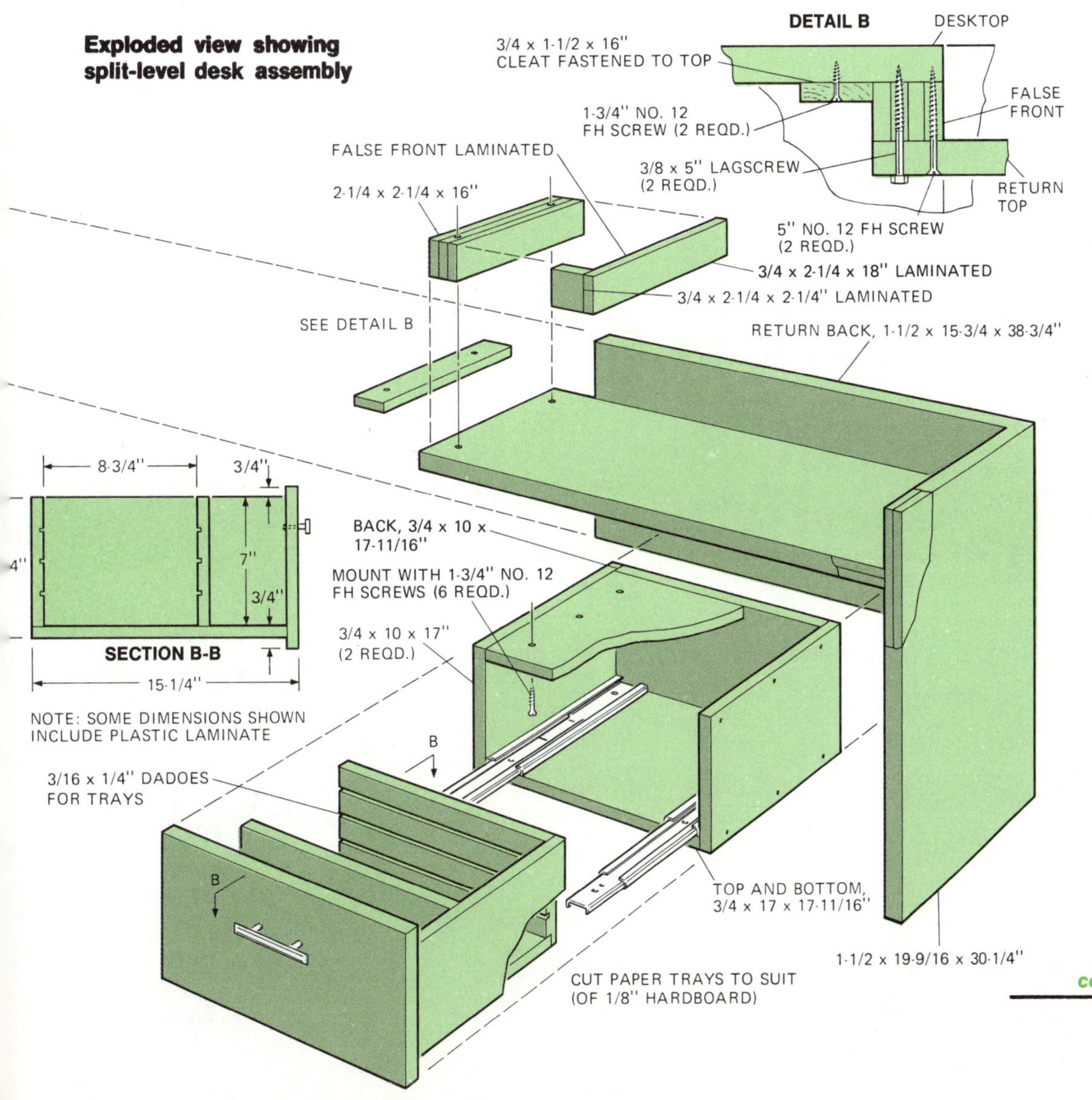


continued

**DRAWER IN SECRETARY RETURN** has hardboard slides that serve as paper-supply trays and compartment for pencil sharpener, office supplies.

the pieces to be cut on the good side. If you'll use a sabre saw that's equipped with a fine-tooth hacksaw blade, lay out the pieces on the back side and provide good support to prevent any chipped edges (from saw chatter and flopping laminate).

With all pieces cut and marked for identification, assemble the desk and return without glue to check for fit. If you're working alone, lay the setup on its back so you will have no trouble supporting the weight while you position and fasten the wells for the two deep drawers.

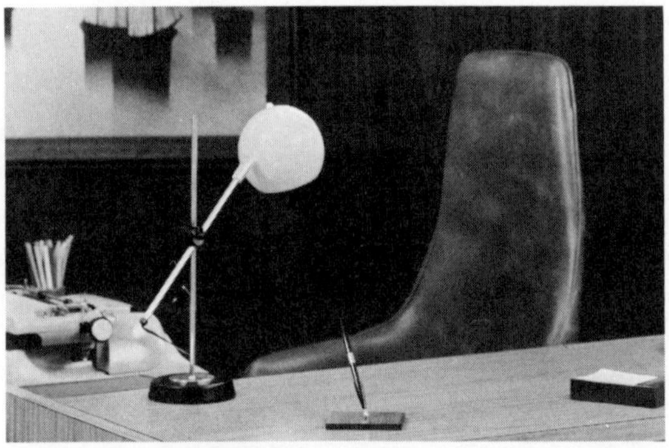

**EXECUTIVE-TYPE CHAIR** with extra-high back is one of many types you'll want to consider.

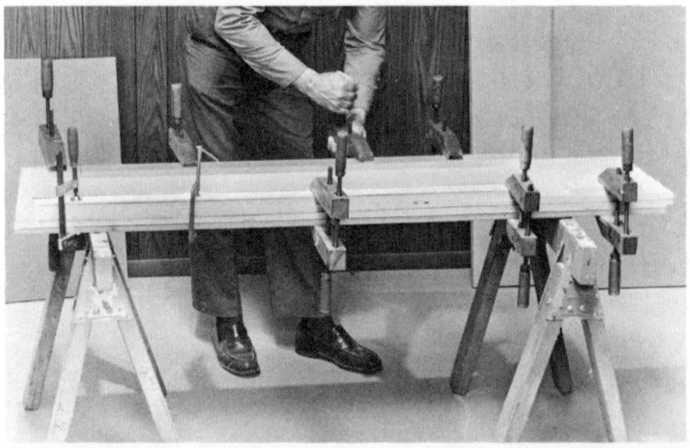

**DOUBLED-UP** plywood panels achieve thickness of 1½ in. To assemble the panels, use screws and glue.

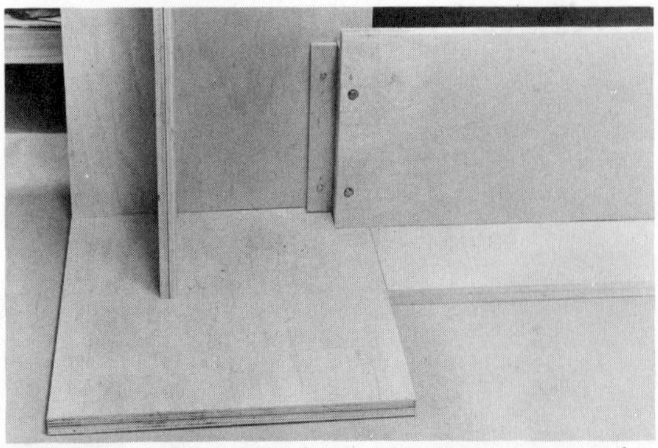

**ASSEMBLE UNITS DRY** for test fit, then take apart for lamination. Underside of desk is shown.

**ASSEMBLE SECTIONS** with lagscrews in counterbored holes after partial lamination; then laminate ends.

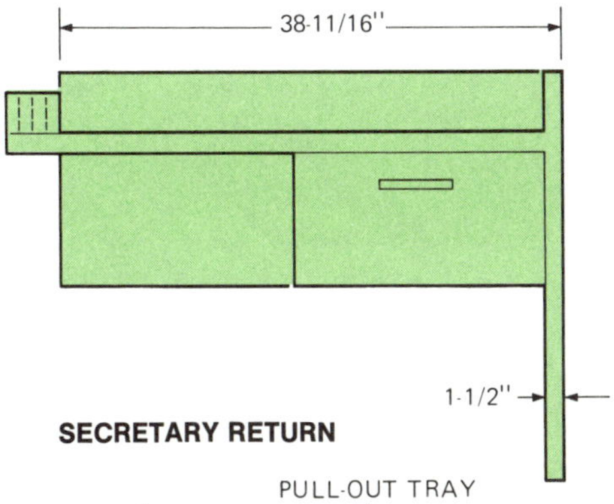


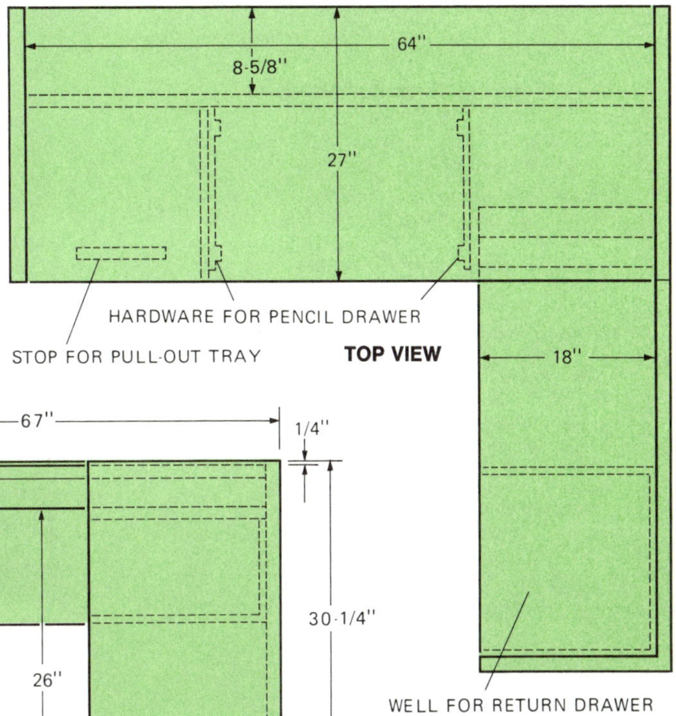


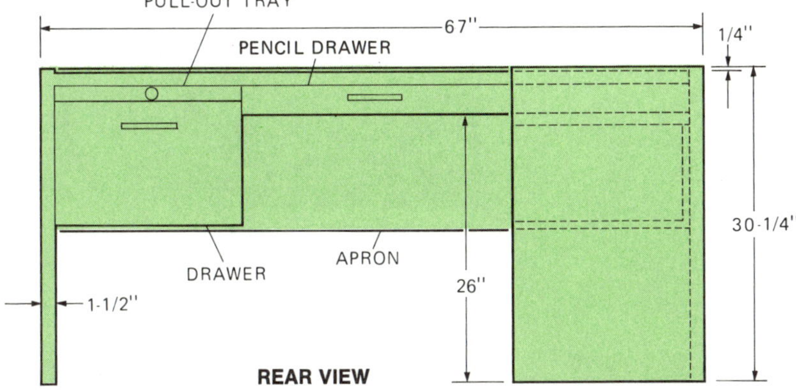


continued

**HOLES** drilled in bottom of drawer compartments aid in mounting to underside of tops with screws.

**DRAWER SLIDES** easily support weight of fully extended drawer. Drawer is then fastened to slides.

**RETURN** with spacer block is shown at left end. Drawer front has not yet been installed.

**UNDERSIDE** view of desktop shows position of pencil drawer slides and stop blocks for tray and return.

**Manufacturers of materials used**

*(Available locally, or write to the maker for nearest source.)*

**Drawer pulls**—Amerock Corp., Dept. PM, Rockford, Ill. 61101. Knob No. 785 AE, pulls No. 185 AE.

**High-back chair**—Sears, Roebuck and Co., Model No. P3 KX 7778N, Tobacco. Order from your local store or through the catalog.

**Plastic laminate**—Formica Corp., Formica Building, Dept. PM, 120 East Fourth St., Cincinnati, Ohio 45202. No. 417 Honeytone teak, suede finish 64.

**Drawer slides**—Grant Hardware Co., Dept. PM, 141 High St., West Nyack, N. Y. 10994. No. 344-16-in. Add-A-Drawer slides for pencil drawer, and two pairs of No. 3320-16-in. slides for the deep drawers.

**DEEP DRAWER** and pencil drawer hold a large supply of office materials. Extra kerfs cut in the drawer slides let you shift dividers as need arises.

Next, the two units can be uprighted for temporarily joining the return to the desk. A simple method here is to use a handscrew (clamp) on the end leg of the desk at the desired height. The apron, or back, on the secretary return can be rested on this clamp while you make final measurements and fit the filler blocks and stop under the desk top. When you are satisfied with all fits, including the three drawers' sliding action, disassemble the piece.

Take time to think out the laminating steps and, in fact, consider jotting down the sequence so you won't run into trouble. (It may prevent a ruined piece of laminate.) Laminate all parts except those which must be left uncovered so that the desk and return can be permanently assembled.

To assemble the desk, again work with it lying on its back. Fasten the ends to the top and the apron, and install the well for the drawer. Remember to install the pullout tray before fastening the well to the desk—because of those fixed stops. Fasten the drawer to the slides and upright the desk so the ends can be laminated.

Construct the secretary return using the same technique. One advantage of this unit is that *the return does not have to be built right away*—it is not an integral part of the setup, as can be seen in the drawings and photos. You can build either one or both units to suit your personal needs and budget. The desk is handsome whether the return is used or not. And you can add it later.

Costs could be kept down somewhat by using laminate on the top only and staining or painting the rest of the desk. But if you choose this course, you will have to use a cabinet-grade, higher-cost plywood. In any event, the top, at the least, should be laminated to provide a durable, trouble-free surface that won't be marred easily by ball-point pens and pencils through paper.

The interior of the desk shown was finished by applying a sealer coat of shellac thinned 50 percent and following that with two coats of semi-gloss harvest gold latex enamel. The pencil tray is a quickie project in itself and is of great value for keeping small items from drifting to the rear of the shallow pencil drawer.

# Build a charming colonial trestle desk

**Because of it's classic simplicity, this desk is easy to make—and just as easy to fit into almost any style of decorating. For casual correspondence or serious study, it's a handsome piece you'll be proud of. Here are complete instructions for building it and for giving it an authentic finish**

By LOUIS J. DILULLO

HERE'S AN EARLY AMERICAN reproduction that you and your family will treasure for years to come—a charming colonial trestle desk. I reproduced it in white pine for about $60, but it has a market value of well over $300.

To copy this fine period piece, start with parts A and B, the desk's top and bottom. Cut six boards ¾ x 8 x 57½ in. Then glue, dowel and clamp them together edgewise to make two ¾ x 24 x 57½ in. panels. When the glue dries, trim the panels to a finished width of 23¼ in.

**Desk ends.** Cut four pieces 5½ x 24 in. from 1¼-in. stock and glue them together to make two 11x24-in. boards, using bar clamps and dowel pins. Next, glue and dowel ⅝ x 1¼-in. pieces (end caps) to the ends of the glued-up end pieces to conceal the end grain. Now lay out the ends, following the shape and dimensions given. Cut to size and shape and round the four outer edges of each.

**Assembly of top members.** The narrow top shelf measures ¾ x 5¾ x 57½ in. After a thorough sanding, position the top, bottom and shelf members against the ends and mark. Allow a 4-in. space between the three to accommodate drawers. Position the top member ½ in. down from the top of the ends and ¾ in. from the rear to leave space for a ¾-in. backboard. Next, drill

SEE ALSO
**Clocks . . . Comb boxes . . . Drawers . . . Dry sinks . . . Gossip benches . . . Varnish . . . Wood finishes**

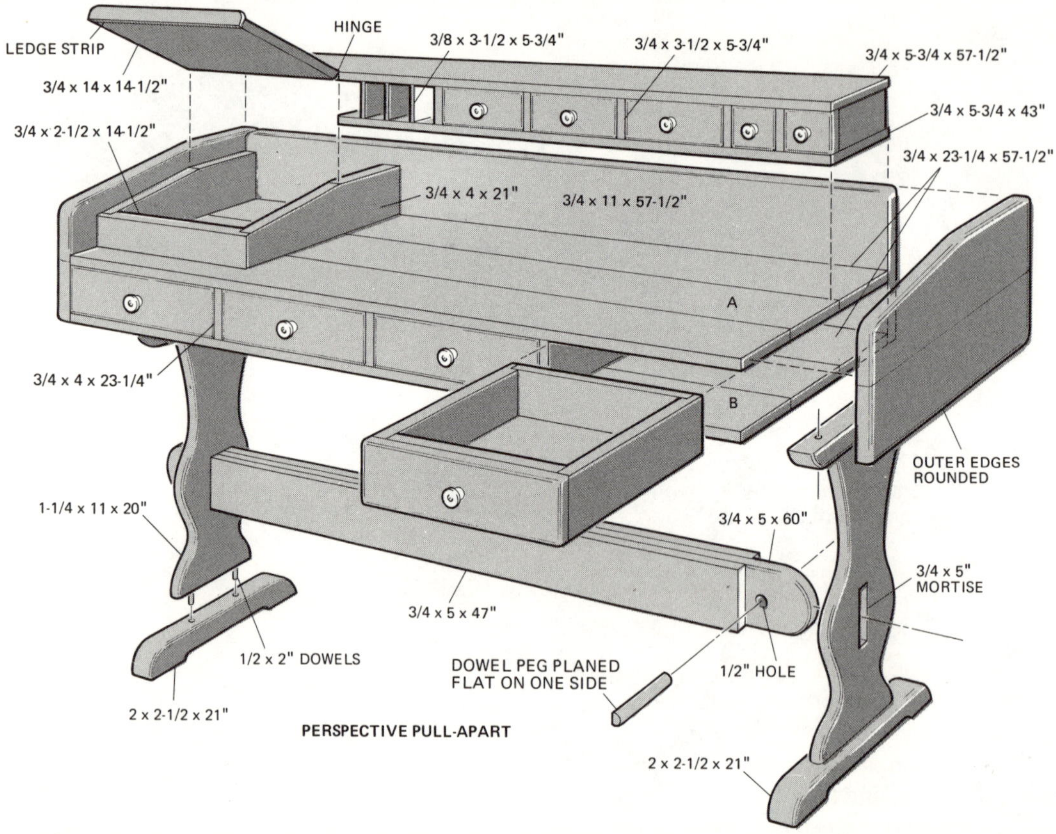


PERSPECTIVE PULL-APART

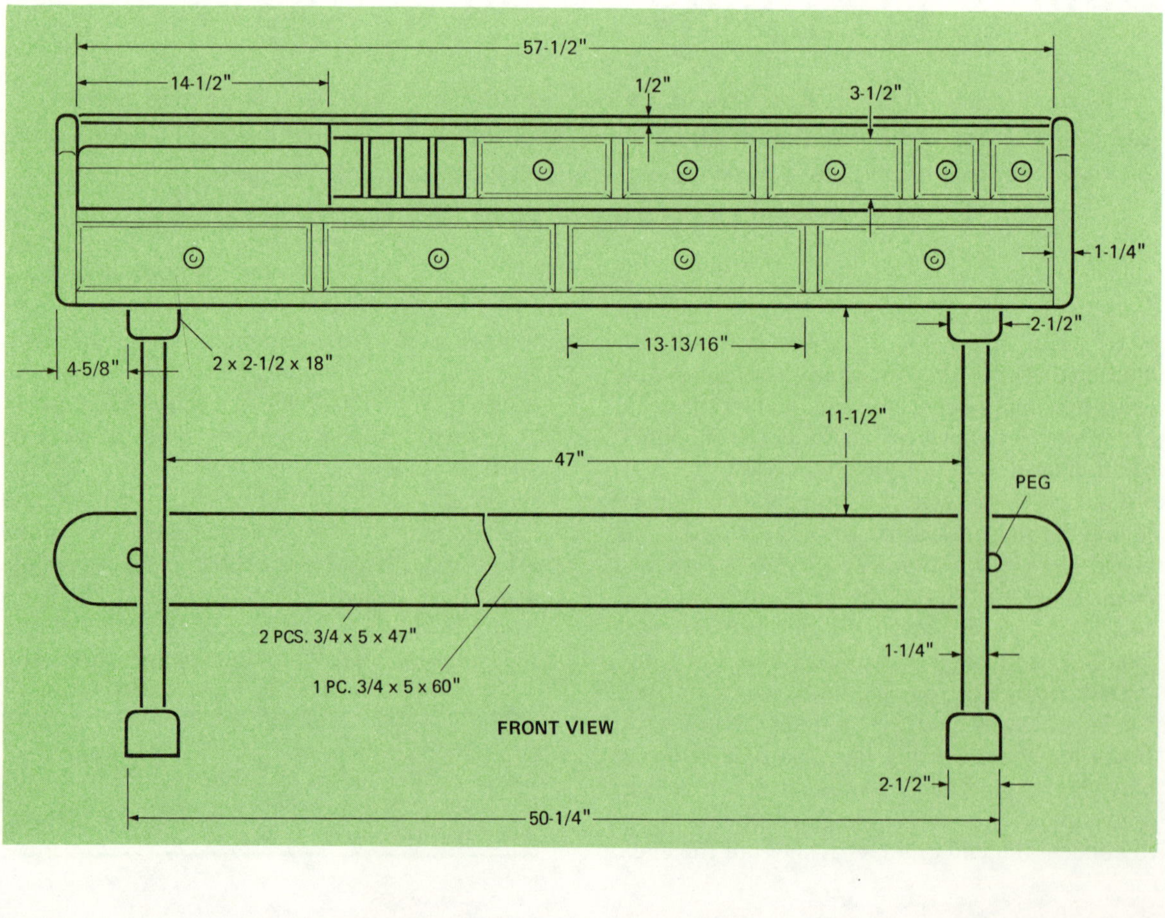


FRONT VIEW

**ACCESS TO** slant-top storage compartment at left side of desk is by its hinged writing surface, which lifts.

and counterbore the ends for No. 10 x 1½-in. flathead (fh) screws, spacing them evenly for attaching the top, shelf and bottom members. Use glue, drive the screws, plug the counterbored holes and sand.

**Hinged-lid compartment.** Cut the front piece ¾ x 2½ x 14½ in. and the two side members ¾ x 4 x 21 in. Preassemble the compartment, then install the members with glue and screws. The

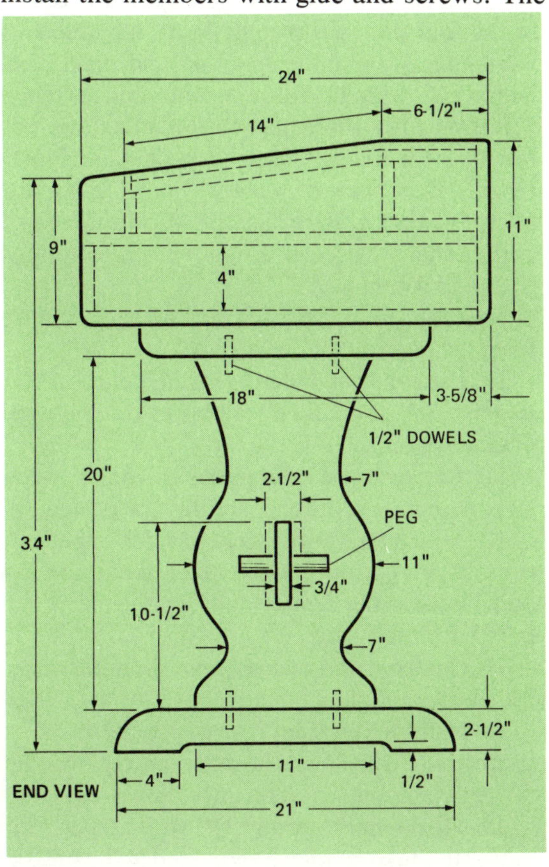


grain of the hinged lid should run crosswise or the same direction as the desktop grain. Here ¾ x 1-in. strips are added to the end-grain edges. Overall size of the lid should measure 14 x 14½ in. including a ⅜ x 1-in. strip added to the front edge. Attach the compartment's lid with a 1¹/₁₆-in.-wide piano hinge.

**Drawer and envelope compartments.** Cut the drawer separators 4 in. wide and glue them in place between the top and bottom members and between top and shelf. Make sure the separators are installed squarely and parallel, using glue and brads. Separators for envelope pigeon holes should be cut from ⅜-in. stock.

Drawers are made following simple rabbet and butt-joint construction and fitted to slide freely in the opening. The sides and backs are of ⅜-in. stock, fronts are ¾ in. and all are grooved to accept ⅛-in. hardboard bottoms.

**Desk back.** Cut a ¾-in. board to size of 11 x 57½ in. for the back. Round the top edge and attach the board from the back and from the end with fh screws in counterbored holes. Plug the holes with screw buttons and sand flush.

Cut two pieces from 1¼-in. stock 12x20 in. for the legs. Lay out the pieces following dimensions, bandsaw them, cut the ¾ x 5-in. rail mortises and sand the edges. Next cut the 2 x 2½-in. head and foot pieces and dowel them to the top and bottom ends of the legs. Note that No. 10 x 1½-in. fh screws are used in countersunk holes in the top cross members to attach the legs to the upper assembly.

Glue together the three members that make up the 2¼-in.-thick rail (trestle); letting the center member project at each end to form a shouldered tenon. Drill ½-in. holes in the tenons for the cross pegs. The latter should be cut from scrap and shaped to rough form.

**Finishing.** The desk is now ready for its final sanding with No. 150 grit or finer sandpaper. After sanding it smooth, I applied Minwax Jacobean, which is a dark stain that tends to enhance the grain structure in pine. Since I prefer varnish to lacquer due to its ability to resist water spots, I next used Valspar No. 11 Soft Glow. I sprayed on five coats, sanded the desk lightly between coats with No. 280 sandpaper and cleaned the finish with a tack rag.

After the fifth coat. I sanded it ever so lightly with the 280-grit paper and then applied four coats of paste wax with a 000 steel-wool pad. Finally I followed this with 10 more coats of paste wax, buffing these coats to a soft luster with a soft cloth.

# For nostalgia buffs— a rolltop desk

By ROSARIO CAPOTOSTO

■ BACK IN THE ERA of the trolley car and Model-T, the rolltop desk was popular in both home and office. Today, it's a cherished antique and you can pay as much as $1300 and more for a store-bought reproduction. Build it yourself in fine cherry at a material cost of about $380. Here's how:

**step-by-step construction**

**1. Rip the strips** for all the frames: upper, lower and center. Use cherry where visible, poplar otherwise.

**2. Cut tongues** in ends of frame side members (use table saw with spacer between two outer blades of dado set to form two parallel cuts at same time). Tenonner or homemade jig should be used.

**3. Cut ¼-in. grooves** in all side and end frame members, ¼-in. deep. Cut dust covers from ¼-in. gum plywood. Make a bit scant to allow space for glue.

**4. Cut the pedestal side panels** to size from veneer plywood.

**5. Use straightedge guide** to cut veneer panels to exact size. Since pieces are too large to handle on the average table saw, a portable circular saw is the best. Use great care in setting up the guide and use a smooth-cutting blade. Cuts must be finish cuts. Note: Tack nails are okay for saw guide because all cutting must be done from the back surface of panel in order to obtain clean, sharp edges on the face of the panel with a portable saw.

**6. Method of notching corners** of front frame members to allow the installation of facing strips on the veneer side panels is optional: Do it with dado cutter or by adding ¼ x ¾-in. strips to the fronts. The strips are cut short at both ends and must be glued perfectly centered.

**7. Use dado head** to cut the four dado grooves in the four pedestal panels. Mark all panels for advantageous grain orientation and make each cut on each panel before repositioning rip fence.

**8. Don't use white glue** or aliphatics; both set too fast for assembling the pedestals. Plastic resin is okay because it allows about 25 minutes assembly time at 70° F. Scrape off all glue run-off with a sharp chisel; use damp cloth to remove traces that remain.

**9. Glue edge strip** to each bottom back frame to form groove for the back panel.

**10. Use brads and glue** to install pedestal back panels. Add solid cherry strips to raw plywood edges at back.

**11. Cut pedestal base pieces** to rough overall size, then miter corners carefully for perfect fit.

**12. Attach long trim pieces** to sides of pedestal first. If you prefer to avoid mitered corners, use butt joints at the corners and lap the side members with the fronts.

**13. Cut front and rear base pieces,** miter or butt the ends, and glue.

**14. Nails driven from rear** with only the points protruding will keep the base pieces in place during clamping—a very important step.

**15. Fit the back apron "Q"** so it sets in ¼ in. closer to the front than is indicated in the full-size

SEE ALSO

**Cabinet furniture . . . Desk accessories . . . Drawers . . . Joinery . . . Modular furniture . . . Routers . . . Shaving cabinets . . . Storage ideas . . . Study centers . . . Wood finishes**

**BLOCK CLAMPED** to rule assures accurate straightedge placement to saw plywood.

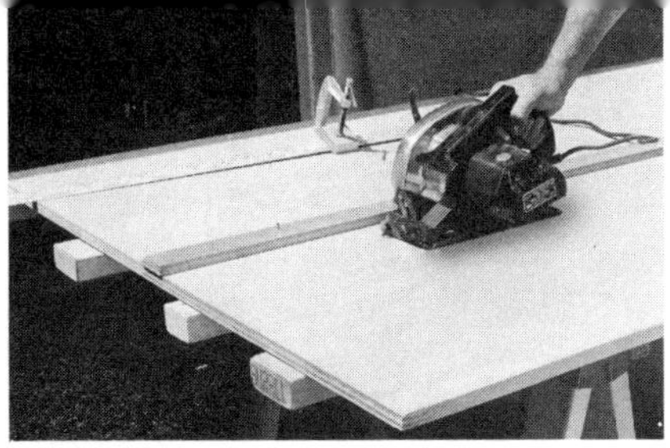

**GOOD SIDE** of panel is placed down and panel is supported by 2x3s on sawhorses.

**IDENTICAL DADO** cuts are made before moving fence. Outboard work support is *must*.

**TENON JIG** and pair of same-size blades with spacer are used to cut frame tongues.

**GROOVED END** members are added to side-pieces after the latter are on dust panel.

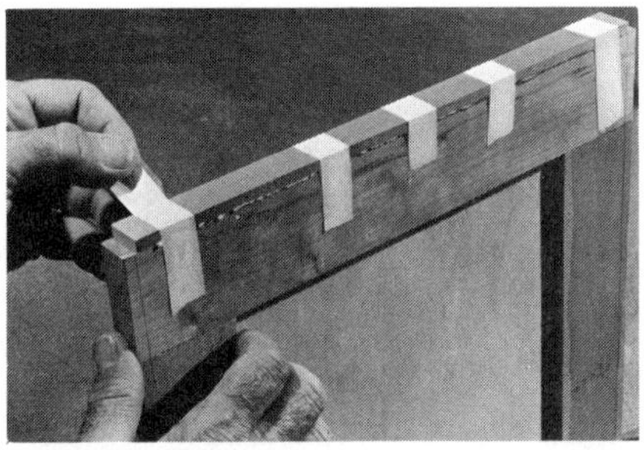

**CORNER NOTCHES** are formed by gluing short ¼-in.-thick strips to the front edges.

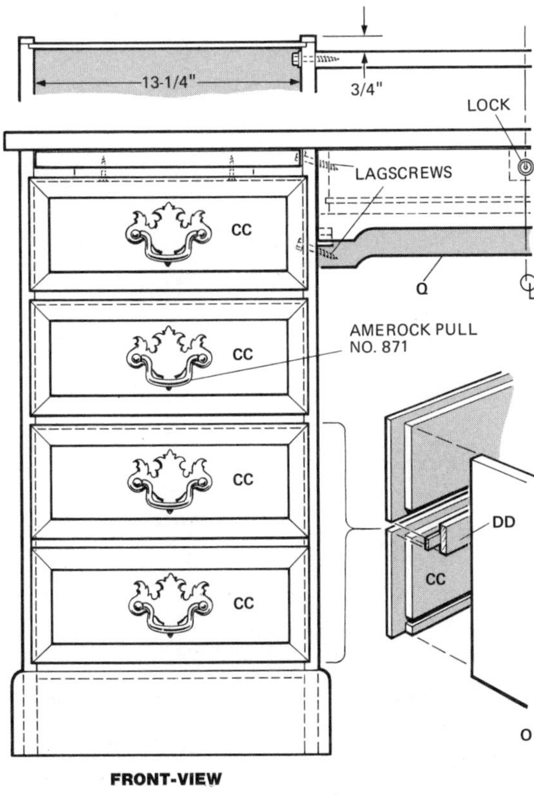


**FRONT-VIEW**

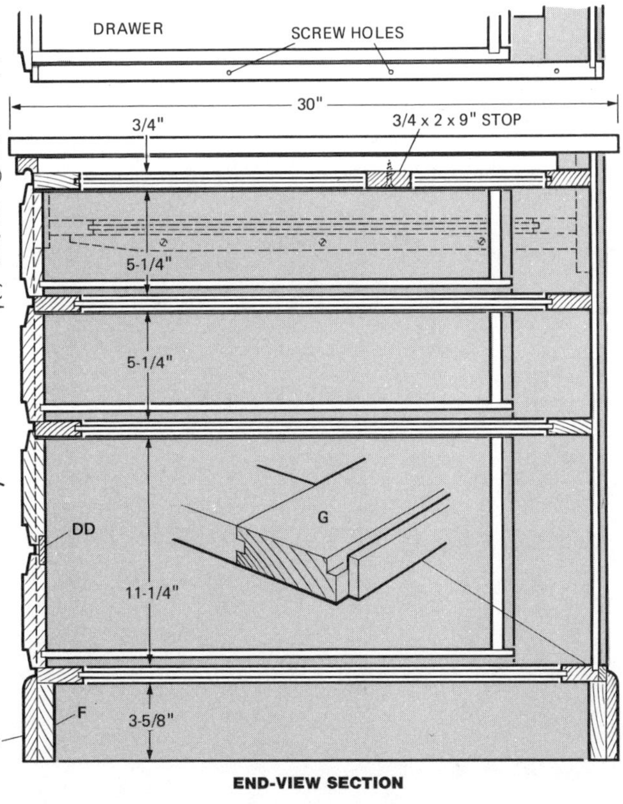


**END-VIEW SECTION**

**USE A SLOW-SETTING** resin glue rather than white to allow ample assembly time.

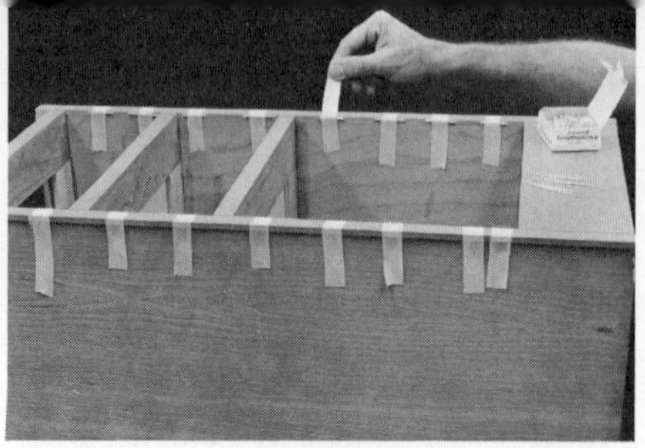

**TOOTHPICK STANDOFFS** keep tape away from glue line on inside pedestal surfaces.

**CENTER FRAME** is set in place without glue, then drilled for screw pilot holes.

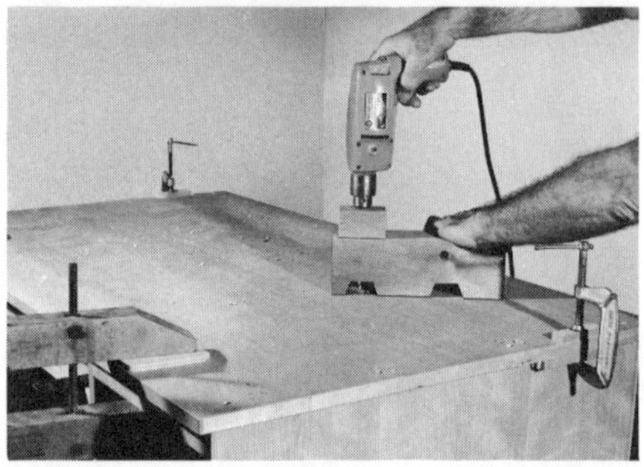

**COUNTERBORED HOLES** for wood plugs are drilled at right depth with homemade jig.

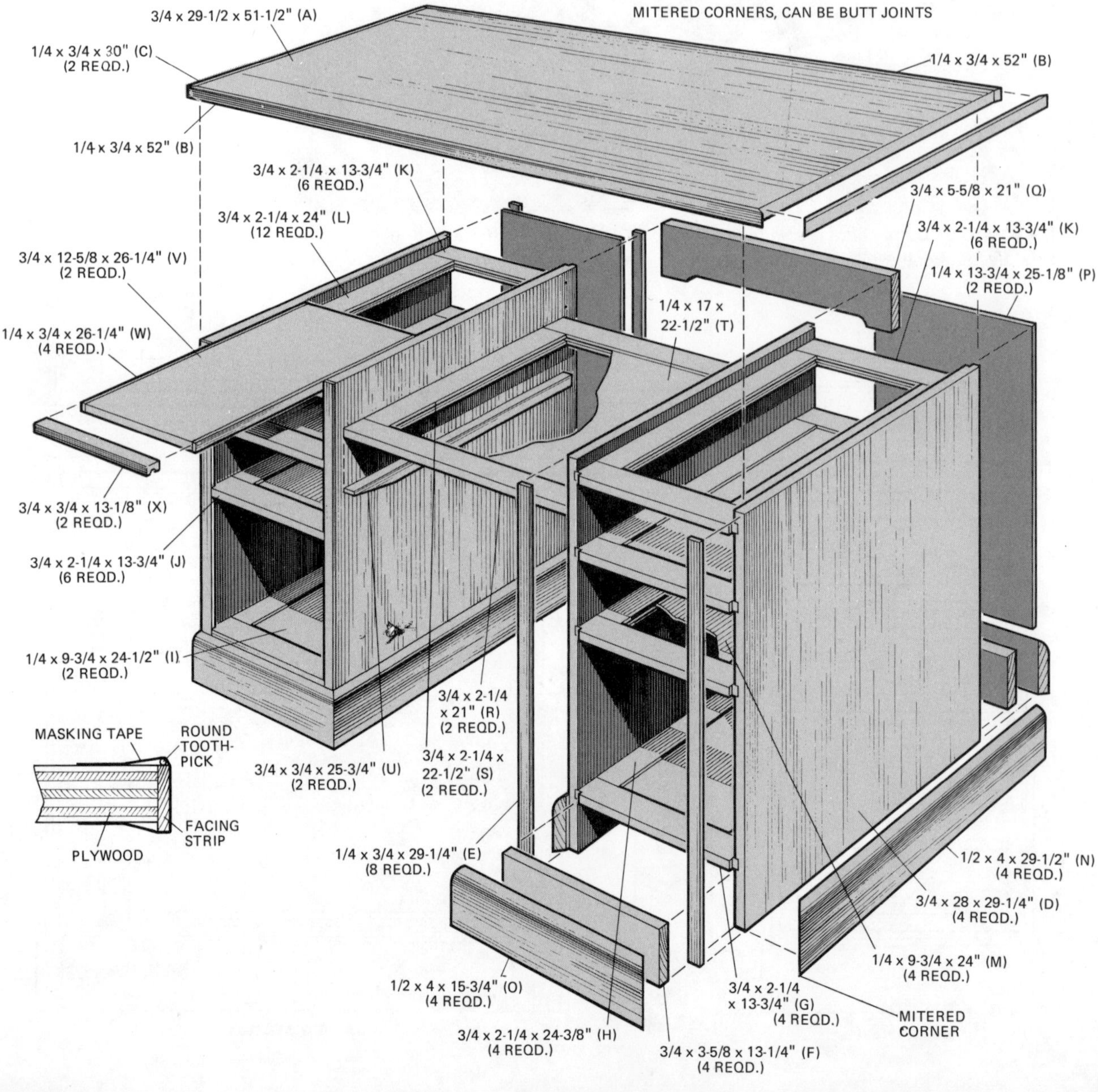

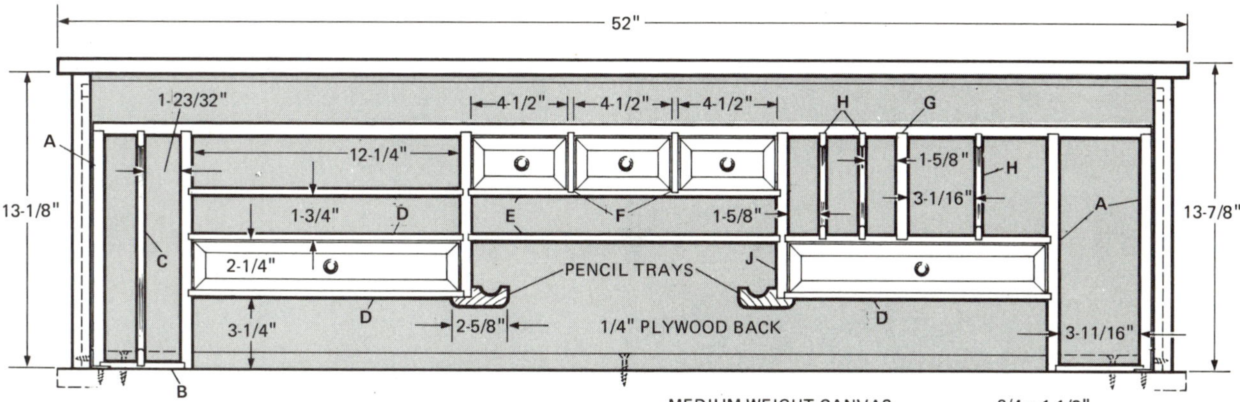


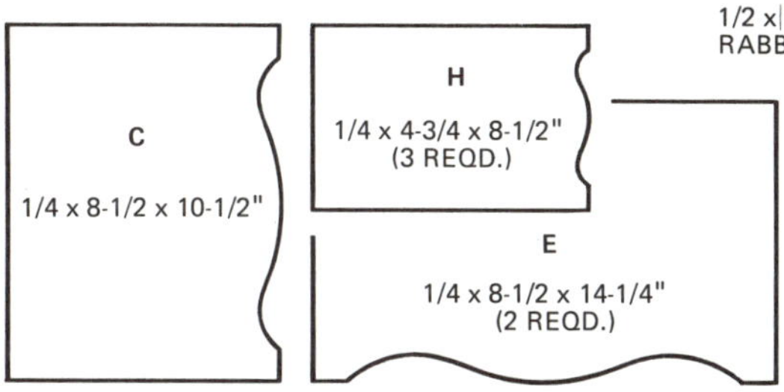


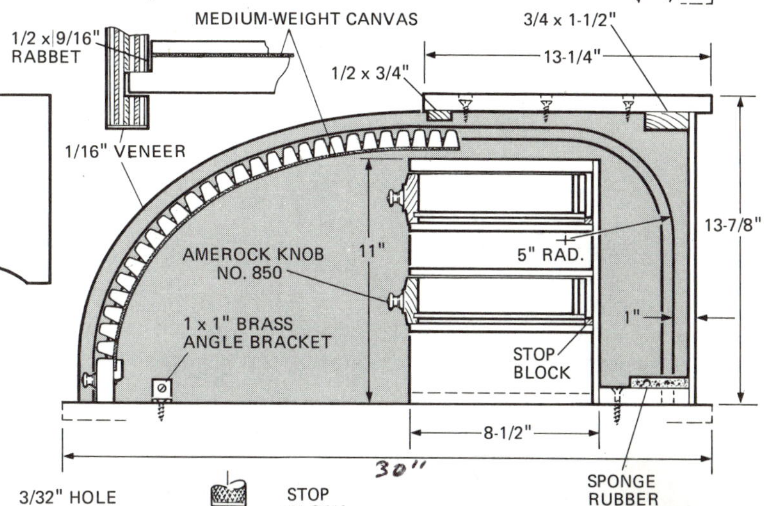


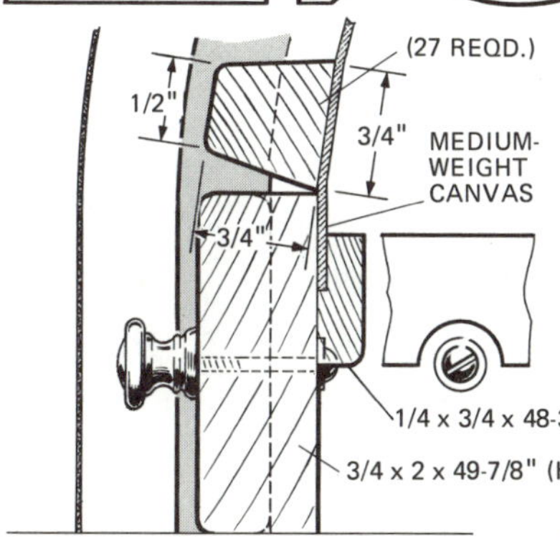


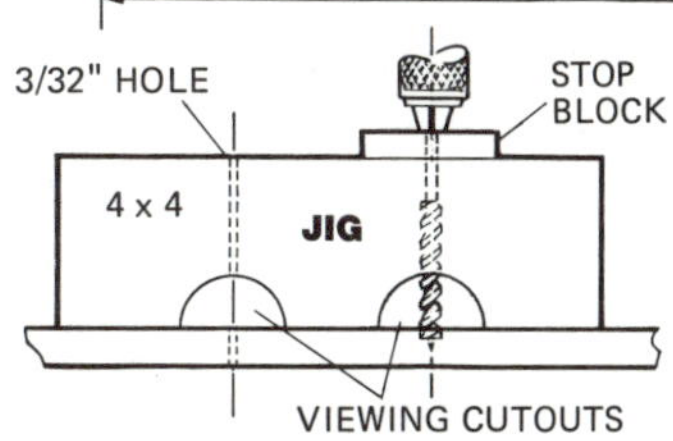


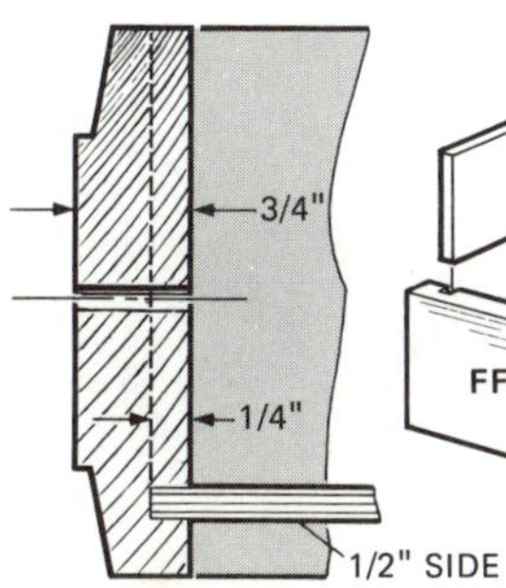


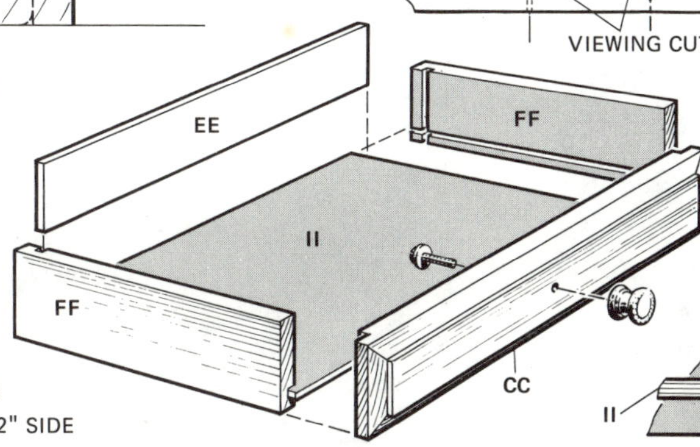


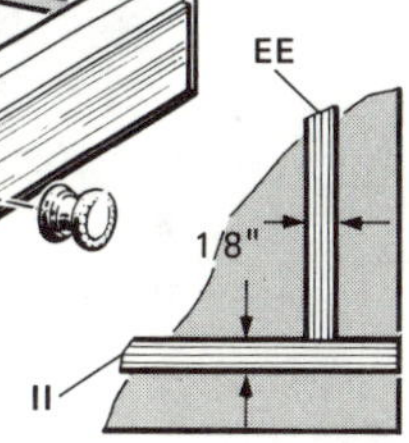

**DRAWER FACES** are beveled with a saw blade set at 8° angle. Keep hands a safe distance from the blade.

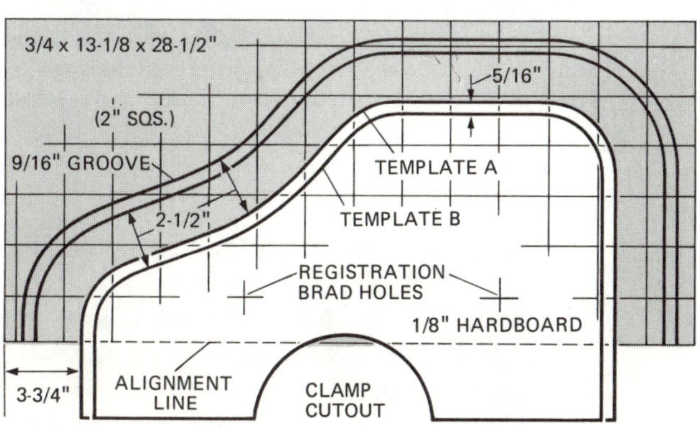


**TWO TEMPLATES** guide the router to form a 9/16-in. groove with a 1/4-in. straight bit. The remaining 1/16 in. between the 1/4-in. grooves is removed cleanly by carefully guiding your router freehand through the area.

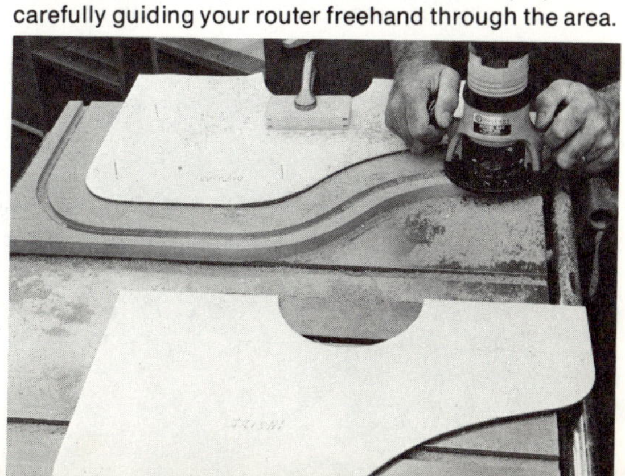

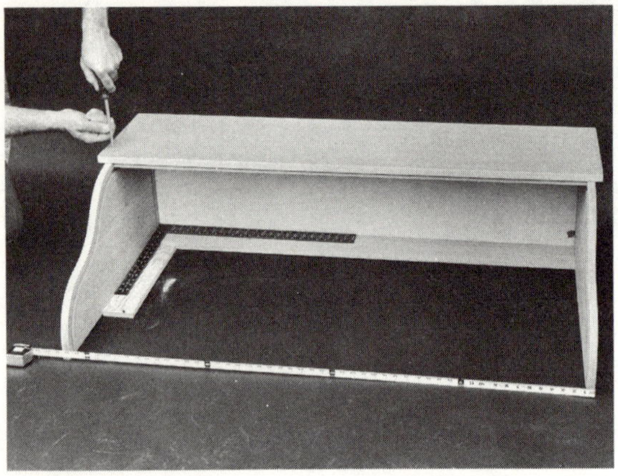

**AFTER THE PARTS** are test-fitted, screws are then driven in the counterbored holes and capped.

**PENCIL TRAYS** are made by passing the stock at a 75° angle across a 10-in. blade.

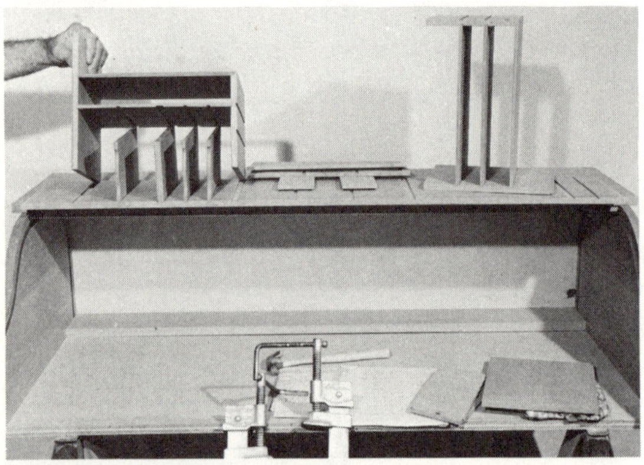

**PREASSEMBLE THE RIGHT** and left section of the cubbyhole unit first, then glue the rest.

**BEVELED SLATS** for tambour lid are ripped with a sharp blade tipped at a 10° angle.

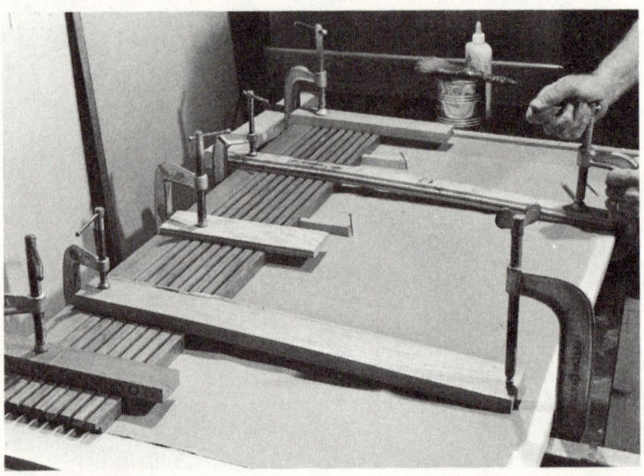

**SLATS ARE** glued to the cloth back 8 to 10 at a time. Apply the glue carefully to the cloth only.

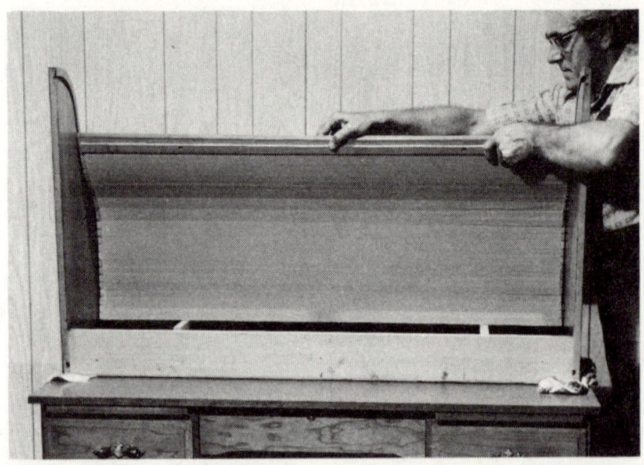

**SLAT ENDS** are waxed, then inserted into the track. Complete the project by screwing the top to the base.

plans. This is to allow clearance for direct drilling of lagscrew pilot holes from within the pedestal. This is an easier and more effective way to secure (rather than to use blind dowels as shown in plan). Use ¼ x 1½-in. hex-head lags and drive with socket wrench.

**16. Screw and glue** center frame supports into place.

**17. Install center frame** and drill holes for screws (instead of dowels) from within the base. Countersink the heads.

**18. Use smooth-cutting blade** to cut desktop

panel. Add ¼ x ¾-in. solid wood strips to ends, then front and rear strips to conceal edges.

**19. If sufficient number** of long clamps are not available to clamp the strips, you can do a good job with masking tape. Apply plenty of strips to insure good contact.

**20. Important note** when using tape to apply the vertical strips to the front edges of the pedestals: Elsewhere the strips are cut a bit oversize so they overhang and later are planed flush. But here the strips must be fitted flush at the start along the inner sides of the pedestals because they would be difficult to trim flush. In this case, it is advisable to use round toothpick standoffs to keep the tape away from the glue line. Otherwise, a gummy residue will result that's hard to remove.

**21. When using masking tape,** it is important to get a good-quality brand.

**22. To drill holes for screws** in desktop, set the top onto pedestals, then draw pencil lines on bottom of the top panel to outline the location of the pedestals.

**23. Drill a 3/32 in. pilot hole** for each screw location. Do this from the back face using the pencil outline as a guide. Since the panel cannot be handled on the drill press, all drilling must be done by hand. Therefore a drilling jig is a must for accuracy. See sketch, page 957.

**position top on pedestals**

**24. When preliminary pilot holes** have been drilled through the top, position the top onto the pedestals and drill through the top to transfer the pilot holes into the top edges of the pedestals.

**25. Use a spur bit** (which has a brad point) to counterbore ⅜-in. holes ⅛-in. deep into the top for matching wood plugs. Use the drilling jig for controlling depth and to assure perpendicularity.

**26. Now proceed to drill** the larger screw clearance holes into the top. Note that if the larger screw clearance holes were bored first, the spur bit would wobble around and tear up the work.

**steps for assembling**

**27. Glue and screw center frame** and apron between pedestals. Apply glue to top edges and to the top and secure with screws. Be sure piece is level on floor or table.

**28. Cut plugs from solid stock** with a plug cutter—orient the grain direction and glue into place. Go easy with the glue.

**29. Drawer fronts.** Set the saw arbor to 8° bevel and slice ends first, then the sides; otherwise, chipping may occur. Pieces can be held firmly against rip fence by hand for this operation.

**30. Rolltop.** Plans call for 9/16-in.-wide groove in the ends for the tambour top. The contoured groove is best cut with a router using a straight bit.

**31. After gluing up solid stock** to get 13⅛-in. width, bandsaw the contours, then prepare to cut the grooves.

**32. A router bit** which will cut a 9/16-in.-wide groove in one pass is nonexistent (so far as I know); therefore, a ¼-in. bit is used—a common size.

**template from hardboard**

**33. A "twin" or two-part template** cut from standard tempered hardboard is used to cut the grooves. The radii vary between the two parts of the template so great care must be exercised to make the templates.

**34. Templates.** Draw the pattern full size onto paper, including the dotted base lines. Rubber-cement the drawings onto hardboard and bandsaw them carefully. Note that the difference between both forms is 5/16 in. and parallel. Tape both forms together with base lines lined up and with smaller form centered side to side over larger form; drill a couple registration pilot holes for nails through both sections.

**35. Center one of the templates** onto the end panel with the base line even with the bottom edge of the stock. Drive in a pair of snug-fitting brads to hold in alignment. Clamp to work table and make the first pass with the router. Take off only a little at a time to avoid burning.

**36. When depth is reached,** remove the first template and install the other using the same nail pilot holes to assure exact lineup.

**37. The two cuts** made with the router will result in two ¼-in. grooves with a space of 1/16-in. from outside to outside; thus a narrow strip of waste will remain in the center of the groove. This is cleaned out by making a freehand pass with the router.

**38. Use a carbide-tip tool** for cutting the tambour grooves and make each pass about ⅛-in. or even less until ⅜-in. depth is reached.

**39. After the grooves are cut** and the inner faces of the end panels sanded, the top and back are assembled. Counterbored screws are used to make glue contact of top to sides. Plug the holes.

**40. Cubbyhole unit.** Make the required dado cuts, then assemble the left and right sections. This will simplify assembly considerably. If an attempt is made to put it all together in one operation, proper clamping would be impossible. Half-inch lumber for this is not usually stocked so you'll have to have it surface-planed at a lumberyard.

**41. Prestain and finish** the face of the back panel, then put it aside and proceed to stain the compartments. The job is tough because your hands won't fit in some of the compartments. Work from both sides (thus the reason for leaving off the back). See finishing steps later.

**42. Tambour lid.** Cut some boards to the required length for the slats, then run a dado cutter over the ends to form the notch.

**43. Use a smooth-cutting blade** to cut the strips. Set the arbor for a 10° tilt, then run each piece through twice to obtain the required bevel on both sides. Use two push sticks for safety and accuracy.

**sand and stain carefully**

**44. Sand and apply the finish** to each piece before assembly. Don't get stain on the bottom surface; otherwise glue will not adhere properly. Use a flat board for a work surface. Lay sheets of kitchen wax paper down to prevent accidental sticking to table. Tape the canvas to the table to keep it flat, then brush a coat of glue on canvas (not the wood). Work about 8 to 10 slats at a time. Most wood warps when cut into thin sections so it is practically impossible to control all the slats in one step. Use sufficient number of clamps to get ample pressure throughout. The use of a thin guide strip nailed to the table at one end will insure accurate alignment.

**45. When tambour is dry,** wax the ends, then insert into the grooves. Wax in the grooves will help. Screw the unit to the desktop.

**46. Finishing.** Presand all components before assembly, then final-sand by hand before applying finish. Use tack cloth to remove all sanding dust.

**47. Apply a coat** of American Lacquer thinned one to one with thinners to seal the wood and to permit better stain spread. Don't brush this on; use a pad of cheesecloth instead. Sand lightly after 10 minutes with fine paper (6/0); wipe with tack cloth.

**48. Mix** 1 part Sapolin Antique Walnut No. 300 and 1 part Sapolin Concord Cherry No. 305 stain. Apply with brush or cloth. Wipe off excess within 10 minutes.

**49. When stain has dried** (24 hours), apply a coat of Satinlac Low Gloss (or Constantine's Wood Glo). Sand first coat with 6/0 paper, then apply a second, final coat. Now stand back and admire your heirloom.

## MATERIALS LIST

**PEDESTAL BASE**

| Pcs. | Size (letter key to drawings), description |
|---|---|
| 1 | ¾ x 29½ x 51½" (A) Top* |
| 2 | ¼ x ¾ x 52" (B) Top edge strips, long |
| 2 | ¼ x ¾ x 30" (C) Top edge strips, short |
| 4 | ¾ x 28 x 29¼" (D) Pedestal sides* |
| 8 | ¼ x ¾ x 29¼" (E) Pedestal facing strips |
| 4 | ¾ x 3⅝ x 13¼" (F) Bottom rails front and back* |
| 4 | ¾ x 2¼ x 13¾" (G) Bottom frames front and back |
| 4 | ¾ x 2¼ x 24⅜" (H) Bottom frames, sides* |
| 2 | ¼ x 9¾ x 24½" (I) Dust panels*** |
| 6 | ¾ x 2¼ x 13¾" (J) Upper frames, fronts |
| 6 | ¾ x 2¼ x 13¾" (K) Upper frames, backs* |
| 12 | ¾ x 2¼ x 24" (L) Upper frames, sides* |
| 4 | ¼ x 9¾ x 24" (M) Dust panels*** |
| 4 | ½ x 4 x 29½" (N) Pedestal base, long |
| 4 | ½ x 4 x 15¾" (O) Pedestal base, short |
| 2 | ¼ x 13¾ x 25⅛" (P) Pedestal backs*** |
| 1 | ¾ x 5⅝ x 21" (Q) Back apron |
| 2 | ¾ x 2¼ x 21" (R) Center frame, front and back* |
| 2 | ¾ x 2¼ x 22½" (S) Center frame, sides* |
| 1 | ¼ x 17 x 22½" (T) Dust panel*** |
| 2 | ¾ x ¾ x 25¾" (U) Center frame supports* |
| 2 | ¾ x 12⅝ x 26¼" (V) Drawboards** |
| 4 | ¼ x ¾ x 26¼" (W) Drawboard edge strips |
| 2 | ¾ x ¾ x 13⅛" (X) Drawboard nosings |
| 1 | ¾ x 4 7/16 x 20⅞" (Y) Center drawer, front |
| 1 | ½ x 2 7/16 x 20⅜" (Z) Center drawer, back* |
| 2 | ½ x 3 3/16 x 23½" (AA) Center drawer, sides* |
| 1 | ¼ x 20⅜ x 23⅜" (BB) Center drawer, bottom*** |
| 8 | ¾ x 5½ x 13¾" (CC) Drawer fronts |
| 2 | ½ x 1¼ x 13¾" (DD) File-drawer front joiners |
| 4 | ½ x 4 7/16 x 12⅝" (EE) Drawer backs* |
| 8 | ½ x 5 3/16 x 23¾" (FF) Drawer sides* |
| 2 | ½ x 10⅜ x 12⅝" (GG) File drawer, backs* |
| 4 | ½ x 11 3/16 x 23¾" (HH) File drawer, sides* |
| 6 | ¼ x 12⅝ x 23⅝" (II) Drawer bottoms*** |
| 2 | ¾ x 2 x 9" (JJ) Drawer board stops* |
| 8 | Drawer pulls, Amerock No. 152 |

| Pcs. | Size (letter key to drawings), description |
|---|---|
| 1 | Lock, Corbin No. K02066 |

**Tambour top**

| Pcs. | Size (letter key to drawings), description |
|---|---|
| 1 | ¾ x 13¼ x 52" Top |
| 1 | ¾ x 1⅝ x 49" Top back rail* |
| 1 | ½ x ¾ x 49" Top front strip |
| 1 | ¾ x 4⅛ x 49" Bottom rail* |
| 2 | ¾ x 13⅛ x 28½" Ends** |
| 1 | ¼ x 13⅛ x 49¾" Back*** |
| 1 | ¾ x 2 x 49⅝" Bottom slat (K) |
| 27 | ¾ x ¾ x 49⅝" Tambour strips |
| 1 | ¼ x ¾ x 48¾" Canvas cover strip |

**Interior of tambour top**

| Pcs. | Size (letter key to drawings), description |
|---|---|
| 1 | ½ x 8½ x 48⅞" |
| 4 | ½ x 8½ x 10⅝" (A) Panels |
| 2 | ¼ x 3 15/16 x 8½" (B) Bottoms |
| 1 | ¼ x 8½ x 10½" (C) Scrolled divider |
| 5 | ¼ x 8½ x 12½" (D) Panels |
| 2 | ¼ x 8½ x 14¼" (E) Panels |
| 2 | ¼ x 2¾ x 8½" (F) Partitions |
| 1 | ½ x 4¾ x 8½" (G) Partition |
| 3 | ¼ x 4¾ x 8½" (H) Scrolled dividers |
| 2 | ½ x 7⅜ x 8½" (J) Partitions |
| 2 | ¾ x 2⅝ x 8½" Pencil troughs |
| 1 | ¼ x 11 x 48⅞" Back*** |
| 3 | ½ x 2 7/16 x 4 7/16" Drawer fronts |
| 3 | ⅛ x 2 1/16 x 4 3/16" Drawer backs |
| 6 | ¼ x 2 7/16 x 8 3/16" Drawer sides |
| 3 | ⅛ x 4 3/16 x 8 3/16" Drawer bottoms |
| 2 | ½ x 2 3/16 x 12⅛" Drawer fronts |
| 2 | ⅛ x 1 13/16 x 11⅞" Drawer backs |
| 4 | ¼ x 2 3/16 x 8 3/16" Drawer sides |
| 2 | ⅛ x 11⅞ x 8 3/16" Drawer bottoms |
| 7 | ⅛ x ½ x 1" Drawer stops |
| 7 | Amerock knobs No. 850 |
| 1 | 21 x 48¾" Medium-weight canvas |

* Poplar wood
** Veneer plywood (cherry)
*** Plywood (gum)

# METRIC CONVERSION

Conversion factors can be carried so far they become impractical. In cases below where an entry is exact it is followed by an asterisk (*). Where considerable rounding off has taken place, the entry is followed by a + or a - sign.

# CUSTOMARY TO METRIC

## Linear Measure

| inches | millimeters |
|---|---|
| 1/16 | 1.5875* |
| 1/8 | 3.2 |
| 3/16 | 4.8 |
| 1/4 | 6.35* |
| 5/16 | 7.9 |
| 3/8 | 9.5 |
| 7/16 | 11.1 |
| 1/2 | 12.7* |
| 9/16 | 14.3 |
| 5/8 | 15.9 |
| 11/16 | 17.5 |
| 3/4 | 19.05* |
| 13/16 | 20.6 |
| 7/8 | 22.2 |
| 15/16 | 23.8 |
| 1 | 25.4* |

| inches | centimeters |
|---|---|
| 1 | 2.54* |
| 2 | 5.1 |
| 3 | 7.6 |
| 4 | 10.2 |
| 5 | 12.7* |
| 6 | 15.2 |
| 7 | 17.8 |
| 8 | 20.3 |
| 9 | 22.9 |
| 10 | 25.4* |
| 11 | 27.9 |
| 12 | 30.5 |

| feet | centimeters | meters |
|---|---|---|
| 1 | 30.48* | .3048* |
| 2 | 61 | .61 |
| 3 | 91 | .91 |
| 4 | 122 | 1.22 |
| 5 | 152 | 1.52 |
| 6 | 183 | 1.83 |
| 7 | 213 | 2.13 |
| 8 | 244 | 2.44 |
| 9 | 274 | 2.74 |
| 10 | 305 | 3.05 |
| 50 | 1524* | 15.24* |
| 100 | 3048* | 30.48* |

1 yard =
.9144* meters
1 rod =
5.0292* meters
1 mile =
1.6 kilometers
1 nautical mile =
1.852* kilometers

## Fluid Measure

(Milliliters [ml] and cubic centimeters [cc or cu cm] are equivalent, but it is customary to use milliliters for liquids.)

1 cu in = 16.39 ml
1 fl oz = 29.6 ml
1 cup = 237 ml
1 pint = 473 ml
1 quart = 946 ml
= .946 liters
1 gallon = 3785 ml
= 3.785 liters
Formula (exact):
fluid ounces × 29.573 529 562 5*
= milliliters

## Weights

| ounces | grams |
|---|---|
| 1 | 28.3 |
| 2 | 56.7 |
| 3 | 85 |
| 4 | 113 |
| 5 | 142 |
| 6 | 170 |
| 7 | 198 |
| 8 | 227 |
| 9 | 255 |
| 10 | 283 |
| 11 | 312 |
| 12 | 340 |
| 13 | 369 |
| 14 | 397 |
| 15 | 425 |
| 16 | 454 |

Formula (exact):
ounces × 28.349 523 125* =
grams

| pounds | kilograms |
|---|---|
| 1 | .45 |
| 2 | .9 |
| 3 | 1.4 |
| 4 | 1.8 |
| 5 | 2.3 |
| 6 | 2.7 |
| 7 | 3.2 |
| 8 | 3.6 |
| 9 | 4.1 |
| 10 | 4.5 |

1 short ton (2000 lbs) =
907 kilograms (kg)
Formula (exact):
pounds × .453 592 37* =
kilograms

## Volume

1 cu in = 16.39 cubic centimeters (cc)
1 cu ft = 28 316.7 cc
1 bushel = 35 239.1 cc
1 peck = 8 809.8 cc

## Area

1 sq in = 6.45 sq cm
1 sq ft = 929 sq cm
= .093 sq meters
1 sq yd = .84 sq meters
1 acre = 4 046.9 sq meters
= .404 7 hectares
1 sq mile = 2 589 988 sq meters
= 259 hectares
= 2.589 9 sq kilometers

## Kitchen Measure

1 teaspoon = 4.93 milliliters (ml)
1 Tablespoon = 14.79 milliliters (ml)

## Miscellaneous

1 British thermal unit (Btu) (mean)
= 1 055.9 joules
1 calorie (mean) = 4.19 joules
1 horsepower = 745.7 watts
= .75 kilowatts
caliber (diameter of a firearm's bore in hundredths of an inch)
= .254 millimeters (mm)
1 atmosphere pressure = 101 325* pascals (newtons per sq meter)
1 pound per square inch (psi) = 6 895 pascals
1 pound per square foot = 47.9 pascals
1 knot = 1.85 kilometers per hour
25 miles per hour = 40.2 kilometers per hour
50 miles per hour = 80.5 kilometers per hour
75 miles per hour = 120.7 kilometers per hour